"*Loss, Grief, and Attachment in Life Transitions* is an essential book for any grief therapist. Securely rooted in the most current concepts and theories of grief, Jakob van Wielink and his colleagues offer both an expansive view of grief as well as a plethora of techniques for therapists aiding clients who are faced with impactful change and transition. Therapists will find in this book useful case studies and dialogues with clients that illustrate their sensitive approach. This is a must-read for clinicians."

—**Kenneth J. Doka, PhD**, professor in the graduate school at College of New Rochelle and senior consultant with the Hospice Foundation of America, USA

"This book fits very well into the growing literature demonstrating the applicability of an attachment-informed grief counseling framework to the understanding of non-death loss and its treatment. The authors make a compelling case for the need to address loss as an unavoidable feature of life that, depending on how it is met, can be an enervating or energizing force, inhibiting or promoting personal development and growth."

—**Phyllis Kosminksy, PhD, LCSW**, counselor in private practice in New York and at The Center for Hope in Darien, Connecticut, USA; co-author of *Attachment-Informed Grief Therapy: The Clinician's Guide to Foundations and Applications*

"Building on a good understanding of current knowledge of the psychology of loss and change, the authors have developed a variety of practical and useful exercises and insights with case studies to show how counselors can help clients to tackle complex and formerly intractable problems."

—**Colin Murray Parkes, OBE, MD, FRCPsych., LLD**, consultant psychiatrist emeritus at the St Christopher's Hospice, Sydenham, UK

LOSS, GRIEF, AND ATTACHMENT IN LIFE TRANSITIONS

Loss, Grief, and Attachment in Life Transitions gives readers an attachment-informed grief counseling framework and a new way of understanding non-death loss and its treatment.

Loss and grief are viewed through a wide-angle lens with relevance to the whole of human life, including the important area of career counseling and occupational consultation. The book is founded on the key themes of the Transition Cycle: welcome and contact, attachment and bonding, intimacy and sexuality, separation and loss, grief and meaning reconstruction. Rich in case material related to loss and change, the book provides the tools for adopting a highly personalized approach to working with clients facing a range of life transitions.

This book is a highly relevant and practical volume for grief counselors and other mental health professionals looking to incorporate attachment theory into their clinical practice.

Jakob van Wielink, MA, is an international grief counselor and executive coach. He is a partner at De School voor Transitie in the Netherlands, a faculty member at the Portland Institute for Loss and Transition in the USA, and is affiliated with IMD Business School's (Advanced) High Performance Leadership Program in Switzerland.

Leo Wilhelm, MSc, is a grief counselor, author, executive coach, and advisor to De School voor Transitie in the Netherlands.

Denise van Geelen-Merks, MSc, is a psychologist, coach, and couples therapist, and is licensed for systemic work in the Netherlands.

The Series in Death, Dying, and Bereavement

Volumes published in the Series in Death, Dying, and Bereavement are representative of the multidisciplinary nature of the intersecting fields of death studies, suicidology, end-of-life care, and grief counseling. The series meets the needs of clinicians, researchers, paraprofessionals, pastoral counselors, and educators by providing cutting edge research, theory, and best practices on the most important topics in these fields—for today and for tomorrow.

Series Editors:
Robert A. Neimeyer, PhD
University of Memphis, Tennessee, USA
Darcy L. Harris, PhD
Western University Canada, Ontario, Canada

Sibling Loss Across the Lifespan
Research, Practice, and Personal Stories
Edited by Brenda J. Marshall and Howard R. Winokuer

Understanding Child and Adolescent Grief
Supporting Loss and Facilitating Growth
Edited by Carrie Arnold

Chronic Sorrow
A Living Loss, 2nd Edition
Susan Roos

Continuing Bonds in Bereavement
New Directions for Research and Practice
Edited by Dennis Klass and Edith Steffen

Prescriptive Memories in Grief and Loss
The Art of Dreamscaping
Edited by Nancy Gershman and Barbara E. Thompson

Loss, Grief, and Attachment in Life Transitions
A Clinician's Guide to Secure Base Counseling
Jakob van Wielink, Leo Wilhelm, and Denise van Geelen-Merks

For more information about this series, please visit www.routledge.com/Series-in-Death-Dying-and-Bereavement/book-series/SE0620.

LOSS, GRIEF, AND ATTACHMENT IN LIFE TRANSITIONS

A Clinician's Guide to Secure Base Counseling

Jakob van Wielink, Leo Wilhelm, and Denise van Geelen-Merks

Routledge
Taylor & Francis Group
NEW YORK AND LONDON

First published 2020
by Routledge
52 Vanderbilt Avenue, New York, NY 10017

and by Routledge
2 Park Square, Milton Park, Abingdon, Oxon, OX14 4RN

Routledge is an imprint of the Taylor & Francis Group, an informa business

Library of Congress Cataloging-in-Publication Data
Names: Wielink, Jakob van, author. | Wilhelm, Leo, author. | Geelen-Merks, Denise van, author.
Title: Loss, grief, and attachment in life transitions : a clinician's guide to secure base counseling / Jakob van Wielink, Leo Wilhelm, and Denise van Geelen-Merks.
Description: 1 Edition. | New York : Routledge, 2020. | Series: Death, dying, and bereavement | Includes bibliographical references and index.
Identifiers: LCCN 2019014162 (print) | LCCN 2019015398 (ebook) | ISBN 9780429277757 (ebook) | ISBN 9780367206574 (hardback : alk. paper) | ISBN 9780367206543 (pbk. : alk. paper) | ISBN 9780429277757 (ebk)
Subjects: LCSH: Death—Psychological aspects. | Loss (Psychology) | Grief. | Bereavement—Psychological aspects. | Counseling.
Classification: LCC BF789.D4 (ebook) | LCC BF789.D4 W444 2020 (print) | DDC 155.9/37—dc23
LC record available at https://lccn.loc.gov/2019014162

ISBN: 978-0-367-20657-4 (hbk)
ISBN: 978-0-367-20654-3 (pbk)
ISBN: 978-0-429-27775-7 (ebk)

Typeset in Minion
by Apex CoVantage, LLC

CONTENTS

SERIES EDITOR'S FOREWORD

To live is to confront an unending sequence of life transitions, whether welcome or unwelcome. At birth, we are delivered from the intimate and protected world of our intrauterine development into an expansive and unpredictable outer world into which our parents and eventually many others beckon us, fostering our growth but also our vulnerability to losses of all kinds. In the course of living we naturally gravitate towards myriad places, projects and possessions, but particularly to people who anchor our sense of self, and confer a sense of connection and continuity as we construct a life story that is uniquely our own. But these very attachments predispose us to grief as we inevitably, at the point of the loss of the cherished person or thing, face the need to relinquish them and reorient to a changed life. Another way of saying this is that grieving entails reaffirming or reconstructing a world of meaning that has been challenged by loss.

It is precisely these themes that concern the authors of *Loss, Grief, and Attachment in Life Transitions: A Clinician's Guide to Secure Base Counseling*, as they winnow the common features that cut across the many contexts of loss and change that living entails. The vision cultivated by van Wielink, Wilhelm, and van Geelen is at the same time flexibly abstract and practically concrete, drawing on the Transition Cycle to recognize the abiding themes that recur in the variegated personal, relational, occupational, and organizational passages we confront, and offering concrete counsel on how to meet them with resilience. Pivotal in the process is the role of meaning reconstruction, as we frequently review, revise, and sometimes substantially rewrite our life stories in the aftermath of life-altering transitions, and in so doing reinvent ourselves.

Ultimately, then, the present volume concentrates on the same universal concerns that attend loss and grief addressed by other volumes in this series, but it does so with a broad, integrative vision of life transitions that includes, but is not limited to, death and bereavement—the focal concerns of the great majority of our titles. It therefore adds a welcome breadth as well as depth, tackling ruptures in attachment in a way that invites our personal engagement with them. As the authors argue, no single abstract model—and this book usefully presents several—can provide an adequate grounding for our work with people facing the challenge of change, unless it is supplemented by a genuine quest to interrogate the lessons of loss in our own lives. Only in doing so, and in developing our own personal philosophy or vision of loss and life, can we authentically accompany others undertaking a similar project. As helping professionals, we, no less than the clients we serve, need wise and compassionate companionship, and in these pages, van Wielink, Wilhelm, and van Geelen provide just that. It is a welcome thing to witness the publication of this work, offering as it does a sophisticated and practical guide to practitioners of many disciplines who accompany people on their quest to reconstruct life in the wake of loss.

Robert A. Neimeyer, PhD
Co-Editor, Routledge Series in Death, Dying, and Bereavement

ACKNOWLEDGMENTS

In 2016, the basis for what became this book was published in the Netherlands. It was the result of an intense and fruitful collaboration between the three of us. We are grateful for the support and encouragement of our Dutch publisher, Marc Appels.

Our spouses and families supported us during the writing process. Thank you so much Svetlana, Larissa, and Jan and our children Vika, Elise, Joy, Jasper, Eva, and Matthijs.

We cannot say enough about our gratitude to Professor Robert Neimeyer, who has conveyed such love in each communication and inspired us through his poetic delivery. He has been a tremendous secure base both in the writing of the book and in the process of translation and adaptation.

Professor George Kohlrieser tirelessly invites us to turn loss into inspiration. His deep knowledge and experience in working with grief have transformed countless organizations, their leaders, and coaches. He has been a great source of inspiration in working on this book.

Dr. Phyllis Kosminksy, Dr. Agnieszka Konopka, and Dr. An Hooghe devoted their precious time and energy to review the manuscript. Thank you for putting so much love into what you do and inviting us to go one step further.

Thank you to our publisher Anna Moore (Routledge) for all your positivity!

We are greatly indebted to all the shoulders in the world of grief and bereavement on which we stand. Nothing in this book would have been written were it not for the scholars and practitioners that were here before us.

We would specifically like to express our gratitude to our Dutch colleagues Riet Fiddelaers-Jaspers and Wibe Veenbaas for their daring leadership in helping us understand the hidden wisdom that lies in grief.

Finally, thank you to all our clients and everyone who has been in training with us: with and from you all, we have perhaps learned the most.

ILLUSTRATIONS AND TABLES

Illustrations

Tables

ABOUT THE AUTHORS

Jakob van Wielink: author, trainer, and counselor

Jakob van Wielink is the co-founder of 'De School voor Transitie' (The School for Transition), as well as an international educator, leadership coach, and grief counselor. He is also executive coach of the (Advanced) High Performance Leadership Programme at IMD Business School (Switzerland) led by professor George Kohlrieser and a faculty member of the Portland Institute for Loss and Transition (USA) led by Professor Robert Neimeyer. Jakob frequently publishes on the themes of the Transition Cycle and has contributed to numerous handbooks. Jakob is considered a pioneer regarding the theme of loss and grief in the workplace and its connection to leadership development.

He was co-author of *Going Berserk. Emotions as a Result of Loss and Change at Work* (2012, Kluwer), *Getting Started on Loss. Coaching During Changes at Work* (2015, Ten Have), *That's How Much I Loved You: Words for Personal Loss* (2016, Witsand Publishers), and *Grief Rules: Tools for Organisations Around Death and Terminal Illness* (2015, Witsand Publishers).

www.jakobvanwielink.com

Leo Wilhelm: author, coach, and grief counselor

Leo Wilhelm is a manager and an (executive) coach, specialized in transition. He has experience in business and with the Dutch government. Leo is a certified grief counselor, has years of experience in a hospice, and gives individual and group-oriented support during or after loss and transition. He is co-author of a large number of articles on loss and grief, has contributed to various books on this theme, and wrote *Grief Rules* in collaboration with Jakob van Wielink.

www.troostcoach.nl

Denise van Geelen-Merks: author, trainer and (organizational) psychologist

Denise van Geelen-Merks has worked on an interim basis in HR positions for various organizations for many years. This work has taught her how much influence earlier experiences with welcome, attachment, intimacy, goodbyes, grief, and meaning have on communication in the here and now. With these themes, she works with individuals, with (married) couples, and with teams. Denise is a certified counselor of family and organization constellations and guides retreats. With Jakob van Wielink, she wrote *That's How Much I Loved You: Words for Personal Loss*.

www.denisevangeelen.nl

INTRODUCTION

This book is about counseling those dealing with loss. Everyone suffers losses throughout life. That is inevitable. On the one hand, it can be painful or sad; on the other hand, it can be a relief, creating space. In each case, loss brings about change, be it large or small. At the same time, change itself also brings about loss. After loss, there is always something that is different from how it was before. Each loss has an impact and needs an answer. The way in which someone finds that answer is very personal. This depends on the circumstances and on how great the impact of the loss is, but it also depends on the way in which a person has learned to deal with loss and on the solace and sustenance that person can find. Sometimes it is impossible to find an answer that fits. Sometimes someone does not realize that something has changed, that an answer is needed, or does not even realize that a loss has been suffered. All kinds of symptoms can then appear and can lead to depression or burnout (Leader, 2008). And it goes beyond that. If no appropriate response to loss is found, personal growth stagnates. For example, these people then often experience conflicts, tension, a lack of inner strength, loss of focus in their work, and so on. These are questions clients ask when they go to see a counselor—questions that conceal underlying loss. It is a loss that requires an appropriate response, so that room is made for grieving and finding meaning.

Change causes loss and loss always leads to change. We[1] call this *transition*: *personal transition* when it leads to inner growth and *professional transition* when it leads to the growth of professionals in their trade or changes in organizations. How people deal with loss and transition is largely dependent on the patterns they developed during childhood. Early in life you learn, while in contact with others, how to best react to others and to experiences. You develop patterns. These patterns, called *attachment patterns*, can be functional. They can help us. But they can also fail, be ineffective, or even hinder us.

When people seek the help of a counselor because they are no longer able to find their own way in life, it is important to understand how their attachment style influences their ability to cope with loss. We therefore reflect on how people connect, on bonding, and on attachment at length. We also highlight how these themes relate to separation, grieving, and finding meaning, modeled schematically on the Transition Cycle (see Figure 0.1).

This cycle is based primarily on the attachment theory of British psychiatrist John Bowlby (1988a, 1988b, 1988c), and it forms the framework for this book. The chapters are built up along the themes of the cycle. We discuss loss, what it is, how to recognize it, and what a counselor needs to be able to guide one through it. You will gain knowledge and learn about the historical development of guiding loss and grief. We also look at various models, and you will find many exercises in this book. These are exercises you can do with your client, but also on your own for personal growth, or during peer-to-peer learning. Each time we connect with another person, especially when a counselor and a client connect, both are touched by the interaction.

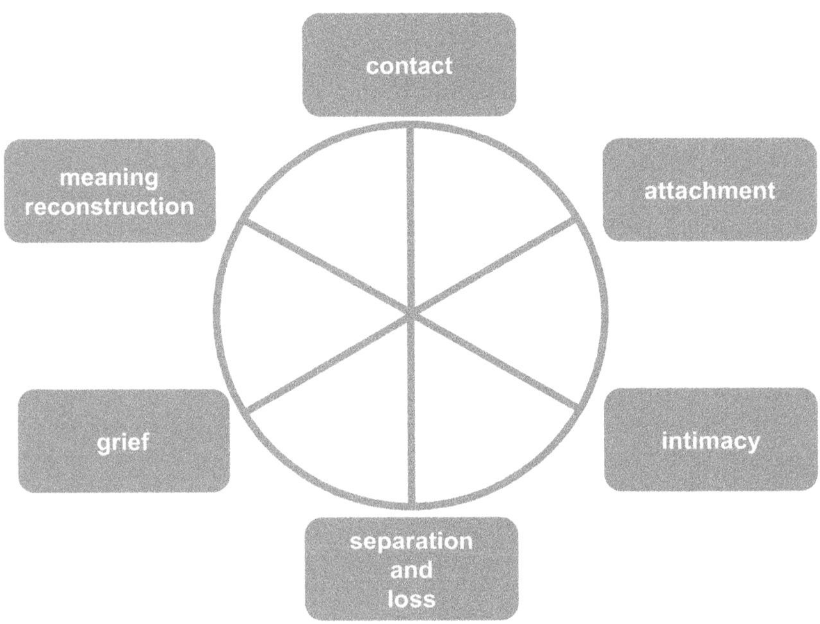

Figure 0.1 The Transition Cycle

We encourage you to examine your own themes by doing the exercises and answering the questions throughout this book.

When approaching grief counseling, we take a broad research area into consideration. We explore the following three contexts:

- The personal and professional history of the client: what does his or her career look like? Which steps did he or she take or not take? Which opportunities did he or she not see? And which line in his or her personal circumstances and events affected his or her career path? Which losses occurred in his past and in the history of the client's parents and ancestors? What are the client's dreams and ambitions? How were losses handled earlier in his or her life?
- The client's present private life: family, partner (or lack thereof), family, friends, children, social life.
- The client's occupation: as source of income, but also as carrier of meaning, the organization as element of bonding, (organization) culture, values, interests, structure, self-esteem, and so forth.

The book continually links theory, reflection, and practice. Each chapter is built in the same way:

- *Case studies*: each chapter starts with an example drawn from life. These case studies are meant to illustrate the subject at hand. They form a common thread throughout the chapter.
- *Dialogue*: by describing actual counseling sessions in the case studies, not only are background and depth added, but the dialogue also gives insight into the design of the personal encounter that could be termed counseling.
- *Knowledge*: each theme is theoretically introduced, readable, and accessible and at the same time scientifically substantiated: what are we saying, exactly, when we talk about loss and grief? Which theory is well known, and which is (still) unknown? What are the various approaches used? How has thinking about and working with loss and grief developed during the course of history?
- *Questions for self-reflection*: to work with clients effectively around the theme loss is only possible if the counselor recognizes his or her own personal history of loss. If the counselor does not consider his or her own loss, it will lead to (unhealthy and obstructive) forms of projection, transference, and countertransference.
- *Skills*: at the end of each chapter, you will find instructions and exercises for daily use. Learning how to counsel someone with loss consists of knowledge, insight, personal experience, experimenting through

exercises, and reflecting with colleagues. On the one hand, the exercises are meant to be used when working with clients around the chosen theme. On the other hand, they are meant for the personal growth, learning, and experience of the counselor him- or herself; it is assumed that the reader has a general knowledge of teaching on professional counseling.

Glossary

In this book you may come across concepts that are new to you or that have a slightly different meaning in this context than in daily interaction or everyday speech. In the rest of this introduction, we explain these concepts.

- *Attention*

  Attention is your brain's selective filter, which enables you to determine which sensory signals are or are not important. You can actively apply the filter by consciously focusing your attention on something. As a result of this, unattended signals are irrevocably ignored. Although your senses register all signals in your environment, signals that do not match your current selection criteria will be actively suppressed. You therefore do not 'see' with your eyes, but with your brain (Van der Stigchel, 2019).

  Attention also means to observe 'what is' instead of what you would like there to be, or what you think there should be. Attention is also about the willingness to postpone judgment about that which presents itself.

  Paying attention is an important part of professional counseling. When attention is combined with presence, the basic conditions are met for a successful encounter. As a counselor, you will need to focus your attention on the client, their story, and their non-verbal signals. At the same time, you will need to keep an eye on your own reactions during the session. 'It takes two to tango': without a truly present counselor, who is conscious of their own sensitivity and reticence, guiding loss is difficult, maybe even impossible.

- *Being present*

  During counseling, we are present when we are fully engaged with our client, yet still in contact with ourselves. Being present means listening, empty-handed with an open heart, without the intention to fix, advise, or help (Baart, 2004).

- *Coping/coping mechanism*

  Coping is the way in which people have learned to deal with adversity.

- *Distance and proximity*

  The same applies here as to 'being touched' (see below). The theme of distance and proximity can be expressed on a physical and emotional level. This is also a relational theme, about the needs, desires, and (in) abilities of the counselor and the client—whether they can and want to stay true to themselves and to the other person.

- *Encounter*

  An encounter begins with the willingness, need, and ability to show your true character, as well as seeing and hearing (observing) the true character of the other person. It is up to the counselor to create the context in which space is created to have this encounter. The counselor who has the ability to open up and show his or her true character leads by example and helps the client to open up in the encounter.

- *Endure (enduring)*

  Both counselor and client will, when working with loss, need a certain type of endurance. You will need to be able to stay with the feeling when you experience unpleasant events or when they come up during coaching. Both will also have to accept that the grieving process has its own pace and dynamics. The pace is determined by the client. This pace needs to be maintained, or tolerated, which can cause inconvenience both for the client and the counselor. This is called enduring loss.

- *Movement/motion/dynamics*

  When we use the term *movement* in this book, we refer, on the one hand, to the physical motion or motor movement—the search for proximity with the other, coming closer—or just the opposite—avoiding closeness and intimacy or keeping a distance. On the other hand, besides this tangible and visible movement or motion of the body, there is the emotional inner movement or motion. This dynamic of wanting to be close or wanting to distance oneself can be tangible, even when one does not actually make the physical movement. It is important to be conscious of this inner dynamic as it forms an effective tool. Once one is able to recognize the underlying need that causes this inner dynamic, the movement can actually be made physically. This increases the chance of the need being fulfilled.

- *Reaching (out)*

  In this book, this term is used to describe the gesture a child makes towards a parent or caregiver when it seeks consolation or sustenance.

Literally, reaching out is the movement whereby the arms are extended to the other person as a signal for the need to be held. Metaphorically, every signal a child gives with which it tries to attract the attention of an attachment figure is a form of reaching out. Even if there are no visible signals, the child may still be reaching out to fulfill its needs. When adults try and reach out to people around them, either with trust for support or the experience of hindrance, both are colored by their early experiences as a child.

- *Resonance/resonate*

  Literal meaning: vibration/vibrate. If, during a conversation or an encounter a deep subconscious knowledge can be accessed, we call this resonance. Emotions may rise to the surface including, for example, restlessness or a sudden surge of excitement, as if something has awakened inside of someone.

- *(Coaching or counseling) space*

  The literal and figurative space in which the counseling or coaching takes place is what we like to call the transitional space. It includes the physical space and the energetic space. The physical space refers to the way it is decorated, or to the outside space in nature. The energetic space emerges in the presence of, for instance, music, poetry, light, symbols, and creative work methods.

- *Story/stories/narrativity*

  The term narrativity refers to storytelling (from Latin: narrare = telling stories). People are narrative, storytelling beings. They also construct meaning in the stories they tell about themselves to others.

  We use these words when referring to the life story of the client. A story is not a dry, factual, historical list of life events. It is a living, ever-evolving story that is only given content and meaning by being told and heard. By sharing the story with someone else, the story is metaphorically given a voice. By actually telling the story, the inner processes of the client are put to work. This is more effective than thinking about or only remembering the story. By giving the story a real voice, there is a better chance that emotions are expressed more clearly. It gives the client a better chance to become aware of his own emotions.

  'Stories' can be used to invite the storyteller to tell, share, and illustrate with a view to making their inner processes audible and visible. Stories also have the effect of retrieval of forgotten pieces, demanding satisfaction, getting the whole story from someone. Storytelling also effectuates retrieving an event in words. It helps a client to come to terms with an experience: to recover, to regain strength, to rest. By applying it in this way, the concept of storytelling can be very helpful to guide others, to recover and rework the sense of it all.

- *System/systemic*

The term *system* in this book indicates the sum of all connections and relationships within groups as found in families and other team constructions or working relationships. In each group, there is always a certain dynamic, of reciprocal influence. On a conscious and unconscious level, patterns, roles, and relationships exist and develop. These may or may not help achieve the 'higher purpose' of the group.

- *Touching/being touched/touchiness*

When we use the terms *touching* and *being touched* in this book, we refer to the physical touch, a hand on the shoulder, an encouraging hug, as well as being touched on an emotional level, for instance, visibly and fully experiencing the emotions of both the client and the counselor. Both types of touching have their own worth and their own healing effect; both also require precise alignment of personal needs and/with the client's needs. The counselor is further required to be aware of their own as well as the client's boundaries: on physical, ethical, and emotional levels.

Being a secure base counselor is all about being able to stay present and be vulnerable with the client in the face of loss.

> *The expectation that we can be immersed in suffering and loss daily and not be touched by it is as unrealistic as expecting to be able to walk through water without getting wet. This sort of denial is no small matter. The way we deal with loss shapes our capacity to be present to life more than anything else. The way we protect ourselves from loss may be the way in which we distance ourselves from life.*
>
> (Remen, 2006, p. 52)

- *Transaction/transactional*

We use the term *transaction* in the same way as used in Transactional Analysis (TA) (Berne, 2016; Koopmans, 2014). It describes the communication between two individuals.

- *Transference, countertransference and projection*

When someone's reaction to a situation in the present is based on feelings, thoughts, and convictions that are connected to situations and people in the past, it is referred to as transference. In the present, this reaction of transference is inappropriate, whereas once, in an earlier context, it was not. Subconsciously the person is still trying to fix or heal the relationship or situation from the past in the present. It is often difficult for the person on the receiving end of the transference to see it as such. Because it is difficult to comprehend, it results in countertransference. Both terms refer to reactions based on behavioral patterns from the past. Both occur regularly during counseling. For example, a client may have a tendency to present helpless behavior because it worked well when used with his parents in the past. This client implicitly invites the counselor to step into of the role of parent. If the counselor is familiar with this role from his or her own past, he or she will easily and unwittingly accept this invitation. Counselor and client may then find themselves in a pattern causing an ineffective process that only confirms old assumptions and patterns. (Counter)transference is in itself a deeply empathic dynamic, since old patterns are activated by being touched upon in the present.

> *Countertransference is a concept that actually beckons helpers to look at their humanness in the face of serious illness, dying, death, and bereavement rather than avoiding it. . . . Countertransference is now regarded as a natural, appropriate, and inevitable emotional response. . . . Armed with education, skills, and techniques, we must be careful not to stay just in our heads. Rather, we must open our hearts to the suffering of others.*
>
> (Katz & Johnson, 2016, pp. 3, 16)

Projection is a transference phenomenon. It occurs when someone unconsciously projects his own feelings or thoughts onto the other person. At that moment, he or she is only able to observe the other person from this perspective. The other person becomes, as it were, a projection screen and can no longer be seen as an individual with his or her own intentions.

- *Transition*

  Transition is the psychological process that people experience when they are faced with profound changes (and thus with loss) at or outside of work (Bridges, 2017). For organizations, change is often complicated, but not as profound as the transitions that employees go through as a result of these changes or reorganizations.

Note

1. In this book, we, the authors, sometimes use first-person plural pronouns to indicate the professional group of counselors, including you as a reader and a counselor.

1

EXPLORING LOSS

You cannot prevent the birds of sorrow from flying overhead,
But you can prevent them from making nests in your hair.

(Chinese proverb)

A Case Study

Emily seems exhausted as she enters the counselor's practice. It seems that everything is weighing her down. A moment later she confirms this. Sometimes it takes so much effort to get out of bed that she calls in sick. The company doctor advised her to seek help. And that's why she made this appointment. A lot has happened in the past six months. The company downsized and the department she had worked in for eight years had been closed in the reorganization. She was transferred to another department. Her colleagues were transferred to other positions in the organization. She has difficulty finding her place in the new team. She misses her old colleagues and the way they divided the work and interacted with each other. When asked how she said goodbye to her old team, she indicated that there was actually no goodbye. It became increasingly empty in the department because there was less and less work and her colleagues were transferred to a new department, one after the other. As a result, she was almost relieved when she heard that she had been given a different function. She left as quickly as she could.

Where do you know this 'leaving, without looking back' from? Have you ever experienced this before in your life? She is visibly startled by this question and is silent for a while. And then she starts to tell her story. She was just a little girl back then. About seven years old. She formed a family with her mother, her father, and two boys from her father's earlier relationship. One day she came home from school to find her mother crying on the sofa. Things had disappeared from the living room and the coat rack was half empty. Her father had left with his two sons. Shortly after, the house was sold and she moved with her mother into a small apartment. She had to go to another school. She only saw her father and her half-brothers once in a while, until they drifted apart completely. When she moved to her own apartment at seventeen, she resolutely decided to focus solely on her future. She banned her father and her half-brothers from her mind and saw her mother only occasionally.

Recognizing, Acknowledging, Exploring, and Enduring Loss

Clients like Emily have a problem, a question, something they encounter in daily life that makes them see a counselor. This is the starting point. Using the starting point as a reference, the counselor examines underlying themes or questions. These are as relevant as the initial question, often unbeknownst to the client. Together they explore. This work can be compared with archaeology or treasure hunting.

> *In almost all types of attachment interventions, emotional recovery from past experiences of loss is going to be the key. Individuals need to work through grief and loss issues, which implies some form of education as to the origin of their feeling. In this archaeological dig for origins, the identification and validation of feelings is important. People need help to understand the cause of their attachment patterns . . ., whatever these might have been, these experiences need to be grieved, otherwise there will be no resolution.*
>
> (Kets de Vries, 2016, pp. 44–45)

Important events and experiences, which have either hindered or helped the client, are to be uncovered in their past and impact their consciousness and most certainly their subconsciousness in the present. These experiences, convictions, and qualities may be 'dug up' and brought to light.

Tip: When guiding someone with loss, we operate on the experience that every question, every problem, and every complaint a client presents is at base always about loss. This is true even if the client is not yet aware of the loss, just as Emily did not connect her past experiences with her father leaving to her present fatigue due to the company reorganizing. Each change the client desires, a change for which the client seeks counseling, is in fact a moving away from something or somewhere, not wanting something anymore, or a moving towards something or somewhere, wanting something else. Both movements are about separating from an old situation. The client comes to us for support and counseling during this process, saying 'I can't do it alone.' As counselors, we work on the assumption that, with every issue at hand, underlying unconfronted loss, unexpressed farewells, and unfinished business is always resonating, regardless of the question or the apparent reason.

During the client and counselor's exploration of the themes of the loss the client has undergone, they may work through the following steps (Fiddelaers-Jaspers, 2010):

- Recognizing the loss
  During the intake, the client tells you his or her story and may have a question. This story evolves in every subsequent meeting, which helps the question to unfold more clearly. As a counselor you always need to listen with healthy curiosity to the client's developing story and on each occasion, make a new assessment of the question. Time and again you invite the client to continue searching within the story. Together you go looking for new starting points, for decisive moments in life. Together you look for choices and decisions that were made, conscious and unconscious, that might have been necessary or even inevitable at that time, but are perhaps no longer helpful in the present. You search for moments of deliberate or subconscious separation in which your client suffered loss.
  A distinction can be made between two types of loss:
  - *Locatable loss:*
    - These losses are easy to recognize. They occurred at a specific point in time and can be connected with or localized in a moment. Examples of such events are death, divorce, having to move, and the like. A precise connection with a date or a period in time can be made. In Emily's case, the moment her father moved out is a locatable loss.
  - *Ambiguous loss:*
    - It is difficult to determine the point in time or the period of ambiguous loss. This refers to less tangible issues such as an

unfulfilled desire to have children, a poor relationship with (one of the) parents, lost hope, lost dreams, illness, and so forth.

In counseling, making this distinction is of great value. For clients with ambiguous loss, actual loss is harder to name, recognize, and acknowledge.

It is also important to define the difference between primary and secondary losses:

- *Primary losses:*
  - These are the losses that are immediately noticeable, the losses that are in clear view or 'in the foreground.' These losses can be the direct inducement of grief. Emily's father leaving was such a primary loss.
- *Secondary losses:*
  - These losses seem to develop in the background as a result of primary loss. Secondary losses are a direct result of primary losses, although not immediately visible. Often, because of this, they aggravate or weigh down the grief. The loss of Emily's half-brothers through her father's leaving could be viewed as a secondary loss, although it also counts very much as a primary loss.

We can divide these types of losses into quadrants (see Table 1.1). These can be useful and help your client gain an overview of and insight into the losses in his or her life.

- Acknowledging loss

During their search together, the client learns to recognize his losses. Once he recognizes them, he will be able to acknowledge them. He can

Table 1.1 A Four-Quadrant Model of the Categories of Loss

	Primary loss	**Secondary loss**
Locatable loss	The parents get divorced when the child is still young.	Loss of sense of security, strained bonds due to the divorce, loss of friends and family who chose or had to choose between the two parties.
Ambiguous loss	Marital infidelity of a parent, which is eventually discovered, causing the marriage to later end in divorce.	Loss of confidence and trust, loss of coziness and ambience at home during the period of conflict leading up to the divorce.

then acknowledge how painful it was, the impact it has or had, and what is missing as a result. In short, acknowledgement is about more than just establishing the reality of loss. Acknowledgement is accepting how the loss changes the course of one's life. Once we have started to pinpoint the losses in the ever-evolving story of the client, part of our role as a counselor is to use our expertise and experience to confirm that the client has indeed suffered loss. You could also say that, as a facilitator, you help interpret and in a way subtitle certain events and experiences. By accepting that there was loss, the client is inevitably invited to assimilate the loss and to feel the grief that goes with it.

- Exploring loss
  When you base your work as a counselor on the life story of the client, by asking questions, doing exercises, or giving assignments, you are together exploring the client's losses. Naturally, the actual circumstances surrounding the loss play a major role. However, the feelings, the (subjective) experience, and the meaning of the loss play the greatest role.

While helping your client to recognize, acknowledge, and explore loss, you will regularly experience that you are touched by his or her story. Perhaps you are shocked by what the other person has experienced, or a memory of a personal experience rises to the surface. You may become annoyed, or feel the need to solve the problem for the other person. Whatever happens to you when in contact with your client, it is important to be aware that it is there. You can then learn to discover when your personal experiences get in the way and cause transference or possibly countertransference. Through training, supervision, and peer-to-peer learning, you will gain more insight into your reactions when your own experiences and sensitivity get in the way. In this way, you learn to allow your experiences to be present alongside those of the client so that you can remain close to him or her and stay present while he or she is working on the loss at his or her own pace and in his or her own way. You offer guidance, exercises and ask questions. And you endure. You endure that you yourself are touched by the intense emotions of the client, that sometimes you have to slow down and that sometimes you have to take one step forward and two steps back. Adapting to this unruly reality, which can cause discomfort for the client as well as for the counselor, is called enduring during loss.

- To endure during loss.
  Loss can have a major impact on the daily life and functioning of the client. He or she has to endure the reality that the disruptive effect the loss has on his or her life can barely be influenced by any conscious choice.

For the counselor, it is important to continuously improve the ability to experience the personal sensitivity, the ability and inability to be present in the background during stories of loss.

The case study, the dialogues, the theory, and the exercises in this book will teach you to recognize the losses your clients have suffered. The exercises, which allow you to explore loss in alternating roles of counselor and client, help you to recognize the themes and explore them further. By reflecting on your feelings and behavior during the exercises, you also experience what grief and loss has brought about in your life and what is touched within you. You may also experience what is meant by the term *enduring*.

Grief

Not only is it important to make a distinction between locatable and ambiguous loss, we also need to discern between loss on the one hand and grief on the other.

> **Definition:** Loss is about permanently missing something or someone, saying goodbye, breaking the connection and the bond with someone or something with which a meaningful relationship had been maintained.

> **Definition:** Grief is about dealing with a sum total of feelings, thoughts, physical sensations and behavior that can be experienced when one separates from something or someone they had a meaningful relationship with, whether voluntarily or forced.

We say 'can be experienced' intentionally. The way in which we grieve is the result of the way in which we choose to deal with the reality of loss. At the same time, grief is an autonomous process. This means that grief can appear all of a sudden, uninvited, as an unwanted intrusion. Grieving can also be done consciously, when the client is aware of the loss and its effect on his or her life. Grief may also come out later, sometimes much later than the moment in which the actual loss occurred. The function of grief is to be able to once again live the ongoing life to its fullest, to be able to reconnect in such a way that the impact of the loss no longer disrupts daily activities. This does not mean that the effects of the loss will no longer be noticeable. Grief has no final station. All feelings, emotions, and sensations, like sadness, anger, and fear, however unpleasant and disrupting for everyday life as the may be, also function as signals of a body that physically, emotionally, consciously, and spiritually has to heal after loss. We have to listen to these signals in order to allow ourselves to integrate the loss in our lives.

There Is No Recipe for 'The Correct Way to Grieve'

Perhaps the most difficult thing in conversations with clients about loss is that the problem cannot just be 'solved.' You cannot simply make the pain of loss go away. In fact, you are left empty-handed. The old situation cannot be restored, the loss is irreversible. It has created a separation between the before and the after. The client looks for a way to deal with this loss. To rediscover himself in the new situation. For both the client and the counselor, it often comes down to enduring when working with loss. Perseverance is needed when one experiences difficult times. On the one hand, grief counseling is about being able to endure the duration and the intensity of the pain, which comes to the surface when the loss is acknowledged. This requires an attitude and state of mindful presence, focused on 'being,' rather than 'doing' (Segal et. al., 2002; Kabat-Zinn, 2003). On the other hand, it means that we should accept that the grieving process follows its own pace and dynamics and that we have no control over its course. The client determines which themes are addressed. It may sometimes be difficult for counselors who are focused on results to follow the pace of the client.

The client also determines the intensity of the process. Perhaps you are inclined to encourage emotions as a counselor and you feel comfortable with a lot of visible grief and tears. Or maybe you prefer it a little quieter and you tend to soften somewhat when the emotions rise. In both cases, it is difficult if your client expresses grief in ways different from yours. That this process can cause discomfort to the client as well as the counselor is part of enduring a loss. It is not only about the discomfort caused by one's own loss, but also the discomfort that the other's loss evokes in you.

The confrontation with loss and the impact of an irrevocable separation often result in a large amount of intense emotional reactions. Both counselor and client are thus forced to face the facts: life is fragile and perhaps not as moldable as one might hope. Loss confronts people with their evanescence and their mortality. Counselors cannot evade these things. The loss and grief of the client will confront us with the manner in which we deal with our own grief. For this reason, it is so essential for the counselor to have explored his or her own experiences with this theme.

Typical pitfalls for counseling people with loss:

- Advising/leading/solving: You should. . . . That will most certainly make you feel better.
- Compare: Do you know who is really having a tough time?

- Trying to change the perspective: That makes you thankful you still have children, does it not?
- Clichés: After rain comes. . . . There is light at the end of. . . .
- Divert attention: Shall we go and do something else?
- Ignore: It is a lovely day, is it not?
- Leading questions: Have you been feeling better lately?
- Not talking about it/silence.

With the aforementioned pitfalls, the other person seems to be able to solve the problem. And yet these interventions do not seem to work. This is because they do not validate the unique experience and pain in one's grief and are based on misunderstandings and myths about grief.

> *Finally, we maintain that mistaken assumptions held about the process of coping with loss fail to acknowledge the variability that exists in response to loss, and may lead others to respond to those who have endured loss in ways that are unhelpful.*
>
> (Wortman & Silver, 1989, p. 349)

These mistaken assumptions can hide the grief from view as so-called 'veils of grief' (Van den Bout, 1997).

Although it seems very apparent when someone is doing it 'wrong,' it is surprisingly difficult to point out when someone is actually doing it 'right.' As a counselor, you may assume that you are doing it 'right' when you are aware of the pitfalls mentioned above and under which circumstances you are inclined to step into any such pitfall. It is important to explore this as these well-meant and seemingly natural reactions often find their origin in our own awkwardness with loss and grief, with the less moldable or inalterable sides of life. At times it is almost impossible to endure your client's loss:

> **Tip:** There is no 'right' way to grieve. All kinds of emotions can rise to the surface, not just sadness, but also anger, relief, and many other kinds of emotion that do not seem to be linked to loss. And not everyone expresses emotions in a set way or at a set moment.

- Grief is much more than just (expressing) emotion, and certainly much more than crying. It is a physical, cognitive, and spiritual process as well.
- Grief is an arbitrary and unpredictable process, during which feelings, thoughts, and physical experiences, past, present, and future, are intertwined.
- The nature and the meaning of the relationship that is connected with the loss is unique. This means that the grief is different for each person. The one who suffers the loss, learns the meaning of what is lost.

- Time will 'do' nothing, if you do not 'do' something yourself. You need to face your grief. The loss will always be present. Even many years and decades later, grief reactions may surface, when least expected.
- There is no measure for grief, neither by time nor intensity.
- Even though there are differences between men and women in the way they deal with grief, there is too great a risk of generalization. 'The' way in which women grieve is not better or worse than 'the' way in which men give shape and form to their grief.

These aspects of grief are reflected in the way the counselor approaches his client. More later. For now, the aforementioned elements can be summed up to describe the starting points for counselors as follows:

> **Tip:** Loss and grief are a part of life. Everyone encounters loss and grief. There are many forms of loss. Loss can occur at any point in time.

- The term *processing grief* can give the impression that on a given day, a person is done with feeling their grief. That then turns out to be an illusion. One can never 'get over' grief. It invites you to integrate the consequences of the loss into your life. The goal of counseling on themes around loss is to eventually enable the client to deal with the situation. 'Processing' makes it sound as though grief is something you can leave behind, or something that will be over somewhere in the future. The new vision of loss and grief suggests that loss remains with people for the duration of their life. They will be able to grieve that loss again from time to time, without the loss and grief defining the rest of their life.
- A client has sufficient resilience: the ability to recover or 'bounce back' after severe adversity, disappointments, and loss.

These general principles are applied as foundation, as pillars to support the approach of this book (see Figure 1.1). At each moment, the counselor can refer back to these principles and convey them to his or her clients to console and sustain them.

A Historical Sketch of the Views on Finiteness

In order to base our work on the new view of grief, we need to learn how views on grief and loss have changed across time. Loss is, of course, as old as life. The oldest known stories, such as the handed-down myths, sagas, religious writings, and philosophical dissertations speak of loss. And yet science, in particular sociology and psychology, has only started to study how people deal with loss in the last hundred years. Psychology is a relatively new

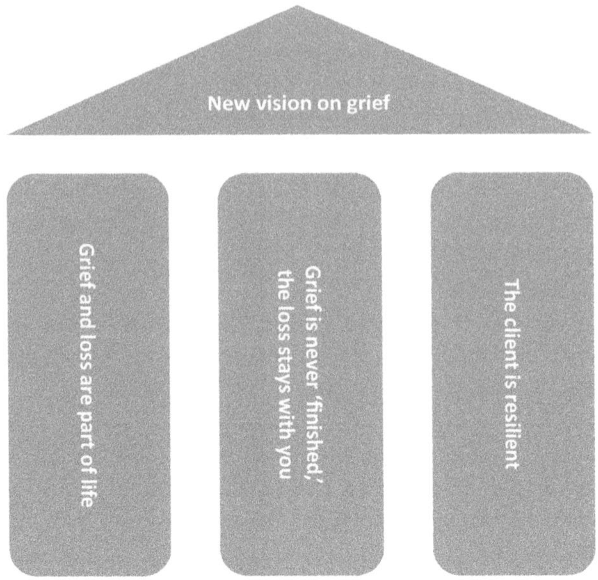

Figure 1.1 Principles of Grief

science. The knowledge has developed rapidly since then and there are many new insights as to how people relate to loss and what could be helpful. In this section, we briefly outline the history of the different views on 'dealing with loss and grief' that have developed over time.

Antiquity and the Classics—Philosophy and Religion

Sociologists distinguish between different cultures and civilizations based on rituals for the loss of loved ones. Well-known examples are the Egyptian pyramids, in which pharaohs were mummified and buried with their riches and possessions, such as boats and hunting tools, to cross over to the afterlife. In Western Europe, the oldest burial monuments, called *dolmens* (built with large stones), date from around 5000 BC. We can deduce from such structures and rituals that, through the ages, human beings have dealt with loss in a conscious and respectful manner.

Around the beginning of our era, the classic Greek and Roman philosophers developed different views on how to deal with evanescence (Dohmen, 2002). According to Epicurus (341 BC–270 BC) life is about happiness in the form of peace of mind and poise. Part of that poise is the realization 'death does not concern us; as long as we are here, death is not, and when there is death, we are no longer here.'[1] Epicureanism, named after him, was the fourth major movement in classic Greece, alongside Plato's Academy,

Aristotle's Lyceum, and the Stoic approach. Plato (approx. 427 BC–347 BC) and Aristotle (384 BC–322 BC) were advocates of so-called dualism, a separation between the physical body and the non-physical soul. Death would separate body and soul from each other, whereby the soul would continue to exist.

The Roman philosopher Seneca (approx. 4 BC–65 AD), who was a Stoic, represented a rational, that is, a reason-based, association with death as part of the cosmos. Because the cosmos in Stoic philosophy was by definition classified as good, reason would also help us to see death as being meaningful. Epictetus (50 AD–approx. 130 AD), another Stoic from ancient Rome, was one of the first to distinguish between death being an event beyond our control, and that which we can control: our reaction to it. 'You die anyway; therefore, focus on what is in your power: that you die in a good way.'[2]

Plutarch's (approx. 46 AD–approx. 120 AD) comforting thought is that

> *Human nature flees from grief. But just as our child was the sweetest and most beautiful in the world, to look at and to hear, so sweet and beautiful should the thought of her be that remains with us. That thought will give us more joy, yes, many times more joy than sorrow.*[3]

The Greek physician and philosopher Claudius Galen (129 AD–216 AD) lost many of his slaves to death during an epidemic and in the great fire of 191 in Rome his practice and library fell prey to the flames. He writes that it was bearable because he looked at what he still had.[4] He does indicate that there are limits to what a person can bear: seeing a good friend tortured or being exiled from your own country would be unbearable events for him (Toebosch, 2012).

From a religious perspective, events of loss are part of the sacred moments in life: the transition rites, such as being born, growing up, and getting married. The social support of a religious community and the support of a religious belief can be helpful when having to deal with loss and grief. People can draw strength from their beliefs, whereby they experience support from a higher power in the event of loss and adversity. The religious community as a group can also be encouraging during the period of grief, whereby rituals can provide support in a time when there is loss of the sense of security. For centuries, religions and religious communities have been supportive of loss for many, due to their deep-rooted role in society.

Religion and the faith community continue to fulfill this role for many people. A loss, however, can also be a shock to otherwise secure beliefs. Faith or trust in a loving, good, or almighty God can come under pressure if the loss is perceived as senseless. The rules of the faith community can also be perceived as restricting, when regulations or convictions are imposed that do not seem to do justice to the personal experience of the person suffering the loss. Faith no longer guarantees peace of mind to everyone in times of grief. When this occurs, loss of faith or the separation from a faith community may cause additional (secondary) loss.

For many people in the Western world, faith no longer plays a significant role. There is no longer a religious tradition or community to fall back on. In part, psychology has become a science to find new answers to the questions of how people cope with loss and adversity. It seems that the religious approach and psychological counseling, for the most part, strive towards the same goal (De Roos & van Wielink, 2015).

Early Years of Psychology—About Letting Go

Modern psychology as a discipline, originated in the beginning of the twentieth century. One of the pioneers was the Viennese psychiatrist Sigmund Freud. He is best known as the founder of psychoanalysis. His theory is based on the functioning of the subconscious, the 'id,' that is driven by basic instinctual drives ('energies'). The 'ego' tries to contain the impulsivity, the goal being eventually to be able to meet the ideal image of the 'superego' (norms and values, conscience). Freud developed a theory on grief that has had great influence on developments in psychology. He saw similar reactions in grief and melancholy (depression), which led him to establish a relationship between the two in his essay 'Trauer und Melancholie' ('Grief and Melancholia'; 1917). Freud viewed depression as an expression of grief over a lost, intangible 'object.' He defined it as the loss of a dream or illusion, rather than the loss of a person. Because the lost object is not tangible, this loss is less visible for the client and the environment, which leads to depression. Freud stated that grief is intended to break the emotional bond with the lost loved-one or object: 'to detach from the lost object of love.' In this way, the limited love energy that people have ('libido') is brought back to the person who is grieving. This should allow the person to enter into new relationships once again.

Freud viewed the recovery of the love energy as hard work. He therefore introduced the term 'grief work' and stated that all memories of the lost loved one or object had to be closely scrutinized. This 'grief work' could be compared with spring cleaning, where all the memories—as if they were photos—are dusted off to be viewed for the last time, after which they should be stored permanently. Once the job was done, the client was ready to close the closet of memories indefinitely and continue with his own life.

Freud's student, Helene Deutsch, continued in his footsteps. She published an essay (Deutsch, 1937) on four clients in which she states that the absence of symptoms of grief was the cause of their illness. Deutsch stated that the symptoms in question, although they were different for each client, could not be otherwise explained than being a result of unfinished grief work. The symptoms, in line with Freud's work, originated from the subconscious and were caused by the suppression of grief. The fact that the clients were not aware of suppressed grief was explained by Deutsch as stemming from denial of the loss. This line of thinking was further elaborated on by Erich Lindemann, who was the first to conduct large-scale research (Lindemann, 1944) on grief after a major fire in a Boston nightclub. Not only did he confirm the image of the absence of grief reactions, he also identified postponing grief or interrupting grief reactions as problematic. Lindemann assumed that the absence of symptoms in people who had suffered loss indicated problems. This formed a variant of the presence of symptoms in people who were not clear on whether the symptoms were caused by a loss. The absence of symptoms indicated an unhealthy denial, which would inevitably cause problems later. As a result, healthy behavior after a loss was deemed questionable. This has been proven incorrect by the current theory, that healthy behavior after loss stems from the natural resilience of people. Chronic grief, the other extreme as opposed to absent grief, was first put forward by Christian Anderson (1949). He diagnosed this phenomenon, in which the grief symptoms persisted for so long that there seemed no sign of recovery.

After the Second World War—The Origins of the Attachment Theory

John Bowlby (1988a, 1988b, 1988c) is the founder of attachment theory. He first studied adolescent juvenile delinquents shortly after the Second World War in England. He concluded that children who had been separated from their mothers during the bombing of London and brought to safety in the surrounding countryside without their parents at a later age became delinquents. He also studied how children reacted to being separated from their parents by a hospital visit. This study gave more insight into patterns of bonding, attachment, and separation (anxiety). Bowlby connected loss with separation from an attachment figure. Grief as a reaction to loss is normal. The person has to adjust to the separation from the attachment figure. Although he also stated that grief often comes in waves, he and Colin Murray Parkes (1970) defined four phases of grief that occur one after the other, but may also overlap:

1. Numbness and bewilderment: these reactions predominate when being confronted by the loss.
2. Intense desire and searching for the person or object that has been lost: after the initial reaction, a period of painful yearning occurs with

conscious or unconscious searching. Most often the person regularly experiences that he meets the other person in the street or sees him in a crowd.

3. Disorganization and despair: with the realization that the loss is definite, people fall prey to despair, thereby being unable to keep his daily life organized.
4. Reorganization: eventually a new chapter begins in which people get their life back together and are then able to continue with their lives.

Lessons for the Living—The Stages of Grief

Elisabeth Kübler-Ross (2014; Kübler-Ross & Kessler, 2014) started her pioneering research in the 1960s on cancer patients who had been told that they would not have much longer to live. She interviewed them about their lives and invited the patients to talk about their upcoming death. She found that many health professionals preferred to avoid discussing death, as they believed dying people should not be confronted with their approaching end. However, participants were happy to talk about their lives and were open about their feelings regarding their imminent death. Kübler-Ross became an authority in the field of research on death and dying. She also became one of the founders of hospices for terminally ill patients. She distinguished five stages that people go through who were told that they had a terminal illness. In her own model, which she later also used as a grief model, she described how people react to their approaching death. She represented the emotional course of grief by a smoothly flowing curved line through the phases. She based this classification on the stages of Bowlby/Parkes:

1. Denial: initially there is denial. This is how people protect themselves against the terrible news.
2. Anger: when it sinks in that the loss has taken place, someone will first display anger as protective mechanism. Certainly, when the death is intentional, rightly or wrongly, anger can be a strong motive for not grieving.
3. Bargaining: when anger subsides and the inevitable is acknowledged and allowed into the conscious mind, someone may go on to bargaining with providence or fate, in an effort to change the outcome. Examples of this are to do penance by changing one's own behavior or to want to take the place of the one they lost, to try to undo the loss. In this stage the worrying and 'what if' thinking occurs. There is a big chance of self-accusation in this stage: 'I wish I had . . . then it would not have.'
4. Sadness/depression: by allowing the loss to finally sink in completely, the client goes through a deep depression (N.B.: by this we do not refer to clinical depression, but the feeling of being depressed or dejection).

5. Acceptance: when the lowest point has been reached, there will be room for the slow and steady road to recovery, acknowledgement, and acceptance.

New Insights—About Waves and Tasks

Modern theories on grief distance themselves from stage models such as the model by Kübler-Ross. As a descriptive model of the course of grief, it is too mechanical, as if grieving were a predictable process. Although we recognize underlying themes, the curve suggests a predictable certainty that is most definitely false. As a result, the model is often used as a rule. In addition, the final phase of 'acknowledgement' or 'acceptance' evokes resistance. It is as if this is the goal of the process or that one should accept the fact that the loss occurred. Be aware of the nuances. It is not a matter of denying the facts, but rather the possibility of being touched and remaining touched by the fact that the loss has occurred.

Robert Kastenbaum was one of the first social scientists to conduct large-scale research on how people adjust after a loss. With his research (Kastenbaum & Costa, 1977; Kastenbaum, 2015), he confirmed Bowlby's belief that grief comes in waves. Nevertheless, the stages model would not yet disappear. In 1983, William Worden came up with an alternative to the phase model of grief with his task model (Worden, 1991). This model fulfills the idea of the grief work that the client must manage. This model consists of four tasks. The grief tasks, as opposed to the stages, can exist simultaneously, are not linear, and sometimes need to be revisited, mostly in a disorderly manner. This is what is meant by 'working through' the loss:

1. Grief task 1: to accept the reality of the loss.
   The acknowledgement and the reality of the loss has the pivotal role here. The fact that it is impossible to turn back time, the acceptance of the altered reality.
2. Grief task 2: to work through the pain of grief.
   For each person and each loss this will mean having to work through a different range of emotions. The—often physically experienced—pain is an expression of these feelings. This mixture of emotions can be extremely confusing. Allowing these emotions to be expressed has a pivotal role in this task.
3. Grief task 3: to adjust to an environment in which the deceased is missing.
   In the beginning the person will be confronted with the loss on many levels and in many moments and this will cause pain. Existing structures disappear or change. The client might have to learn a wide array of skills and tasks that, in the past, were done by the person who is no longer there. In addition, the input and the feel of the person are missed.

4. Grief task 4: to find an enduring connection with the deceased while embarking on a new life.
   To continue life after the loss, in a meaningful way, also means that one needs to find a different sense of connection to the person who has died. If successful, it means that the person is able to find an appropriate, ongoing connection in his or her emotional life with the loss, while allowing themselves to continue living, opening up to others and to change.

Weijers and Penning (2016) later added task 0 to the original four tasks. This task documents the systemic influence of the upbringing.

0. Grief task 0: including life and death in the upbringing.
   During the upbringing, many 'messages' are passed on, including those about how to deal with loss. By becoming aware of these messages, one is given a great deal of insight into the way loss is dealt with. (Un) pronounced views will be revealed not only around (being allowed to express) feelings and emotions, loss, and separation, but also in asking for and accepting consolation and sustenance.

Therese Rando (1991) has introduced an alternative stages model that she calls the Six Rs of grief.

1. Recognize the loss: this means acknowledging, admitting and allowing oneself to recognize that one has suffered a loss.
2. React to the loss: emotionally reacting to the loss, experiencing the pain.
3. Recollect and re-experience: remembering and commemorating.
4. Relinquish old attachments: leaving the loss behind, accepting that the world has changed and the situation is irreversible.
5. Readjust: returning to a daily life, in which the pain is less sharp.
6. Reinvest: eventually moving out into the world once again and entering into new relationships and attachments. Leaving the loss and the change behind.

Latest Insights—Space for Duality and Individual Experience

At the end of the twentieth and the beginning of the twenty-first century, important changes occurred in our views on grief, influenced by the increasingly scientific approach to psychology. These changes are so radical that we would like to describe them as seismic.

There have been major breakthroughs through expanding the definition of 'normal grief.' There are now many more reactions and expressions of grief that are classified as 'normal' or 'healthy.' This concept of 'normal' grief also includes two extremes on the grief spectrum. On one end of the spectrum, expressions of grief are categorized that may have a disruptive effect on people and their environment because of their emotional intensity, but which can still be classified as normal grief. On the other end of the spectrum, there is now agreement that denial and avoidance, albeit temporarily, are also seen as coping mechanisms. Behaviors such as denial and avoidance of the loss were regarded as 'unhealthy' (pathological) reactions in the previous century. If a loss is intolerable, or if the client would otherwise be overwhelmed, postponing grief until the person has recovered somewhat and has more reserves to draw from is an excellent strategy. In counseling, this broader view of 'normal' grief means that many more reactions become normal for the client. However disruptive it appears to the client, it is part of the process.

An important addition to the new vision of healthy grieving is that loss and grief do not have to 'go away.' The relationship (you could also call it the bond) changes shape, but will continue to exist. We call this 'continuing bonds' (Klass et al., 2014). A part of this continuing bond may be that the contact (with someone or something) continues to exist in a certain way after the loss. In the event of death, clients sometimes see or hear the other person, or they feel a presence. Clients often indicate that this form of permanent connection is extremely supportive to them. When needed, clients can be comforted by the reassurance that these manifestations of continuing bonds are not 'hallucinations' or symptoms of a psychic disorder. The phenomenon of continuing bonds can also be helpful in the context of changes at work—people in organizations can be given more space when they are able to talk about old departments, brands, or a manager who has left a lasting impression.

Because of the broader view of healthy grieving, we have gained more insight into the possible personal and various reactions. We have since been able to pay more attention to the diversity and the individuality of grieving, which was neglected in stage models. An important model that fully illustrates this personal form of grief is the Dual Process Model of Margaret Stroebe and Henk Schut (1999, 2010). Grieving is illustrated by a wave motion, such as Bowlby and Kastenbaum had already described. This wave characteristic of grief can be seen as an interaction between an orientation towards loss and an orientation towards recovery. Within the duality of both orientations, there are tasks for the client, aimed at dealing with the loss, and at taking action that contributes to the recovery. The wave or pendulum motion between loss and recovery will not necessarily decrease in frequency or severity. The loss is no longer seen as something that has to go 'away,' but more as something that will always stay with you and possibly move more into the background. In Chapter 6, this important Dual Process Model will be further elaborated on and explained in the context of the theme of 'grieving' on the Transition Cycle.

Kenneth Doka (1989, 2002) discovered a new variant of grief: disenfranchised grief. This type of grief differs from delayed or absent grief in that it is present, but not seen or not recognized by the environment. Usually, this type of loss is not acknowledged. It may, for example, be grief from a miscarriage while those in her environment did not yet know that the woman was pregnant, or the death of a loved one with whom the person had an extramarital or otherwise secret relationship. The environment is either not aware of this, or does not recognize the relationship (as meaningful), denying the person their grief.

George Bonanno (2010) is considered one of the main critics of old and outdated insights into grief. He emphasizes that 'resilience' is essential for people to be able to deal with loss and adversity in life. Older studies are mainly focused on people who have become stuck in their grief and have sought professional help. Bonanno shows that most of the people who are confronted with loss learn to deal with it on their own. In Chapter 8 on the brain and trauma, the work of Bonanno will be discussed in greater detail.

William Bridges (2017) and George Kohlrieser (2006; Kohlrieser et al., 2012) explore the theme of loss and grief within the context of work and the organization (change). Bridges emphasizes that organizational changes, reorganizations, and mergers not only create changes in the formal hierarchy, but also have a psychological and emotional effect on people. He calls this transition management. Psychologist George Kohlrieser, a former hostage negotiator for the police in the United States, illustrates the stages of attachment, separation, and grief through a cyclical model ('bonding cycle') that he uses in leadership development. This model was introduced in the Netherlands as an 'attachment or contact cycle' by Piet Weisfelt (1996) and Wibe Veenbaas (2007) and was then expanded on by Riet Fiddelaers-Jaspers (2011b) and Sabine Noten (Fiddelaers-Jaspers & Noten, 2015). Jakob van Wielink and Leo Wilhelm (2014) have named this model the Transition Cycle to emphasize that changes evoke loss, in which the themes of the Transition Cycle present themselves automatically.

> **Tip:** The Transition Cycle (Figure 1.2) is the center of the subject matter when guiding loss.

An important element of the Transition Cycle is the theme 'meaning reconstruction.' Dr. Robert Neimeyer (2005, 2006, 2016; Neimeyer & Thompson, 2014), a Memphis-based psychologist, uses narrativity, the telling of stories. Through the story, we can reconstruct meaning after an impactful loss. By telling their life stories time and again (and by being heard), people are given the chance to integrate the loss in their lives. Grief is a social process that requires a community of trustworthy witnesses with whom these stories can be shared. Meaning reconstruction, as we will see in Chapter 7, goes

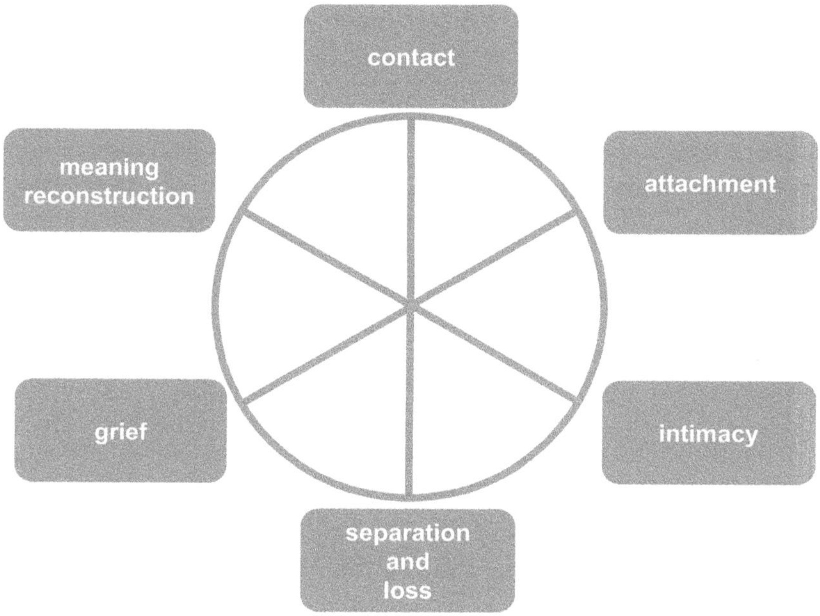

Figure 1.2 The Transition Cycle

beyond merely sharing stories though. Narrative techniques and other practices that help meaning reconstructions are aimed at reinterpreting both past and present events in order to integrate loss in our life stories.

A recent development takes place around the medicalization of grief. Grief is a part of life. However uncomfortable grief may be, by far the majority of grief reactions is normal and should not be labelled as a mental disorder. Even though symptoms during grief sometimes seem to indicate depression, grief remains an ordinary reaction, including all the melancholy, to an often unwanted loss. Symptoms during grief, therefore, do not have to be treated with medication. The risk of medicalization of grief has increased since adjustments were made to the most recent edition of the American psychological handbook *Diagnostic and Statistical Manual of Mental Disorders* (*DSM*) (van Wielink & Wilhelm, 2012d). The *DSM* describes disorders in such a way that diagnoses can be determined unambiguously. In many countries, the *DSM* is also used to determine whether treatment is covered by health insurance. Mental illnesses that are not listed in the *DSM* are not covered. Grief has, rightly, never been included as a 'disorder' in the *DSM*. In fact, in the earlier versions of the *DSM*, grief was included as an exclusion criterion to arrive at the diagnosis 'depression.' This was linked to a period of two months after loss: only if the depression symptoms persisted for longer than two months would the physician make the diagnosis of 'depression.' With the latest version of the *DSM*, the

DSM5, this exclusion criterion has been cancelled. A physician can now come to the diagnosis of 'depression' in the case of grief, if symptoms persist for some time and severely hinder the client's functioning.

The advantage of omitting the two-month period as exclusion criterion for grief is that it is now implicitly recognized that grief does not have to be over after two months. A disadvantage however is that there is a greater risk of unnecessary prescription of medication to treat grief, when time, support, and/or therapy would be more appropriate. The diagnosis is made by the attending physician based on the client's symptoms.

In addition to this change in the *DSM5*, a 'candidate' disorder was also created, namely, Persistent Complex Grief disorder, which is listed in the appendix. Based on several criteria, a lengthy period of severe grief symptoms could lead to such a diagnosis. Although this decision has not yet been made on the status of this candidate disorder, this discussion may be revisited leading up to the next version of the *DSM*.

New Vision of Shaping Personal and Professional Change

With every change a person makes, there are earlier changes in their lives that precede this one. There is life experience preceding the loss. In their personal history, many events have taken place before this person gets a job and then loses it, or before someone gets married and then divorced, or before leaving home and then emigrating, and so on. These are formative or life events, which co-determine how someone reacts or behaves at each moment when confronted with (far-reaching) change and loss.

A loss experience is never an isolated incident. Previous life experiences will always touch on the present in a direct and indirect manner. It is always with an entire inner framework that one reacts. In the background one always and constantly finds themes resonating, such as feeling welcomed, attachment and bonding, sharing intimacy, separating, grieving, and meaning reconstruction. These themes are part of a repetitive pattern. They take shape in early childhood and are continually repeated during one's life, including during adulthood. These themes play a role in one's personal life, at school, during college, and at work. The repetitive pattern of these themes on a timeline, is represented in a cyclical model.

This cyclical model is referred to as the contact, attachment cycle, or cycle of loss that sheds light on the specific themes. The term Transition Cycle (see Figure 1.2) indicates that all themes in the cycle play their specific role in shaping (personal) change and that no single theme should be considered more important than any other in advance.

The Transition Cycle is a powerful tool to help the client become aware of the themes relevant to loss and change. The counselor plays a unique part in exploring these themes together with the client. Not every client comes to the first session with a specific question about a loss experience. If someone has a request for help, it is often not immediately clear that there is any (form of) loss. The request for help can be very nonspecific. Clients always wants something to change: something is bothering them or is difficult to do. The task of the counselor is to explore the question with the client. By taking alternating steps of recognition, acknowledgement, and exploration, client and counselor will dig deeper and deeper into the problem. The themes of the Cycle of Transition help to better understand the underlying patterns of the client that resonate with the request for help.

The counselor continually moves through his or her own cycle of transition. All these themes also pertain to the counselor and his or her personal history of attachment and loss. Specific concerns may be present at the time of counseling. In a certain way, all the themes of the Cycle of Transition are also present in the therapy sessions between professional and client (e.g., transference, countertransference, and projection). The counselor builds a relationship of trust with the client during the sessions. The relationship entered into with the counselor, because of its special nature in terms of confidentiality and security, is comparable to the relationship the client has had/has with previous attachment figures. All experiences, both positive and negative, will be transposed onto the relationship with the counselor.

Dialogue

Emily, the client in the case study discussed earlier, came to see Catherine for counseling on problems she is having at work. The following dialogue[5] unfolded at their first meeting.

Catherine: Hello Emily, welcome, please have a seat. How are you doing?
Emily: I am so exhausted. Sometimes I don't know how I am going to get through the day . . . so tired.
Catherine: That sounds intense. What is causing you to be so tired?
Emily: I don't know exactly. It has been troubling me for a while now, a couple of months I'd say. The occupational physician thinks it might be a psychological problem and advised me to come here.
Catherine: And how was it before, before you became so tired?
Emily: I had no problems. I am a very practical person, always busy doing something. That's why it is so weird that I am so tired now.
Catherine: Has anything happened in the past few months?
Emily: A lot! Our whole department has fallen apart. I have been assigned a position in another department and many of my colleagues have been relocated as well.

Catherine: Well, that is actually quite a lot. Can you tell me more about it? What happened as the department fell apart?
Emily: Last year, we were told that there was going to be a reorganization and that our department would be phased out.
Catherine: Describe to me exactly how it happened.
Emily: Our manager issued a statement during the team meeting. She didn't know any details, nor did she know how it was going to happen. Except that the department would be phased out. She had no idea how we would be impacted.
Catherine: What was it like to hear such news?
Emily: At first, I was really calm. As if this didn't concern me. I did hear it, but it didn't sink in. That lasted about two weeks. During that time, I told no one. Strange really, is it not? It was like sticking my head in the sand. Acting like it wasn't happening.
Catherine: And when did it start to sink in?
Emily: When my manager told us she was being transferred to another department as a supply chain manager. She told us that she wasn't planning on abandoning us just yet, but we hardly saw her after that. All her attention was focused on the new job. From that moment on, I became restless. I still remember wanting to ask her a practical question, but not being able to reach her. I almost panicked. That was a shock to me. I picked myself back up after that, but started having trouble sleeping. I often lie awake worrying and have vivid dreams. All that makes a person really tired.
Catherine: And what happened with the department afterwards?
Emily: Well, several colleagues left the organization. They were offered a severance package and were able to leave almost immediately. Others found a position in a different department.
Catherine: So that's how the department slowly disintegrated?
Emily: Yes, it just got emptier and emptier. And there was less and less work. I was glad when it was my turn to leave.
Catherine: And how did you say goodbye to your colleagues?
Emily: Actually, I didn't really say goodbye.
Catherine: No goodbyes. How was that for you?
Emily: I don't really know. Nobody said goodbye. Not even my manager. I didn't even really think about it. I was glad to leave.
Catherine: Have you ever experienced anything like this before in your life? Leaving without looking back?
Emily: (Is quiet for a while.) I have never thought about it like that. My father also left without looking back.
Catherine: (Nods but says nothing.)
Emily: I was seven, I think. I came home from school and he was gone. My mother was crying. I saw that all kinds of things were gone from our house. My brothers too.

Catherine: Were your brothers gone too? Did they leave with your father?
Emily: Yes, they were my half-brothers, from my father's earlier relationship. They lived with us. All of a sudden it was just the two of us, my mother and I. (Silence.)
Catherine: (Remains silent, sees that the story of what happened then is being recalled by the client and waits.)
Emily: My mother was completely overwrought. She didn't know what to do.
Catherine: And you?
Emily: I could not do much. I was still small. I tried to stay calm. Yes, that I remember. That I decided to stay calm. As if I flipped a switch.
Catherine: Do you remember which switch you flipped?
Emily: I shut off my emotions.
Catherine: You shut off your emotions, your mother panicked and there was no room for your emotions.
Emily: Yes, I think that that's how it went.
Catherine: What a huge sacrifice for such a little girl to have to make.
Emily: (Eyes filling with tears.) Yes.
Catherine: Who was there for you?
Emily: (Shakes her head.) Nobody.
Catherine: (Remains quiet, stays close.)
Emily: (Blows her nose.) Yes, that was actually some pretty heavy stuff. I have never given it any thought. Pretty intense for a seven-year-old.
Catherine: Do you have a picture of yourself when you were seven?
Emily: Yes, I do actually . . . somewhere.
Catherine: Would you be willing to look for it and put it somewhere in clear sight? Somewhere in your home? Then you can think about her now and again, when you pass her by.
Emily: I will do that, that's nice, I think.
Catherine: And the next time you come, we will focus on saying goodbye.

Questions for Self-Reflection

- Think of an event from the past that has had an impact on you.
- What made this event impactful?
- How did you react to the event at that time?
- How do you look back on it now?
- Can you discover links between your reaction to this event and your reaction to the event you are currently experiencing?
- What locatable losses were there in your life? Were you able to grieve?
- Do you recognize any ambiguous losses on the timeline of your life?
- How was loss and grief dealt with in your home, when you were young.
- How did you discover that there is always more loss hidden under the other losses in your life?

Exercises

When doing these exercises, please note:

Tip: We would like to invite you to practice often and find wholesome ways to experiment with these exercises.

How to work with loss during counseling is best learned by being completely aware of your own experiences and emotions and dealing with them at the same time. Some of the exercises can be practiced on your own, others require small groups of two or three because of the various roles involved. All exercises benefit from sharing your views, experiences, and self-reflection with others. We would like to encourage you to participate in a peer group to study these themes and practice these exercises.

Exercise—Recognizing the Losses

Instruction: According to the case study in this chapter, Emily sees her counselor for the first time. What is her initial question? Which underlying losses and questions rise to the surface during the course of the conversation? Make a distinction between locatable loss and ambiguous loss on the one hand and between primary and secondary loss on the other.

Which sentences would you use to acknowledge Emily's loss?

Share your thoughts in pairs.

Exercise—Personal Loss

Instruction: In a group of three: A is the counselor, B is the client, and C is the observer. Question each other by making use of the first five Questions for Self-Reflection listed in the previous section. Evaluate briefly and then switch roles.

Exercise—Lifeline

A lifeline is the visual presentation of the timeline with the client's life events. It is helpful in making the moments or periods of joy and success or periods of loss and failure visible. These can then be marked on the lifeline. You can also draw parallel lifelines, one for the client's personal life and one for his or her career. Or both can be combined in one line. By marking these moments separately, the client is able to feel and see the positive and negative shifts along the way on a single trajectory. Which of these moments impact the issue your client has a question about? Take plenty of time to do this exercise with your client or ask him or her to do it as homework to be discussed in the next session.

For this exercise, start with an empty piece of paper, as large as possible (A3 or on a flipchart) and draw on it breadthwise. Draw a line from left to right. This line is the time axis of the client's personal history. On the left, the client marks his or her birth. The line runs through to the present on the right of the page. The client then marks the ages at which major events took place and describes these moments briefly next to the mark. They can be joyful as well as sad moments. The client can also mark them symbolically with a plus or minus sign if he wishes. In this way, a chronological picture of significant events is created (see Figure 1.3). During each of these events, a coping mechanism was addressed and possibly strained. You can also ask your client to make the lifeline at home.

For Emily (the woman presented in the case study at the beginning of this chapter and in the dialogue), the departure of her father and her two half-brothers, the divorce, moving to the small apartment and the new elementary school were milestones on her lifeline around the age of seven. The number of events in such a short time is indicative of the impact on her young life. At seventeen, she leaves home. Although becoming independent felt like a positive experience at the time, as a step towards freedom, it is also a step that cannot be disconnected from earlier loss experiences.

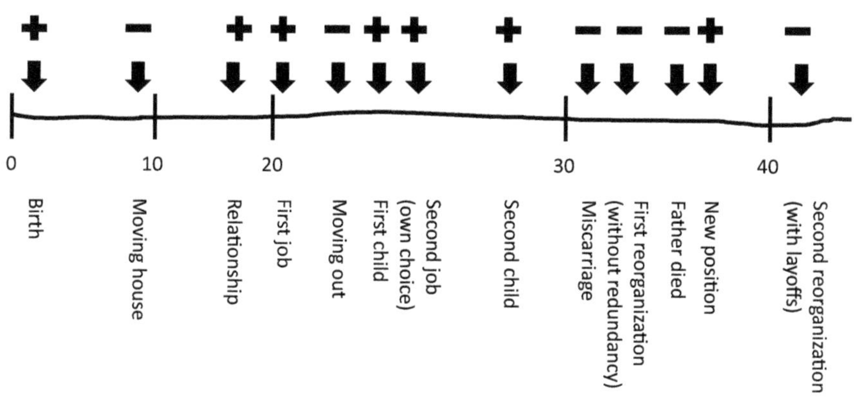

Figure 1.3 The Lifeline

The themes on the lifeline can relate to career or personal life. Examples of these themes are:

- Birth;
- Brothers or sisters being born;
- Miscarriages;
- Divorce/relationship(s) ending/new relationship(s); new relationship(s) of (grand)parents or carers;
- Passing away of (grand)parents/brothers/sisters/classmates/friends;
- Moving away;
- Changing school/repeating a year;
- Beginning/ending of friendships;
- First/new love affair(s);
- Leaving home/living alone for the first time;
- Part-time jobs;
- First job/new job(s);
- Reorganization(s)/changes at work;
- Dismissal/redundancy;
- One's own divorce(s)/relationship ending(s);
- . . .

Looking back, some moments can be rated with a plus as well as a minus at the same time, but the client needs to think back to how it felt at the time it happened.

When discussing the lifeline with your client, ask questions such as the following:

- What made this period or this event so positive or negative for you?
- Who was important to you during these periods or moments?
- Did you say goodbye?
- What influence do these events or this period still have on your life?

Tips for the counselor:

- Be curious. Your questions will lead the client towards new insights and perspectives. Ask pertinent questions as to the choices that led to the decisions or effects of events. For Emily the basis for her decision to leave home and live on her own was the choice to want to leave everything behind. The effect was that she tried not to think of her father and her half-brothers after that.
- Add years or approximate ages to the lifeline. Start by dividing the line into blocks of ten-year periods and then refine it from there.

An alternative approach is to first have the client draw the lifeline with only specific work-related events. This variation offers a less threatening starting point because it is less personal. After that, the client is asked to draw a lifeline under the first with the same time format but adding in specific personal events. The combination of both lifelines gives a more complete picture. It helps to see the relation between career and personal events (see Figure 1.4).

A variation on the exercise above is to ask the client to indicate the intensity of the events by marking a plus above the time axis if the experience was positive and marking a minus underneath the line if the experience was negative. The various highlights and all-time lows will show the measure in which the client considered key events to be major. As the points are joined together chronologically, the highs and lows emerge as well as the steep declines and ascents (see Figure 1.5). This is most effective visually, when career and personal events are combined on one line.

Instruction: Draw up your own personal history with regard to departures and losses on your lifeline: draw a line from your birth up to the present and mark events of departure and loss on the lifeline. Add years and a brief description of the event. All losses may be added (ambiguous and locatable): deceased loved ones, divorce or separation, failing a class, changing schools, end of friendship, being bullied or bullying, death of a pet, you or your friends moving away, (r)emigration, childlessness, disease or disability, accident, and so forth.

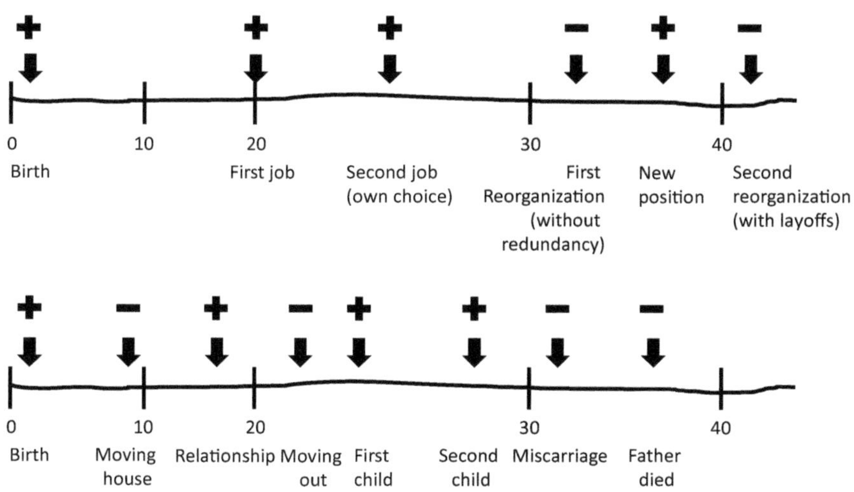

Figure 1.4 Separate Timelines for Career and Personal Life

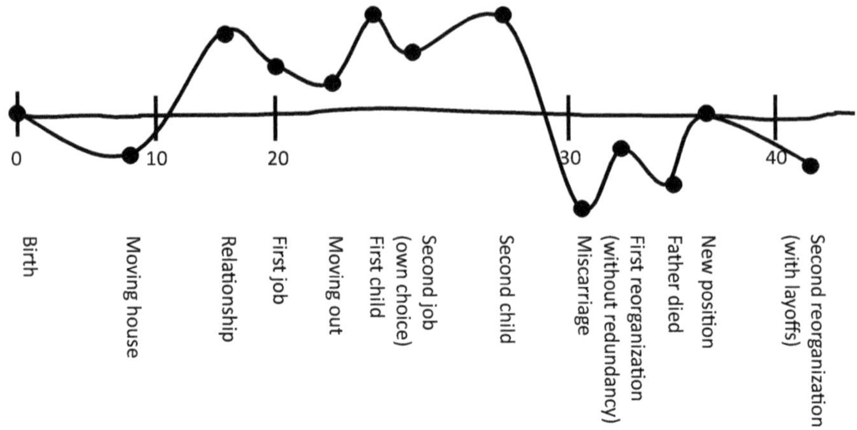

Figure 1.5 The Lifeline With Highs and Lows

Instruction: In a group of three: A is the counselor, B is the client, and C is the observer. Question each other by making use of the last three Questions for Self-Reflection and the questions found in the exercise about the events on the lifeline. Evaluate briefly and then switch roles.

Notes

1. From his 'Letter to Menoeceus.'
2. Epictetus: 'The Good Life Handbook.'
3. From the '*Letter of Consolation*' by Plutarchus to his wife.
4. In his text 'Avoiding distress.'
5. The dialogues in this book illustrate the theory. They stem from real-life guidance sessions, although they are anonymized and can be shortened and adapted to fit the purpose of the addressed theme.

2

TO WELCOME AND CONNECT

A Case Study

Emma had completed her bachelor's degree in Social Work a while back. Her grades were good and her supervisor was very pleased with her thesis. Her school career had always run smoothly. She was well-liked by teachers. Her work was always finished on time and she never disrupted a lesson. She was always friendly and polite. But now it was time to find a job. In the six months that followed she applied to several organizations, but was unsuccessful. In many cases, she was informed of her rejection by written notification only. She was invited for an interview twice and in both cases did not make it to the next round. For the first interview, she was very tense. She had hardly slept the night before and felt nauseous. During the interview, she was hardly able to utter a word. The second interview was even more difficult. The receptionist had misunderstood her and said that she could not reach the person Emma was looking for. Much later the misunderstanding was cleared up, but by that time, Emma was in such a panic that she could not seem to comprehend the questions that she was asked. Unsuccessful, once again. The mother of one of her friends referred her to a counselor. She wanted to learn how to hold her ground more firmly during interviews. At the beginning of the first session, the counselor noticed immediately that Emma was very reserved. Her handshake was limp, her breathing was shallow, and she looked at the ground or out the window as she spoke. It took a few sessions before Emma felt safe enough to open up and the counselor could ask about her youth. Emma told her about her biological father, who had an extramarital affair with her mother. He was furious when he discovered she was pregnant. In the sessions that followed, the story of her life slowly unfolded. Her father did not want to know her. In the beginning, he came to visit a few times, but eventually informed her mother that he did not want to see her again. He wanted to focus on his own family. Her mother fell apart and, even though she never said it out loud, Emma always had a feeling that it was all her fault—that, because she arrived, everything was ruined. Subconsciously, Emma had made sure that she caused no disturbance, trouble, or problems. She had learned to always put others first. Together with her counselor, she looked back at her youth, her history. Only then was she able to feel how badly she had missed feeling really welcome. By allowing herself to feel how much pain this had caused her and by grieving over it, she was able to welcome herself back into her life and be more present in contact with others. Although applying for jobs still created tension, she was able to find a nice job and was hired.

Stories of Loss Need a Sanctuary

Working through the themes of the Transition Cycle usually begins at the top, at 'feeling welcome' or 'making contact.' Even though this seems to be a natural starting point, a circle has no beginning or end. For counseling this means that there is no fixed point at which to start. While exploring the client's question or issue the themes will naturally appear. The counselor can work with the theme that arises from behind the question of the client, working backward on the cycle addressing previous themes, or moving forward addressing following themes. This is not a fixed process. To create a workable structure in this book, we will, however, start at the top of the Transition Cycle and work clockwise.

The 'first' theme on the Transition Cycle is 'contact' or 'welcome.' By 'contact,' we mean every form of contact the client makes in his or her life. In each new contact all the old contact experiences are also present. This includes the contact at birth, the first welcoming in life. Each encounter during and since childhood counts. Each new contact refers to feeling welcome in life in general. The theme will be revisited with each new encounter in the present, also between counselor and client. In the very first encounter and in the very first moment of contact, the entire history is present too. The client and counselor will decide almost instinctively whether there is enough of a 'click,' that is, sufficient basis on which to build security and trust in the relationship. Each subsequent encounter also starts off with a moment in which there is a first connection and a new experience in being welcomed. In this welcome, the basis for the relationship is formed. It is therefore important for the counselor to know his or her issues on the subjects of feeling welcome and contact.

From the first moment of contact between partners in intimate relationships—parents and children, brothers and sisters, managers and colleagues, teachers and students, friends, counselor and client—a psychological contract is formed. This contract sets the dynamics of a relationship in a collection of unspoken rules, needs, and expectations about how these people will relate to each other. What they discuss, and what they do not.

How will they approach each other: formally or informally? How vulnerable will they be in the presence of another person, who is in the lead? The basis of the social engagement is determined in this moment and is needed to shape the attachment. The question is how to keep suitable distance, be polite and respectful. Such a contract is invisible, implicit, unspoken, and based on the life experiences of both people. On the one hand such things are included as disappointments in attachments, moments in which needs were not fulfilled or expectations were not met. On the other hand, the beautiful and joyful moments of real connection are also present, which strengthen the faith in other people and in oneself.

Counseling the Other Side of Contact and Welcome

When people come for counseling, they have a question they need answered. Mostly the question is about how they can do something differently: they have a problem they want solved or they want to change some aspect of their behavior. The themes on the Transition Cycle are fundamental and unavoidable when guiding people towards such answers or when going through such change. Themes of loss and grief are always present in the background, even when they are not (yet) part of the question. Each theme intensifies when people are faced with loss. Only when a new loss is faced will it become apparent whether someone has mastered the theme.

To not let yourself be affected by the themes on the Transition Cycle comes at a high price. If you shut down your feelings or push them away, you become side-tracked and cannot experience the themes on the Transition Cycle. There is a risk that the grief solidifies these fluid emotions. Each theme on the Transition Cycle constantly interacts between the forms of 'normal' grief and 'frozen' or 'solidified' grief. The themes each have two sides (opposites) and both sides play a role in dealing with loss. Solidified grief, the other side of grief as it were, is a 'negative' view of the same theme when one is unable to let grief run its course. It is often an attempt to avoid feeling the pain of the loss by avoiding new contact. The price of the illusion of getting off easy is, however, not only keeping your feelings at a distance, but also keeping others at a distance. Solidified grief obstructs the ability to connect with others. When this occurs, the other themes on the Transition Cycle also turn into the negative version of the themes (see Figure 2.1).

On the other side of being welcomed and of contact, there is isolation and withdrawal. This is what someone in grief can choose to do when it seems to be the safer choice and there is a risk of not feeling welcome. To avoid attachment seems to offer protection from the pain of being rejected or ignored. For the counselor it is important to be able to recognize whether the client is trying to avoid the themes, so that he can invite the client to pay attention to that particular theme. Along with each of the themes below, we will also examine the possible consequences when someone is avoiding the theme at hand.

Someone who is grieving constantly oscillates between either side of the themes, of normal and solidified grief on the Transition Cycle, constantly moving from one view of the theme to the other, and back again. With each theme, there is a risk that the client who is willing to explore the theme ends up experiencing its flip side. The theme on the Transition Cycle rotates around its axis, as it were. When someone avoids the theme at hand on the Transition Cycle at any given point in time and ends up stuck on its 'negative' side, the result will eventually be solidified grief.

And yet we would be oversimplifying by describing the themes of solidified grief as purely 'negative.' At any given moment, this dynamic can once again rotate towards its healthy counterpart (see Figure 2.2), in the same way as there is constant oscillation between the loss orientation and the restoration orientation in the Dual Process Model of coping with grief

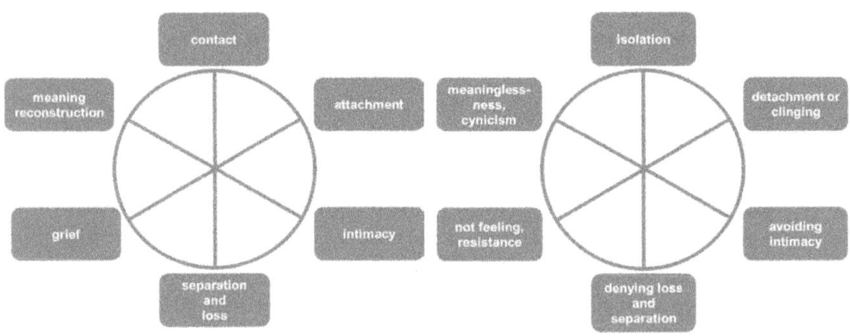

Figure 2.1 Both Sides of the Same Coin for the Transition Cycle: Healthy and Solidified Grief

Figure 2.2 Both Sides of the Same Coin for the Theme 'Contact'

(see Chapter 6). It may be necessary once in a while, to withdraw emotionally or isolate oneself, to protect one's ability to cope. Only when this happens often and during every step in each theme does it become problematic. As long as there is an oscillation between both orientations in each theme, it can be regarded as a healthy course.

The counselor has the task of recognizing this oscillation and exploring it together with the client. He or she starts off with the theme 'contact' versus 'isolation.' This is also where the psychological contract is exchanged between counselor and client, which is a necessary and unavoidable aspect of counseling. The psychological contract, which arises mostly and implicitly in the subconscious, is a dangerous pitfall here. For it is here that a decision is made on what can and cannot be discussed during the sessions. We call this the hidden contract. It is not an easy task to unravel psychological and hidden contracts as they contain just as many unconscious and instinctive behaviors of the counselor as of the client. The client discloses a great deal of the person he or she is in this contract. The counselor requires substantial observational skills and self-awareness to unlock and use this information to help the client.

The client also has psychological contracts with the people in his or her life. These can differ from relationship to relationship, but there is often a discernible and corresponding structure in the expectations and needs of the client and his or her attitude to others.

It is precisely the unconscious character of this psychological contract that causes intense emotions when the contract is altered or violated. These alterations have a direct impact on our sense of security or predictability. The place in the relationship feels threatened. And that brings back earlier incidents—incidents from youth. Which position did someone have in his family? What was his birth order? Did he have older or younger siblings? Brothers or sisters? Who or what did he take care of, and who cared for him? At and before birth, children experience these encounters and they absorb them into their own psyches, brains, and bodies. The parents and caregivers play an important role as attachment figures. In the Transition Cycle the psychological contract and the occupied position in the family will be further elaborated on in the following chapters on attachment and sharing intimacy.

Dialogue

Emma, who was introduced in the case study at the beginning of the chapter, has been seeing Ashley for therapy for quite some time now. Emma is trying to find a job, but she is dreading the interviews after two very unpleasant encounters. In earlier conversations, Ashley noticed that Emma needs time to feel at ease.

Ashley: Welcome Emma, it is good to have you back.
Emma: (Does not look Ashley in the eye.) Thank you.
Ashley: Lead the way. You know where to go.
Emma: Yes.
Ashley: Have a seat. Would you like a pillow for your back, to support you? And place your feet firmly on the ground. Take a few slow, deep breaths. Relax your shoulders a bit more and take your time to look around a bit. Take in your surroundings. Stay focused on your breathing. (Is then silent for a while.) Welcome Emma.
Emma: (Looks Ashley in the eye now.) Thank you!
Ashley: That makes you feel good, does it not? Taking the time to actually arrive and be present.
Emma: Yes, that's true. I am making a conscious effort to practice that, but it is quite hard. I am inclined to pay little attention to myself and not at all used to taking up any space. It seems as if I keep having to take the same hurdle time and again.
Ashley: That's understandable. And you describe it clearly. It shows that you are aware of how difficult it is for you and admitting this to yourself is a huge step. Keep practicing! It will also help you with your job interview.
Emma: That would be nice, because I have been invited for another interview.
Ashley: That's good news! Tell me more.
Emma: It is a government job as Community Liaison Case worker. The job requires you to improve living conditions in the community. It is an opportunity to meet all kinds of people, also people who don't normally go looking for help. That's what I love about it.
Ashley: And why do you love that about it?
Emma: Well, I actually have thought about it. I like it when people are given attention who would not normally ask for it, I think.

Ashley: Why does that make you emotional?
Emma: (Is quiet for a while.) I think that I am also someone like that . . .
Ashley: Someone who . . .?
Emma: Someone who does not ask for much attention, but does actually need some.
Ashley: So, you want to give others something you never had?
Emma: Yes, I believe I do.
Ashley: I think you are very good at that. That these people will feel seen and heard. You have a good eye for that.
Emma: Do you really think so? That's good to hear.
Ashley: Yes, I really think you have a lot to offer them. These people will be in good hands with you. And do you think there are any pitfalls?
Emma: Um. . . . My biggest pitfall is once again being afraid to take up too much space and that I pay too little attention to myself.
Ashley: How are you planning to deal with this in this job?
Emma: Well, that's a good question. I had not thought about that yet. In any case, I need to take time for me.
Ashley: A good idea. And maybe you can find a peer group and take a further look at this theme with them. It will keep you active and aware of your pitfalls.
Emma: That's a really good idea.
Ashley: Is what we have talked about going to be helpful to you in preparing for your interview?
Emma: Yes, I think it will. I already feel steadier, because I have thought it through better. And I am going to make sure that I feel present and welcome before the interview starts. I may even say something about it to them.
Ashley: I have a good feeling about this! Will you let me know how it went?
Emma: I will! See you next time!

Questions for Self-Reflection

We have formulated questions for each theme, which you can also use during a counseling session.

- Where was your crib?
- What did your welcome into this world look like?
- Do you have siblings? How do you feel about that?
- What is your birth order? (Were you the first-, middle- or last-born?)
- How did the members of your family deal with attachment and feeling welcome?
- How do you get emotionally attached to others?
- What do you need to feel welcome?

- How does it feel when you do not feel welcome?
- What do you do when you do not feel welcome?
- Can you identify any themes in your personal history that explain these reactions and feelings?

Exercises

Exercise—Getting Acquainted/Intake Interview

As a counselor, you will meet many clients for the first time during the intake. You know little or nothing of their background, neither of their story nor why they have come to you for help. Sometimes you cannot imagine why they have come to you. During the intake interview, you get acquainted with each other and you make sure you get a clear picture of the question the client has for you. Everything that occurs in this session will resonate with the theme of feeling welcome. From the very first moment of contact, the first version of the psychological contract is drawn up and these conditions lay down the framework in which counseling will take place. The following exercise is to make you aware of the conditions you add to a psychological contract and teaches you to recognize the conditions the client draws up. Make use of the questions for self-reflection listed above.

Instruction: Divide into groups of three (A is the counselor, B is the client, and C is the observer). A guides B by asking the self-reflection questions listed above. The observer focuses his or her attention on the psychological contract between counselor and client.

Review this exercise by making use of the questions listed below:

- How does it feel to talk about these things?
- Are you feeling welcome in this conversation? What helps and what hinders you from feeling welcome?
- What is it like for the counselor?
- What aspects of the psychological contract were noticed by the observer?

Continue switching roles until everyone has had their turn.

Exercise—Make Your Own Birth Announcement Card

Use colored paper, coloring pencils, and felt-tip pens, scissors, stickers, and so forth to make a birth announcement card that expresses your view of how you were welcomed into this world. The goal of this exercise is to learn the way in which your birth (story) was told to you, how it plays a major role in encounters in the present, and whether you allow yourself to feel welcome or be welcomed.

Instruction: Divide into pairs (A and B). A talks about his or her birth announcement card with the help of the following questions:

- What were the circumstances around your birth?
- How were you welcomed by your father? How by your mother?
- What stories do you know about your birth?
- What impact did the way you were born have on your life?

B listens and asks A questions to clarify.

Variation:

Divide the group into pairs and decide who is A and B.
Stand or sit facing each other.
A takes the birth announcement he or she made and shows it to B in silence. B looks at the card and says nothing.

After some time, A says:

- 'This is the way I am being born again, each time I come into contact with others.'
- 'This is the way I feel others are looking at me.'

Then B welcomes A in a way that comes to mind at that moment.
A takes in how it is to be welcomed and describes to B how it feels.
A and B switch roles.

Exercise—The Genogram

A genogram can be used to gain an understanding of how the emotional systems in your client's family operate. A genogram is a type of family tree, a diagrammatic representation of a person's family history (see Figure 2.3), making use of a number of symbols to identify the nature of relationships (see Figure 2.4). Miscarriages, premature births, or stillborn children are included in the genogram because these are important for the family composition and the history of the birth order of the children in the system.

The genogram is a diagram of the system in which someone grows up. This does not always have to be the system of the biological parents and ancestors. When someone is adopted or grows up in foster care, the person is part of several systems. Family systems can be mapped and work along

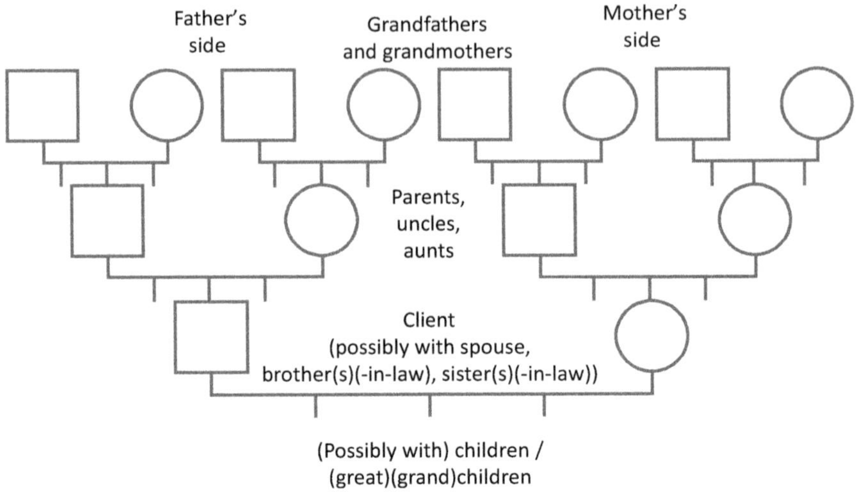

Figure 2.3 The Genogram

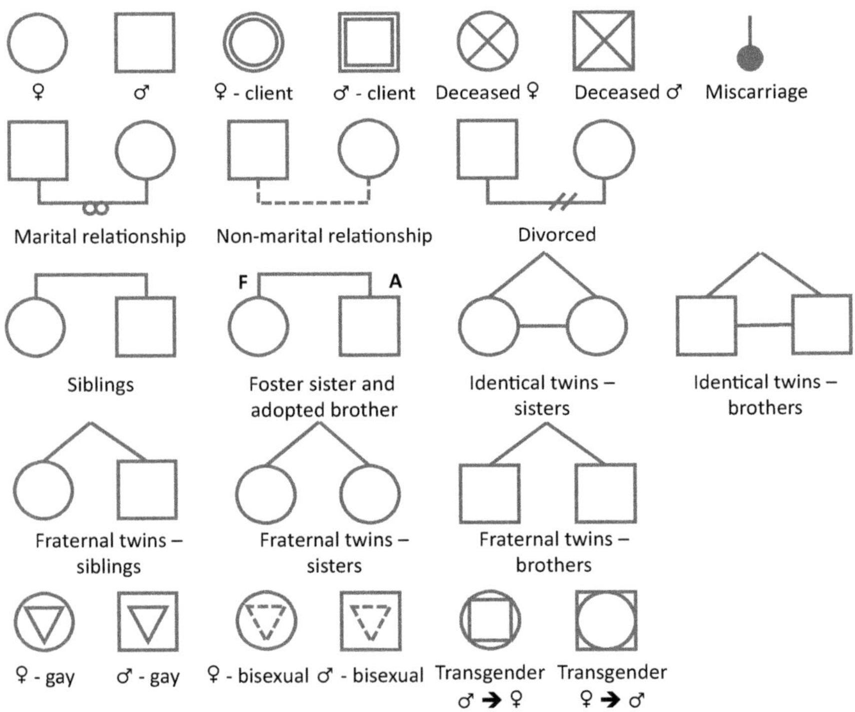

Figure 2.4 Symbols of the Genogram

the lines of both nature and nurture. It is best, if possible and if there is any information, to draw up both systems.

Use a large piece of paper (A3 if possible) and draw the symbol for the client in the center of the paper: a circle for a girl or woman, a square for a boy or man. Add their name and date of birth. Then draw a v-shaped line above that symbol and draw a square as symbol for the biological father on the left top of the 'v' and a circle as symbol for the biological mother on the right. Ask their names, dates of birth, and the nature of their relationship. Did they get married? If so, mark dates or ages in the relationship on the connecting line between the parents. A divorce is symbolized with a line and two small lines crossing (disconnecting) the line. In the event of a new partner, a new connecting line is drawn to the father or mother. A non-marital relationship (or any intimate relationship) is connected by a broken line.

Work from the client's parents upward to the grandparents on both sides (father and mother). Using the same questions, fill in the details. Any uncles and aunts, brothers and sisters of the client's father and mother, can be added to the genogram in chronological order (by date of birth). Deceased family members have an x drawn over their symbol and the (approximate) date of death. You can help the client place the event in time by asking questions such as 'how old were you when it happened?'

Also draw in older and younger siblings in chronological order. If there are stillborn siblings and miscarriages they are to be given a place in the genogram. Finally draw in the client's own family: sons and daughters and the partner. Once again, every symbol should be drawn in chronological order and stillborn sons and daughters as well as miscarriages should be given a place in the genogram.

If Emma's mother (Emma being the woman from the earlier case study), after Emma's birth and Emma's father ending the extra-marital relationship, had started a new relationship, Emma would have had a stepfather. In that case her genogram would have looked like the diagram in Figure 2.5.

- In this manner, the genogram is a visual rendition, an analogue of the family tree, of the personal history of the client. The diagram itself, including all the relationships, dates of birth and death, attachments, and divorces, provides a helpful perspective. To get deeper insight you can ask questions about things that were not discussed openly in the system of origin.
- How did relationships start, how did their (grand)parents meet?
- Was the relationship approved by their (grand)parents? What did the (grand)parents think of the relationship?

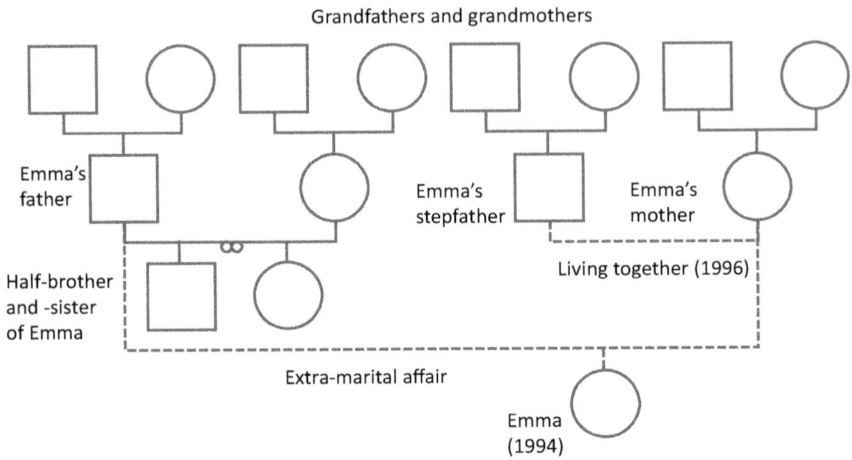

Figure 2.5 Genogram of the Case Study

- Who was the favorite, who received preferential treatment, in the parent's families or ancestors? How do they influence the client's system?
- Which problems did the family members face in the parents' families (or ancestors)? How do they influence the client's system?
- Who took care of whom in the families of the parents or ancestors? How did that influence the client's system?
- Were there any divorces, and how do they influence mutual relationships?
- Did anyone emigrate or move away?
- How does faith, education, profession, or country of origin play a role?
- Were there any taboos or secrets? If so, what were they?
  - Were there any secret (first) love affairs, clandestine or extra-marital affairs or children?
  - Were there any miscarriages, stillborn babies, or children who died young? Were they brothers or sisters?
  - Was there violence or abuse?
  - Were or are there any problems due to homosexuality or sexual orientation?
  - What role does faith or belief play within these taboos or secrets?
  - Were or are there any problems with respect to roles of 'good' or 'bad' sides in war(s) or armed conflict?

Instruction: Make your own genogram, putting yourself in the center, and work upward towards the top of the page by drawing the families of origin of both your parents.

Divide into groups of three (A is the counselor, B is the client, and C is the observer) and discuss the impact of the genogram using the questions listed in this chapter to guide you. Evaluate the session after each turn and switch roles.

3

ATTACHMENT AND BONDING

A Case Study

'Can you see us sooner?' Susan calls. Her relationship with Kevin is going through a crisis. 'I really don't know if we are going to make it, but it would be really nice if we don't have to wait another two weeks before we can see you.' Luckily, we are able to find a moment in the coming week.

Kevin and Susan have been together for three years. Since that time, they have broken off their relationship once. After a few months they got back together. It went well for a while, but now the tension appears to be mounting again.

'I think she's fantastic, but I often feel that I have to tiptoe around her. Sometimes, when she calls me, I hear something in her voice that warns me to watch my words. Like the other day. She almost exploded because I didn't understand what she was saying.' Kevin sighs deeply and looks almost apologetically at Susan, who is looking defeated. A tear rolls down her cheek. 'I don't know why I do these things. I feel so restless then. At those moments I want him to listen to me and give me his full attention. And at the same time, he irritates me and I feel the urge to push him away.'

Susan is the eldest of four children. She has a younger brother and two sisters. Her parents had split up when she was fifteen. She said that she was relieved when it happened, because there was a lot of arguing going on all the time. Susan decided to live with her father, leaving her brother and sisters with her mother. It was no easy time for her. Her father was away at work a lot and was hardly ever home. He left Susan to her own devices. She loved having the freedom, after all those stifling years of arguments and intense emotions. Her mother's breakdowns and anxiety attacks had exhausted her. But once alone, she often felt lonely a lot of the time and spent much of her time staying in contact with friends. That gave her peace of mind for a while, until they started to lean on her and would appeal to her to support them. She would then distance herself from them. The process was often accompanied with conflict. It was always a process of attracting and repelling, which is now repeating itself in her relationship. Looking back, Susan saw this pattern of behavior in her parents during her youth. Her father was quite aloof. He showed little emotion and was inclined not to interfere with Susan's life. Susan's mother on the other hand, was often more affectionate and often sought validation, also from Susan. In stressful or tense situations, her mother clamped onto Susan. Susan has learned how to distance herself somewhat from her father. Her mother, on the other hand, has taught her to stay close to the other person when there is tension. For a long time, she managed to combine these two extremes and to handle the tension between her parents in their relationship, but she is now slowly starting to recognize how much energy it costs her. She wants to learn how to do it differently.

The Importance of Secure Bases

In the 1950s, the psychiatrist John Bowlby laid an important foundation for contemporary knowledge on attachment between children and their parents, and later with other (attachment) figures. We have already briefly mentioned this subject in the historical overview. We cannot emphasize enough the importance of his work as the founder of attachment theory.

Bowlby first studied the effect on children of being separated from their parents during a hospital stay. In those days it was quite normal for hospitalized children to be separated from their parents.

The anxiety and distress caused by the separation, as the child is forced to part from his or her parents, was back then seen as normal and surmountable. As long as the parents came for the child afterwards, it was believed that the child would suffer no lasting emotional damage. Bowlby noticed however that some children were very detached on being reunited. These children did not fall into their parent's arms, nor were they ecstatic to see them. They needed a considerable adjustment period before the attachment with the parents was restored to some extent.

The research that led to the Attachment Theory model explained certain patterns of attachment, bonding, and separation (anxiety).

> *Attachment behaviour is any behaviour that results in a person attaining or maintaining proximity to some other clearly identified individual who is conceived as better able to cope with the world . . . for a person to know that an attachment figure is available and responsive gives him a strong and pervasive feeling of security, and so encourages him to value and continue the relationship.*
>
> (Bowlby, 1988d, p. 29)

Bowlby is the first to make the connection between the breaking of attachment and loss. According to Bowlby, grief is a normal adjustment reaction to the loss of the attachment. Bowlby's Attachment Theory and his views on separation anxiety challenged the Freudian-based theories. According to Freud, the development of a child was determined by his 'dependence' on the parents, mostly the mother. This dependence has to be overcome in order to grow and develop.

Bowlby describes attachment as a natural instinct, which exists in all mammals. Attachment is a motivational and behavioral system that directs an infant to seek the safety and care of its parents or caregiver for as long as it is dependent on them for its survival. Also, a secure attachment ensures that the child or young animal can examine its world step by step. Attachment offers a safe point of departure to explore, to experiment, and take risks. The attachment figure (parent or caregiver) in this description is the *secure base* (a term first used by Mary Ainsworth), to which the child can always return, and then once again set out on another adventure and explore the world.

Bowlby makes a major distinction when it comes to 'safety.' On the one hand there is 'feeling secure' and on the other hand the safety of the actual situation, in the sense of absence of threat factors or 'being safe.' Feeling secure and being safe are clearly not the same thing. From an attachment point of view, feeling secure is the most important of the two. This subjective feeling of security is created when the attachment figures are close by and available, even though this may not lead to objective safety. This is where the term *secure base* comes from: attachment figures give a feeling and a sense of security. But even secure bases cannot always guarantee that the situation is actually safe. We use the expression 'safe haven' as a metaphor used to describe the feeling of safety and security. The safe haven is where people are welcomed in, where people seek safety when feeling threatened. This safe haven refers (only) to what Kohlrieser calls 'caring.' Secure bases are not only about the security people experience when they receive support while exploring the world, but also about being encouraged to face challenges, do research, and discover. So, this is not only about caring, but also about daring.

Bowlby developed his theory based on careful observation and experiments. He took a different approach to others before him. He conducted research on 'healthy' individuals: how 'normal' children and parents react to separation. It is now hard to imagine that his work was controversial in his time. Because the effects of the upbringing of children only become visible at a much later age—and therefore in the long term—it took much longer to prove the irrefutable accuracy of Bowlby's theories.

Bowlby's work was supported by studies of American psychologist Harry Harlow (1959). In an experimental setting, he studied how, when new-born rhesus monkeys were separated from their birth mothers, they react to their surrogate mothers. The prevailing thought at that time was that children only needed sufficient warmth and food to grow. The infant monkeys were placed in cages with two wire monkey mothers. One of the wire monkeys held a bottle from which the infant monkey could obtain nourishment, while the other wire monkey was covered with a soft terry cloth so that they could cuddle, but not obtain nourishment. To prove the prevailing theories, the infant monkeys would have had to give preference to the wire monkey with the bottle because the only thing necessary to survive should be food. To Harlow's surprise, although the infant monkeys would go to the wire mother to obtain food, they spent most of their days with the soft cloth mother. When frightened, the baby monkeys would turn to their cloth-covered mother for comfort and security. When Harlow gave the infant monkeys a scare, before giving them the choice between the two surrogate mothers, without any exception, they all fled to the soft cloth mother.

Attachment and intimacy are conditions necessary to live, develop, and grow. Children cannot survive without a form of attachment and intimacy. To feel safe and secure is essential for our coping, to deal with adversity (see Chapter 8). How the feeling of being secure is achieved varies from an active approach to a passive waiting and seeking support, to trying to solve it alone. That the lack of secure bases in the development of the infant monkeys has major consequences is proved when Harlow frightens the infants who grew up in complete isolation, without surrogate mothers. These monkeys did not flee when threatened. They just sat there, paralyzed with fear, intensely disturbed.

Working Models

In Bowlby's theory, he distanced himself from the vision of Freud, that people are driven by their urges. Freud considered the dependence of children on their parents as negative, but necessary for growing up. From this point of view, childhood dependence is something that must be overcome. Bowlby replaces the theory on dependence with the theory of attachment, in which attachment is both a necessary tendency and a natural need. Attachment allows people to enter into long-term relationships, to take care of others, and allow themselves to be cared for; this sense of safety and security allows them to develop and grow. The basis for how people enter into attachment relationships is laid down during the earliest period of attachment. During the first attachment phase, children develop working models, as Bowlby calls them. These working models are internal representations that children develop based on experiences they gain in relation to their parents and caregivers. They create a working model of their outside world (external working model), of how others react to them as well as a working model of their inside world (internal working model), of how they see themselves.

Children build up these working models based on their experiences, while at the same time, using them to make predictions of the reactions they will receive from others. In other words, the internal working model is a cognitive framework comprising mental representations for understanding the world, self, and others based on a set of expectations about the availability of attachment figures. When the prediction and the outcome match, it endorses the assumption, internalizing the working model even more. The working model can only have one of two effects, a positive or negative outcome. A positive outcome can empower the child and the positive image of the attachment figure. Seeking closeness to an attachment figure (for example the parent or caregiver) will be answered by that figure's availability and appropriate responsiveness to the needs of the child. The child is positively reinforced in his or her belief that there is support available when desired. The ratification of a negative outcome, however, will fortify a negative image of the self and of the other person, when the attachment figure (consciously or subconsciously) is either unavailable or does not react appropriately to the needs of the child. It will also strengthen the (self-)belief that the child is not worth that support.

Humans develop a sense of security and the ability to deal with fear in two phases. From earliest childhood, the actual physical presence and the supportive reaction of attachment figures are vital to develop a sense of security. When a baby cries for a reason other than hunger, thirst, or pain, the most effective ways to console him or her (in decreasing degree of effectiveness) are by the sound of the voice of the attachment figure speaking in a soothing tone, sucking on a pacifier, and lastly, being picked up, held, and rocked. Children begin to realize that because of the calming effect of attachment figures, when available, they can endure threatening situations. As the child develops, this learning experience leads to the second phase in which the child learns to trust. They will learn that if the attachment figures are not physically present, they will be available if and when necessary. In the early years, the physical presence of the attachment figures determines the sense of security. Later on, whether this sense of security grows or lessens depends on whether the child has the expectation and the ability to correctly assess if the attachment figure will be available, even if they are not physically present.

For the above-mentioned development to take place, it is essential that people not only see their attachment figures as people who are prepared to offer help and support, but also, and more importantly, that they judge themselves to be someone to whom help and support will be given, especially by their attachment figures, when they ask. These two assessments could be seen separately. Yet they influence each other during our development. The external and internal working models affect each other as we grow up because our subconscious mind is continually registering events and experiences that confirm both models. If attachment figures repeatedly reject a child, it will create an external working model based on the message 'people will reject you.' At the same time, the child creates an internal working model based on the message 'you are undesirable and not worth loving.' These become important values with which the child approaches and experiences the environment. Of course, there is also a positive version: the child is validated in his or her contact with attachment figures, develops an external working model in which he or she receives positive reactions, developing an internal working model with the view that he or she is loved and has value as a person.

Unexpected outcomes, both positive and negative, challenge our working models. We then have two options, either review the working model, or ignore the unexpected outcome and park it somewhere, waiting for confirmation at a later moment. Because the brain has a cognitive filter, people tend to ignore unexpected outcomes or attribute them to specific circumstances, so that they do not have to adapt their working models. As a result, working models are more often confirmed than revised. Beliefs are then empowered, despite the fact that in actuality, other attachment experiences are being offered. This makes it difficult, but does not rule out that it is possible to change the attachment style later on in life.

Children have a hard time understanding mixed messages from their attachment figures. When the behavior of an attachment figure causes a child to develop an external working model, in which it cannot seek closeness and cannot expect support, while at the same time the attachment figure says that they love their child, then there is a mixed message. The words are incongruent, not in line, with the behavior of the attachment figures. This can confuse the child. What should it believe? The words or the behavior? This confusion can cause the child to develop double external and internal working models. Depending on the situation, the child will show behavior that seems to be required by the behavior of the parents, and the next moment it will show behavior that suits the way they behave. A teacher at school, for example could notice that a child will sometimes come very close, will show positive behavior and ask for confirmation, while at other times it will show negative behavior, make it impossible to talk to him or her, and seem aloof and unattainable.

Susan, the subject of the case study at the beginning of this chapter, also received mixed signals/messages from her parents. The signals from each parent separately were quite congruent, but the parents differed greatly from each other. Susan was offered totally different examples in the behavior of her father and that of her mother: her father was more aloof, her mother more affectionate. When developing an external model as to how one should approach the 'other,' this is very confusing to a child. Out of loyalty to both parents, it is almost impossible for the child to make a choice and two such different styles cannot be combined into one working model. The child will eventually develop its own preferred style, but remain dependent on the reactions of the parents. In a way, Susan 'chooses' the more aloof style belonging to her father, because the affectionate manner of her mother feels suffocating to her. At the same time, she remains aware that her need for proximity has not disappeared.

Rejection or the threat of abandonment has quite a negative effect on the ability to bond. This happens, for example, when attachment figures threaten to stop loving the child when it misbehaves. Sometimes this is a latent threat, lurking just under the surface, but some parents actually say this in an effort to impose discipline. Such conditional love and care for a child prevents it from being free to develop as it needs to. The emotional availability of the attachment figure, the appropriate reaction to the child's innate need, the responsiveness as their child reaches out to them, is withdrawn. The (repeated) threat of being abandoned, either by being left behind somewhere or by its parents threatening suicide, for example, has a much greater, sometimes devastating effect. For the child, the attachment figures are then completely out of reach and become permanently unavailable. It goes without saying that, especially if the threat is physically carried out through, for example, divorce, fleeing from a conflict or war zone, someone going missing, or (chosen) emigration, it can cause long-term serious disruption.

Attachment Styles

Attachment styles describe the way in which children attach to their parents or caregivers. Based on Bowlby's working models these can be divided into two groups: secure and insecure attachment. Insecure attachment has a number of variants. Various terms are used in contemporary literature. In this book we will be referring to the most common terminology and we will point out similarities with other models.

Attachment styles are usually represented as opposite poles in a coordinate system where the y-axis is the measure for avoidance of intimacy, closeness, and attachment, and the x-axis is a measure for separation anxiety. In this manner four quadrants are created: one quadrant represents secure attachment when there is almost no avoidance of intimacy and little fear of abandonment. In the other quadrants in this model, three insecure attachment strategies arising from combinations of avoiding intimacy and separation anxiety are identified. An alternative classification using the same polar coordinate system makes use of the 'model of other' on the y-axis and the 'model of self' on the x-axis. The x-axis with the 'model of self,' runs from a positive self-image (secure) on one end and fearful/tense on the other. The y-axis runs from high avoidance at the bottom to low avoidance or, in other words, represents having a positive view of others on one end of the scale and avoiding others on the other. In Figure 3.1 we have combined the quadrants of both models.

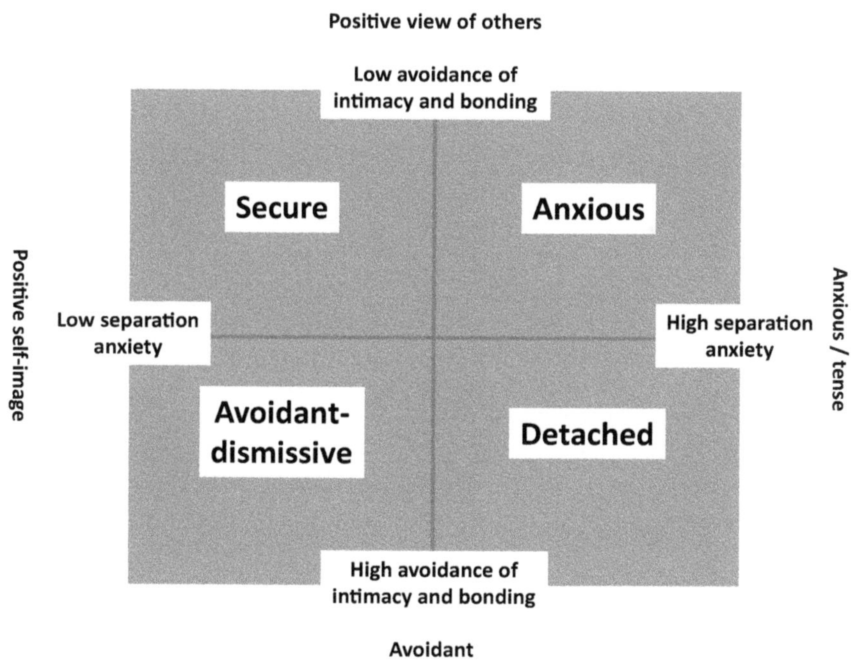

Figure 3.1 Matrix of Attachment Styles

Secure Attachment Style

The secure attachment is the 'healthy' variation of attachment, which exists when there is a combination of a positive self-image and a positive image of (the) other(s). This is regarded as the 'successful, normal' attachment, when someone has the ability both to connect with others and to say goodbye. People with a secure attachment style have positive views of themselves and their attachments. In general, they have warm, responsive, and stable relationships, feel at ease, and are content with them. These people are comfortable with intimacy and with independence. They have no trouble being alone, they are not afraid that they will be abandoned. There is a good balance between independence and dependence. The majority of people are securely attached. It is estimated that 60–80% are securely attached. Incidentally, people who are mainly securely attached also sometimes recognize some of the characteristics from the other styles, at certain times or in certain relationships. In the same way, people who have a mainly insecure attachment style are able to feel secure at times or recognize aspects of other attachment styles (see also Figure 3.2, which shows the overlapping attachment styles).

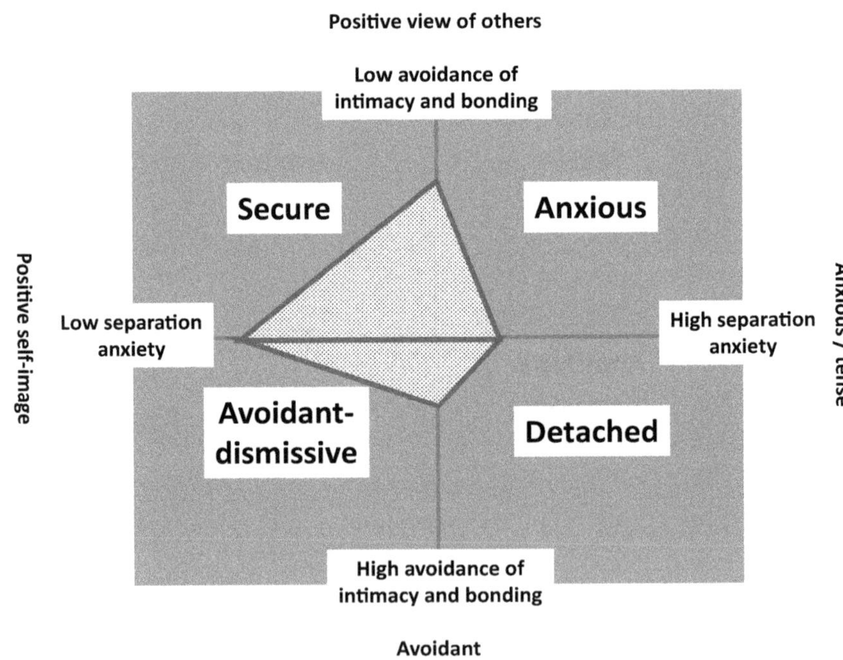

Figure 3.2 Overlapping Attachment Styles—Predominantly Securely Attached

Insecure Attachment Styles

Insecure attachment styles develop when a child reaches out to an adult and has to deal with the adult being inconsistently attuned to it. A child reaches out to an adult to be consoled and needs that adult to be sensitive and responsive. This is the primary strategy of infant mammals. If the attachment figure constantly responds inadequately, the child develops secondary strategies also called deactivating strategies. These secondary strategies help the child to experience a sense of intimacy, even though limited. There are two types of secondary strategies: hyperactivation or deactivation of the primary attachment style (Kosminsky & Jordan, 2016). When hyperactivation of the primary attachment style occurs, the child will attempt to elicit the involvement, care, and support of the attachment figure through clinging and controlling responses, and cognitive and behavioral efforts aimed at minimizing distance from them. When this attempt finally succeeds and feels like it has been rewarded, the child's feeling that this secondary strategy is the right one to use will be validated. If there is no response however, or the response feels like a punishment, then the child has no other option, in its dependent position, than to resort to deactivation of the primary attachment style. The child will then hold back, no longer reach out, and withdraw. If the punishment then stops, or the child is rewarded for its adapted behavior, the child will then be validated in this secondary strategy.

Please note: even though the child needs to deactivate the primary attachment style, as it is appraised as nonviable, the need for attachment itself does not disappear, but rather is hidden behind the secondary, insecure attachment style. Not only does this cause the observable behavior of reaching out to disappear from sight, it also leads to the denial of attachment needs, avoidance of closeness, intimacy. The need as such, however, is still present, only the child can no longer feel it. As Brené Brown comments on her research on attachment:

> *Scientists agree that we are neurologically programmed to connect with each other. We are made to give, to care, to be empathetic. But what does this mean exactly, and especially, what prevents us from doing it? Something that kept popping up, was the fear of the lack of connection. The stress we experience when we do something or do not do it, that results in withholding of love and appreciation, can be described as shame. There I was. Shame is not exactly an ideal study object. No-one wants to talk about it, just because it is such a powerful, painful and complex emotion. . . . Shame is that intensely painful feeling that we are not worth being seen or belong somewhere. It is the most human and primitive emotion we know, and above all, an emotion with a memory. Everyone is able to recall a specific event and immediately feel ashamed*

> *again. . . . Shame is deadly and we are neck deep in it. It creeps into every corner of your life, it dictates everything.*
>
> (Ongenae, 2015)

As shown in Figure 3.1, insecure attachment can be divided into three different attachment styles:

1. Anxious (also anxious-preoccupied or anxious-ambivalent) attachment style
   People with an anxious-ambivalent attachment style combine separation anxiety with the need for proximity and intimacy. They have a more positive view of others than of themselves. They would love to totally immerse themselves in their relationship and have an intense fear of abandonment. This strategy is based on thoughts about whether they are worthy of receiving love. Children with this attachment style hardly ever play, because they feel they have to be vigilant in case they are left alone by the parent. They will demand a lot of attention and act clingy and desperate. They react strongly to separation from the parent, but will behave ambivalently with them, seeking proximity, but at the same time express anger and be difficult to comfort.
2. Detached (also fearful-avoidant) attachment style
   The anxious-avoidant attachment style is found in the quadrant that combines separation anxiety and avoidance of intimacy. People with these attachment styles pull away from needing anything from anyone else and are self-contained and independent. They have little need for intimacy and attachment. Also, they keep feelings and intimate personal thoughts to themselves. Children with an anxious-avoidant attachment style avoid emotional contact as often as possible. They do not exhibit stress upon separation, or when the parent returns. Such a child will hardly react or respond to physical contact. This child would like to connect emotionally with someone else, but pulls back when the opportunity arises. The separation anxiety in this person is expressed by an aversion to attachment. People with this attachment style find it difficult to be vulnerable and express their feelings. They also have difficulty with physical and sexual intimacy.
3. Avoidant-dismissive (also known as disoriented or disorganized) attachment style
   The dismissive-avoidant attachment style is found in the quadrant that combines low separation anxiety with high avoidance of intimacy. People with this attachment style are highly independent and keep their distance. They are sure of themselves, but have a negative image of others. Children with this attachment style have learned to keep their feelings to themselves. Their parents were inconsistently attuned to them or sometimes even punished them for any sign of emotion. Children with a

> dismissive-avoidant attachment style have learned that in the end, when all is said and done, they will have to face everything alone. They have learned to survive and no longer expect affection or love.

People's attachment styles can also overlap somewhat. An attachment style rarely falls into a single category. People react (slightly) differently in some relationships and situations than in others.

> *'It can also be possible that people should be viewed as along a continuum in all categories,' said Glenn I. Roisman, the director of the Relationships Research Lab at the University of Minnesota in Minneapolis. It's worth noting that just as people in the insecure categories can become more secure when they form close relationships with secure people, secure people can become less so if paired with people who are insecure. 'You need social context to sustain your sense of security,' said Peter Fonagy, a professor of psychoanalysis at University College London.*
>
> (Murphy, 2017)

In general, however, one of the styles predominates and usually this is the style activated when loss occurs.

The work of developmental psychologists such as Mary Main (1996; Main, Hesse & Hesse, 2011) and Peter Fonagy shows that the quality of the attachment relationship also determines the development of the child's ability to regulate its emotions and deal with stress, and the level in which the child becomes aware that it can influence some things. Recent research shows how the development of our brain and neurological system support Bowlby's working models (Schore, 2001, 2012; Cozolino, 2010). The hormone oxytocin, which is produced in the brain (also see Chapter 8), helps this process. The production of this hormone is stimulated by the first skin-on-skin contact, immediately after birth. This physical experience, which takes place at such a young age (in the preverbal stage) and is stored in the unconscious memory, indicates whether approaching someone is safe. In a new relationship, oxytocin is again produced, but the very first experience determines whether someone will allow it in automatically or still has some discomfort to overcome. These emotion-regulating skills form the foundation of the child's psychosocial development. A secure attachment makes a positive contribution to the development of these skills whereas insecure attachment hinders that development (Kosminsky & Jordan, 2016).

As previously mentioned, attachment styles are developed during early childhood and continue to wield influence throughout the course of one's life. The attachment style of a child can be observed in its behavior, for instance, when it plays with the parent present, but because attachment is a pattern of behavior, it cannot be determined after a single observation. A child's attachment style defines its development. People take their attachment style with them wherever they go. Secure attachment allows people to bond and enter into new intimate relationships. Insecure or avoidant attachment causes all kinds of problems that stand in the way of 'healthy' and fulfilling relationships and bonds.

Attachment styles can, however, still change during the course of one's life. It is possible for people to evolve from an insecure to a secure attachment style (or the other way around). Life experiences and access to a network of attachment relationships can change the internal working model, in the positive as well as negative sense (Sroufe et al., 1999).

For an insecure attachment to change in a positive sense depends mainly on whether there are secure bases available during (impactful) experiences later on in life. Main (1996; Main et al., 2011) calls it 'earned' secure attachment.

When an insecure attachment develops during childhood, a stable relationship during adulthood can heal attachment insecurity to some extent. The most securely attached partner then becomes the secure base and has the greatest influence on the development of the attachment style in the relationship (Vonk, 2013). Losing an attachment figure, an otherwise important relationship or a meaningful object or thing later in life, can evoke the same feelings that belonged to the separation (anxiety) from an attachment figure during childhood (Kosminsky & Jordan, 2016).

> *If we accept that someone is irreplaceable, we become so dependent, we create insecurity for ourselves. I remember thinking as a child, if my mother is irreplaceable—she threatened to leave, and sometimes to commit suicide—I would have to find a replacement. And I think that I have been doing that ever since. I am attached to people and at the same time, I am always thinking: I need to have a replacement ready, just in case. I always need to have an alternative ready, which of course is not a very good idea in relationships. These are survival strategies meant to help you in the relationship, that have very perverse side effects as they are actually putting the relationships at risk.*
>
> (Grunberg, 2016)

People can revert to their earliest attachment style, even though they have learned later in life to make healthy attachments.

Attachment in Adults

The attachment style of a child to its parent can also be observed in various close adult relationships. On the road to adulthood, children internalize the attachment figure and do not need them to be present physically to feel secure. This is true for as long as their attachment figure is indeed available, so that they can be contacted if they need consoling, for instance after an exam or troubles with friends. Also, everyone develops extra coping strategies to deal with difficult situations in life. But when people are confronted with potentially threatening situations, they are inclined to revert back to the strategies that are connected with the attachment style from their childhood (Mikulincer & Shaver, 2010; Kosminsky & Jordan, 2016). At a certain level, people are continually scanning their environment, on the lookout for possible dangers and threats. When these signals appear, they activate their attachment mechanism:

1. The first reaction will be to seek the proximity of an (external or internalized) attachment figure to push away or remove the danger. This primary attachment reaction is followed by a second step.
2. This second phase consists of an evaluation of whether the attachment figure is available for and responsive to their need for support.

    - If so, then the availability of the attachment figure is not only comforting, but there is also confirmation that this approach works: when people receive positive feedback to their act of reaching out, it endorses their belief that the attachment figure is available to them and that they are worthy of receiving support. This positive acknowledgement increases self-confidence.
    - In the event of the attachment figure not being available, because he or she is unreachable or non-responsive, it will lead to an insecure attachment reaction. This insecure attachment reaction in turn leads to a third phase.

3. In this third phase, people estimate whether looking for proximity for support is an achievable option:

    - When a decision has been made that the option is not achievable, it leads to a strategy in which the person will no longer seek proximity to an attachment figure and chooses to push away the danger of rejection and keep it at a distance altogether. This too, is an confirmation, but a negative one, arising from the decision that you will have to manage on your own.
    - When one decides that closeness is still a viable option, but not from the attachment figure one was expecting and had received it earlier, it leads to a frantic search for other attachment figures, increasing the stress. The result is a paradoxical direction of movement. On the one hand, the person feels unprotected and on the alert for signals of potential threats. On the other hand, the person is searching for attachment with other attachment figures, which makes them vulnerable.

The Difference Between Attachment and Bonding

Bowlby, the founder of attachment theory, introduced the term *attachment* into psychological language use. Kohlrieser (2006; Kohlrieser et al., 2012) added another term to this cycle: *bonding*. Attachment and bonding are distinct concepts.

Attachment describes the unconscious process of emotional connections in relationships, and bonding refers to the conscious behavior and actions presented when in contact with others, in the attempt to exercise being open and vulnerable in new relationships. Attachment is the foundation underlying the ability to bond. Bonding is also essential for intimacy, the next theme on the cycle of transition.

The Counselor as a Secure Base

In this chapter, you have been able to read about how attachment determines the way in which people are connected with each other. Especially in significant or major situations, tensions, conflict or (the threat of) loss, they grab hold of the old working models for support. Often, however, these working models are no longer very helpful. This is a key reason for people to seek guidance from a counselor or coach.

Initially many clients will look for confirmation of their old working models, since these constitute their vision of reality.

> *Each time we make the journey of personal change, we need to understand our attachment patterns. . . . Our attachment scripts influence the nature of our personal relationships, how we manage our emotions and our outlook on life. It is never easy to overcome dysfunctional attachment. As I have already indicated, it takes a lot of work and effort. . . . The only way to restore attachment is by looking ourselves straight in the eye and face our attachment styles and inner demons to become free of false perceptions. We can only heal when we are prepared to face up to what has caused us trouble and find new solutions.*
>
> (Kets de Vries, 2016, p. 46)

The counselor represents the old attachment figure. Subconsciously they invite the counselor to 'join in' in their working models. This is called transference. When the counselor unwittingly accepts this invitation, it confirms all the assumptions of the client's working models. As part of this dynamic the client may develop a strong dependency on the counselor continuously telling him what to do. Or the pertinent subject is never really addressed, because the counselor does not probe a client who is used to figuring out everything themselves. Temporarily, it may feel good that the client is reassured and has had their working model confirmed, but the client does not actually learn anything new.

True learning then is not about reaffirming the working models of the client. On the contrary, the client's self-awareness and self-confidence can only develop further when he or she acquires new convictions about attachment and thereby adjusts his or her working models. The counselor is key in this process.

Bowlby (1988d) used the term *secure base* in a broader sense of the word than merely pertaining to the parent-child relationship. He also used it to refer to the counselor-client relationship. The counselor performs the role of the attachment figure in a way different from what the client is used to, namely, as a secure base. The concept of secure bases clarifies how the relationship between client and counselor is critical to the therapeutic process.

Kohlrieser et al. (2012) added two other aspects to the term *secure base* that are important in counseling. He writes about the balance between caring and daring.

> **Definition:** 'We define a secure base as: a person, place, goal, or object that provides a sense of protection, safety and caring and offers a source of inspiration and energy for daring, exploration, risk taking and seeking challenge' (Kohlrieser et al., 2012, p. 8).

Caring consists of the security and trust the therapist provides and that are necessary as a basis from which the client can be dared: challenged to take new steps and grow. To succeed in counseling, it is essential to maintain a good balance between caring, security, and daring/challenge. The professional who aims to be a secure base for their client offers them security and trust and challenges them to grow at the same time.

In Chapter 10, we will elaborate further on the counselor as a secure base.

Counseling the Other Side of Attachment and Bonding

A secure or healthy attachment provides an important basis for dealing with loss and grief. In other words, when there is solidified grief as in detachment of clinging (see Figure 3.3), you will often see aspects of insecure attachment.

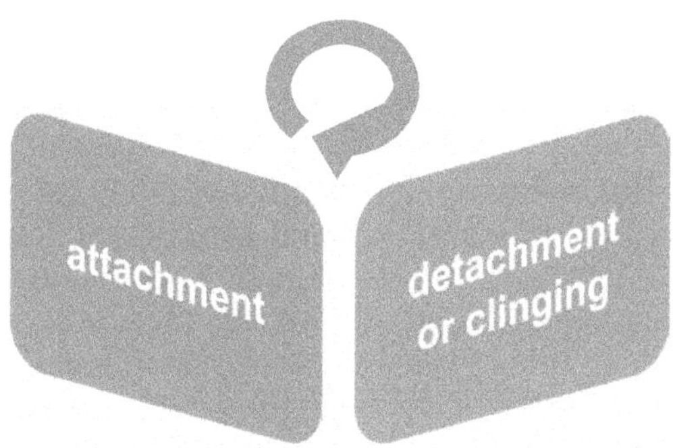

Figure 3.3 Both Sides of the Same Coin for the Theme 'Attachment'

Inability or refusal to attach, or its opposite, clinging, causes someone to avoid actually having to say goodbye and, thereby, as it were, leaves out grief. The client will feel isolated and disconnected from his or her surroundings. Learning to trust a new secure base is an important step for the client to take.

Dialogue

The case study at the beginning of the chapter was about the relationship between Susan and Kevin. Susan chose a new, short series of individual counseling sessions to gain more insight into her attachment dynamics.

Barbara: It is good to see you again, Susan.
Susan: Thank you. It is good to be back, but also a little strange being here by myself.
Barbara: What do you mean by 'strange?'
Susan: Well, it makes me a bit nervous actually. Even though we fight and argue a lot, I like having Kevin around. At least I am not so alone then.
Barbara: You say 'at least you are not alone.' What does it mean to you, 'to be alone?'
Susan: That's a difficult question. I am not exactly sure what it means. The minute I am alone, I always call or text someone, or something of the sort.
Barbara: So, when you are alone, you always immediately look to make contact again.
Susan: Yes, that's correct. I have never thought about it like that, but it is true.
Barbara: And do you know why you do that?
Susan: No, I have no idea. It's almost automatic.
Barbara: Would it be okay with you if we do a little experiment here, now?
Susan: Yes, okay.
Barbara: Close your eyes. (She closes her own eyes too.) And imagine that you are completely alone. In reality I am here with you, but imagine that you are alone. We are going to sit here like this for a few minutes. Just relax and sit with your eyes closed.
In the minutes that follow, Susan's breathing rate increases. She becomes restless and starts to fiddle with her fingers.
Barbara: When you are ready, you can open your eyes again and come back into the present.
Susan: Wow. . . . That was really unpleasant. I began to get really restless.
Barbara: So, you felt restless inside. And what was it your hands wanted to do?
Susan: I kept grabbing my hands. Almost like I was looking for something to hold onto.

Barbara: So, when you imagine that you are alone, you feel restless inside and you look for something to hold onto.
Susan: Yes, that's exactly what I do. That might be what I am hoping to find in Kevin. Something to hold onto. So that I am not alone. But at the same time, I keep pushing him away, as if I am also afraid when he comes too close. (Visible emotion.)
Barbara: So, you are looking for something to hold onto and you cling to it, and then push it away again when it comes too close. How is that similar to the relationship you have with your parents?
Susan: That clinging reminds me of my mother. But that is mostly how she does it. She clung onto my father and also onto me. And now she is clinging even harder onto my eldest brother. Always trying to draw attention. She can't do anything herself. Needs help with everything. Well, my dad . . . he just let go. It was like he moved beyond her reach. She kept trying to grab him, but could not. She had no grip on him any longer. It sometimes made her almost hysterical. (Stares into space.)
Barbara: That must have been really intense for you. To be a witness to all that.
Susan: Yes, it really was intense. Usually she took it out on me. Or I would have to console her and stay with her for hours. I seemed to be the best at calming her down. I knew what would help her and what would not.
Barbara: And where was your father then?
Susan: At work or at the gym. Or just not around.
Barbara: Who supported you? Who was there for you?
Susan: My grandmother. My mother's mother. She came around regularly. Sometimes she would take me out shopping, to buy things for school and things like that. That was nice. When I was with her, I didn't have to watch out all the time.
Barbara: So, you could be a kid again for a while.
Susan: Yes, something like that.
Barbara: Is she still alive?
Susan: Yes, she's still alive, but when I went to live with my dad, I hardly ever saw her. She had a hard time trying to understand that too. And now she lives on the other side of the country, close to my uncle. She has difficulty walking and suffers from dementia. My uncle and aunt take care of her. (Then, suddenly, tears.) I miss her so badly. It was also awful to hardly ever see her after the divorce.
Barbara: I can imagine. She gave you the security that a child needs in an environment that was unsafe for the most part. Your parents could not give you that security. It was good that she was there for you when you were young. I can imagine that you must miss her.
Susan: (Nods and wipes her tears.)

Barbara: And how painful it must have been for you to have to let go of the one person that made you feel safe. That is hard to comprehend when you are a child.
Susan: I have never really stopped to think about it. But I believe that it could be the reason why I keep having to keep a certain distance in relationships.
Barbara: That may very well be possible. Do you think it would be possible to visit your grandma?
Susan: Yes, I do actually. I could call my uncle sometime.
Barbara: I think that's a very good idea. Do you think you could manage to do that before our next session?
Susan: I am certainly going to try my hardest. (Smiling through her tears.)

Questions for Self-Reflection

- How do you deal with asking for help? When do you ask and when do you not? Who do you ask for help? Who do you not ask?
- Who or what makes you feel safe?
- Who or what supports you? In what way?
- Who or what carries you? How?
- Have you ever missed security, support, or being challenged? When? What happened?
- Are you anybody's secure base or would you like to/could you be that for someone? In what way?

Exercises

Exercise—Recognizing Attachment Styles

In the role of counselor, explain the four different attachment styles to the other person and let that person tell you what he or she does and does not recognize in him- or herself and in others in his or her system. As counselor, you may help with the inner search by asking pertinent questions.

> **Instruction:** Divide into pairs and do the exercise described above. Decide together who is going to be counselor and who client. Switch roles after 15 to 20 minutes. Which points were raised during the role play?

Exercise—'Inquiry'

Sit quietly with the client. Ask the client, during the course of five minutes, the same question over and over again: 'tell me, what is so good about not bonding with someone?' After the client's answer, no matter what it is, you say 'thank you.' Then repeat the question: 'tell me, what is so good about not bonding with someone?' You can change the intonation of the question, put the emphasis on other words in the sentence, or repeat the question in an identical way. With every repetition of the question, the client is invited to dig a little bit deeper and come up with answers possibly previously unknown to himself. In this way, the client (also) explores the flip side of bonding and is possibly confronted with (perhaps unacknowledged) elements of his own insecure attachment styles.

Instruction: Divide into pairs and do the exercise described above. Decide together who is going to be counselor and who client.

Switch roles.

What have you gained from this exercise?

Exercise—To Physically Experience Different Attachment Styles

This exercise is designed to allow a client to experience the direction of the motion of his or her attachment dynamics physically. In this way the client learns to recognize the reactions of his or her own body, in situations in which the client's needs are or are not fulfilled.

Attachment experiences are stored in our so-called body memory. They are formed at such a young age before there is any lingual ability to verbalize the experience. The memory can therefore not be cognitively reproduced. There are literally no words for it. The memory can however be recalled by the body by placing the client in a similar attachment situation. This exercise consists of several different responses given by the counselor when the client consciously reaches out to him or her. These reactions can be compared with the reactions the client experienced at a young age with attachment figures. The goal of the exercise is to give the client insight by experiencing in the present what happened in the original situation.

Instruction: Divide into groups of two (A is the counselor, B is the client). Decide together who is going to be counselor and who client. The counselor asks the client to stand opposite at an arm's length.

- Ask your client to recall a situation from early youth in which he or she reached out to a parent in need of support and ask the client then to actually hold out his or her arms to you.
- The counselor reacts from the parent's position successively in the following ways:
  - By taking a step back as the client holds out his or her arms.
  - By not responding.
  - By pushing the client's arms away.
  - By welcoming the client and holding him or her firmly.

- After each step, make sure the client returns to the present. The counselor asks the client to move around, change his or her pose to confirm that the present is safe and secure and that you are there for the client if need be.
- After each part of the exercise, ask B how it felt to get such a response and what feeling it elicits.
- Ask your client to once again recall a moment from his or her youth and repeat the steps as above.
- Afterwards discuss briefly how it was for both of you to do this exercise.
- After that, switch roles.

Exercise—The Secure Base Map

Secure bases can be people, places, events, experiences, goals and much more:

- Examples of people who can be secure bases include (grand-, step-, foster-, adoptive-) mothers, (grand-, step-, foster-, adoptive-) fathers, brothers, sisters, uncles, and aunts. (N.B.: parents cannot give their children the role of secure base, as long as the parent is in the caregiving role.) At the end of a parent's life, the roles may be exchanged, but not during childhood as there is risk of parentification (see Chapter 4; in the latter case, the child can in no way be a secure base to a parent).
- Examples of places that can be secure bases include country, house, nature, city, and town.
- Examples of events than can be secure bases include marriages, funerals, (sports) games, catastrophes, and accidents.
- Examples of experiences than can be secure bases include a deep friendship, being rewarded for an extraordinary achievement, receiving an unexpected compliment, getting the opportunity to do something special, becoming a parent, and a good marriage/relationship with a partner.
- Examples of goals than can be secure bases include business targets, being promoted, becoming a parent, running the marathon, and organizing a charity event.
- Examples of other categories than can be viewed as secure bases include pets, faith, standards and values, ideology, and symbols.

Secure bases may differ for each phase of life. Have the client make an inventory of secure bases for three time periods (Figure 3.4):

- Then—past
- Now—present
- Later—future

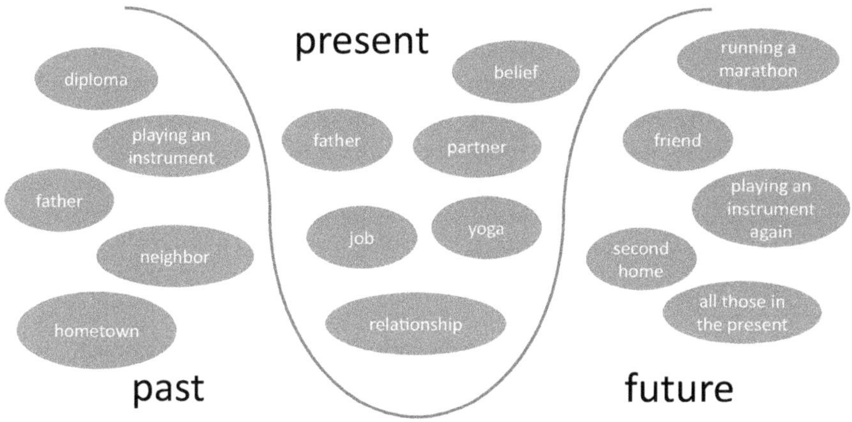

Figure 3.4 Example of a Secure Base Map

This inventory can be done as a simple summary, but the client can also be encouraged to be more creative, by drawing or symbolizing figures, places, and events.

> **Instruction:** Divide into groups of three (A is the counselor, B is the client, and C is the observer) and guide each other to make your own secure base map.
>
> Discuss your findings together and keep switching roles until everyone has had a turn.

Exercise—Constellation Using Mats

In addition to the genogram described in the exercise found under the topic 'feeling welcome,' a family constellation can offer a lot of insight into the different relationships within the system, in this case, the family of origin, by means of the physical experience it gives. For a constellation, the client starts with a question about something that is bothering him or her, and instead of finding the answer by talking about it, the answer is found by putting representatives of family members in the constellation. Several people are needed to do a constellation. The client arranges the representatives of his or her family members in the space according to what feels right in the moment. The members represent someone's father, mother, brother, sister and so on. These people may be alive or deceased. They do not need to have physical resemblance to play the role, it is more a matter of being able to perceive the energy of the position he or she is placed in.

Because there is not always a group available when doing individual sessions, you can also work with mats in different colors, to mark the places of the family members in the system. The client will go with his gut and place the mats on the floor of the room. The distance between the mats and their positions (facing each other or facing away) is of importance. By standing on each mat in turn and attuning to the position, the client can feel what dynamics are at work in that place in the system. The client can feel what it is like to stand in that person's shoes.

Keep in mind:

- The client first must put a mat down to represent him- or herself.
- Subsequently, every person in the system must be given a place, whether alive or deceased, stillborn or miscarriage.
- The differences between the mats, where they are placed, and the directions they are facing in relation to the other positions must feel correct to the client.
- That the mats symbolize actual people must be clearly and unmistakably recognizable to both counselor and client.

When the client has finished placing the mats, the counselor asks the client to begin on his or her own mat and then stand on each of the other mats taking note of physical feelings. To help, ask questions like the following:

- What is it like to stand in this place?
- How does it affect your relation as seen from the place where you are standing to the other members of your family?
- What does this position, the place, the demeanor, the direction in relation to the others, mean, especially in relation to you?
- What are you feeling while standing in this place?
- What changes do you wish for in the relationships within the system?

> **Instruction:** Divide into groups of three (A is the counselor, B is the client, and C is the observer) and help the client to get a clear picture of the family system. Use the theme-related questions described to guide the client.
>
> Discuss your findings together and keep switching roles until everyone has had a turn.

Exercise—Reaching Out and Withdrawing in Attachment Strategies

This exercise aims to let the client physically experience the push or pull dynamic of the attachment style. It will teach the client to recognize how his or her body reacts to situations in which needs are fulfilled or not.

Attachment dynamics can be considered as two distinct movements: reaching out and pulling back, that is, reaching out and expecting that help is available, and pulling back when help is expected to be unavailable. Once an action is well learned, we automate it and it disappears into our subconscious. People have a natural tendency to do this to a high degree (in other words, we all do it, all the time). Once automated, they lose sight of the direction of the movement they made in the behavior and how it related to their needs. When such a need is threatened, they will have already (almost instinctively) made the movement before realizing it.

- When someone assumes that they need to solve something by themselves, because they are on their own and help will not be available, they internally pull back. In doing so, they shut down and keep everybody out, which will not bring the fulfillment of their need any closer. In this exercise the client will make this inner motion visible on the outside by, in the case of the above example, physically taking a step back.
- When someone is able to reach out to someone because he or she expects that help will be available or simply wants to connect with that person, he or she actually moves towards them. Normally this is only an inner motion. The client will make this movement visible on the outside by following their inner intention and taking a physical step forward.

The basic setup: have the client stand in the middle of the space. The client may close his or her eyes to increase concentration and stay in touch with what he or she is feeling. The counselor reads one of the sentences below and invites the client to move in the direction that his or her inner feelings point towards. In other words:

- A step forward when the question gives rise to reaching out to the other.
- A step back when the question gives rise to wanting to pull back and keep at a distance.
- If the client cannot decide whether the movement should be forward or backward, he or she may take a step to the left or the right. In this manner, the client will learn that even when there is 'freezing' it is always possible to make a movement.

The counselor speaks for a meaningful person from the client's network. These people may be living or deceased. The counselor starts the sentence by introducing the person in question: 'I am . . .' followed by the sentence inviting the client to make the movement that the sentence calls for. After each movement especially the pull back movement, since this one is primarily triggered by fear, the counselor asks what the client needs to come/go back to the starting position.

To do this exercise, it is necessary that the counselor has gotten to know some of the people from the network of the client through the client's stories. The sentences spoken in their names always start with naming the relationship of that person to the client, to make the movement visible that the relationship evokes. Examples:

- I am <name of the father/mother>. I am your <father/mother>. You are my <child/son/daughter>.
- I am <name of brother/sister>. I am you <brother/sister>. You are my <brother/sister>.
- I am <name of partner>. I am your <partner>. You are my <partner/husband/wife/friend/boy-/girlfriend>.
- I am <name of child/son/daughter>. I am your <child/son/daughter>. You are my <parent/father/mother>.
- I am <name of friend/boy-/girlfriend >. I am your <friend/boy-/girlfriend >. You are my <friend/boy-/girlfriend>.
- I am <name of another meaningful person>. I am your <name of the relationship>. You are my <name of the relationship>.

Each meaningful relationship can be explored along the whole spectrum of emotional involvement, from joy to sadness, fear, and anger. You will be able to tell which attachment dynamic the client is used to, particularly when sentences are spoken that are contrary to the client's need/longing. Examples:

- I love you.
- I am so glad you are in my life.
- I miss you.
- I want to spend more time with you.
- You should try harder.
- You should try to fit in.
- You should behave.
- You should think about the others.
- I am mad at you.
- I am afraid of you.
- I am sorry.
- I do not want you to be mad at me.
- I do not want you to be afraid of me.
- Can you forgive me?

The attachment dynamic can be intensified by asking the client to make a pull-back movement by crossing their arms in a defensive motion, at the same time protecting the heart. When making a movement of reaching out, let the client reach out with their arms as well as well as by taking a step forward.

Instruction: Divide into groups of two. Decide who is going to play the role of the counselor and who the role of the client.

- Do the exercise described above.
- Discuss briefly what it was like for both parties to do this exercise.
- Switch roles.

4

SHARING INTIMACY AND OUTLINING SEXUALITY

A Case Study

Amanda is desperate. She is thirty-four and single. All her friends have already settled down. They all have partners and most of them have kids too. Amanda feels increasingly lonely lately. At times when others are all with their families she is mostly alone. Holidays and Sundays are the worst. She longs for a cozy home and a nice, stable relationship. Amanda is the eldest daughter. Her mother was only eighteen when Amanda was born. She knows who her father is but the relationship between her parents never really amounted to anything. When her mother discovered that she was pregnant, they had only just met and they were not really compatible. Her mother decided to have Amanda and raise her alone, against her parent's wishes. They refused to support her. In the beginning, it was hard. Amanda's mother was totally unprepared for motherhood. At times she left her alone in her bed for hours, while she was out shopping or drinking coffee with her friends. As Amanda got older, her mother would take her with her wherever she went. She often found herself sitting on a bar stool until late at night drinking a Coke, while her mother enjoyed herself with her friends. Sometimes Amanda actually had fun. She got plenty of attention and was allowed to drink anything she wanted. But more often, she dreamed being the child of a mother who read her stories at home, on whose lap she could sit, who sent her to bed on time, and who insisted she finish her food. Amanda grew up to become an independent young woman and was completely self-sufficient at an early age. She hated having to depend on others and still has difficulty letting others support her. She prefers to keep others at a distance. The thought of intimacy scares her, but at the same time she longs for it—for someone she can trust.

The Very First Moment of Intimacy

Intimacy and feeling secure are closely linked. Emotional intimacy is generally defined as a closeness and deep connection. It is letting someone see you for who you really are and letting them in. It is being touched, nurtured, and carried without having to stay alert. Intimacy is the longing to be touched on the boundaries of your being: your physical or external boundary being your body and your skin, and the internal boundary. Being touched on your internal boundary means that you are completely vulnerable, that your deepest thoughts, doubts, and feelings are seen and felt by the other.

> *It has cost me a year of therapy to realize that vulnerability is the only door to intimacy.*
>
> (Brené Brown, quoted in Ongenae, 2015)

And so, intimacy follows closely after bonding. The way in which attachment develops has enormous consequences for how close a person is able to let someone else come and whether someone can truly bond with goals and challenges in life and to groups (such as sports teams or other kinds of teams and organizations). The ability to truly bond with someone has everything to do with the level of intimacy you are able to handle.

A child's first experiences with intimacy are in contact with parents and caregivers, the child's first secure bases. From birth on, they are the examples and attachment figures who have the greatest impact on the development and molding of the child through the way they behave and their use of language. The manner in which they deal with intimacy when in contact with each other and with the child plays a major role in the development of a healthy intimacy experience on a physical and an emotional level.

Within the family system, there is a structure and an order. First, there are parents. Then come the children. The parents take care of the children. And the children accept the care of the parents. A secure attachment develops and the parents are a secure base for the children. They learn that they can trust and be vulnerable at the same time. That their boundaries are respected and that it is appropriate and enjoyable to be hugged and cuddled, rocked and carried.

Sometimes however, there is a shift in the family system, family members leave their natural place and end up in someone else's place. A child, for example, will then take on the care for his parent. Or a parent discusses adult subjects with one of the children instead of with his or her partner.

The cause can lie inside the family. Events such as the chronic illness of a parent or their departure through divorce or death bring changes to the interactions in the systemic relationships. It upsets the balance of giving and taking. In other instances, the cause is harder to pinpoint. An insecure mother could for example seek support from her daughter. Or a son sensing that his parents have great difficulty dealing with daily life after their war experience may therefore try to take as much off their hands as possible, often without even realizing it. When the natural order of caregiving roles changes in a family, and children take over parents' roles, (systemic) role confusion occurs.

Common forms of role confusion are parentification and triangulation:

- Parentification occurs when a child takes over tasks from the parent that are too heavy or not age appropriate. The child grows up too quickly, which disrupts emotional development. For instance, this might occur when a ten-year-old child takes care of her younger siblings because their parents are fighting all the time. Their mother is an emotional wreck from all the fighting and is unresponsive to her children. The young girl is not yet emotionally ready to take on the responsibility of this caregiving role. There is often a dual dynamic in parentification. The parents can appeal to the child for help, or the child can offer unsolicited care, which is accepted by the parents. Because children are loyal, they need their parents to do well, and may be inclined to offer help beyond their emotional capabilities. When parents allow this to happen or even demand it and when this continues during a longer period of time, it is detrimental to the child. Of course, children need to learn to help around the house and be given tasks to perform, as long as the parent stays in the role of the parent. It is important to keep in mind that the nature, weight, and duration of the task is age appropriate and that the child is acknowledged for finishing it. Parentification is always a combination of an excessive burden and age-inappropriate duration of the task in an unsupportive environment.
- There is another form of parentification. When a child takes on or is obligated to take on the parent's life-fulfilling dreams, it is equally detrimental to the child's autonomy. The child is then expected to achieve that in life that which his or her parent could not, making it impossible to build his or her own life. Nagy (Boszormenyi-Nagy & Spark, 1984) studied this form of parentification. Simply put, he states that such a child feels it only has the right to exist on condition that it achieves the dream of the parent, causing it to grow up with guilt.
- Triangulation describes a triangular relationship in which a child is made the ally of one of the parents against the other. The other parent is excluded and the child is put in an age-inappropriate role and position

where it does not belong. The parent forms a coalition with the child against the other parent, whereby the first parent will not communicate with the other directly (insofar as there is still any form of communication left), but will use the child to relay communication to the other parent. This forces children to choose between their parents and results in loyalty conflicts. Divided loyalty has serious consequences for the attachment strategies of children

Intimacy and Touch

Touching and being touched on the boundary of longing for connection and fear of rejection, feels vulnerable. This is why intimacy and vulnerability have so much in common. Feelings of vulnerability bear directly on experiences in early childhood. The child is vulnerable because it depends on the parent for nourishment, care, and physical contact. When the parents are present and available, the child learns to trust that others will not damage him or her while vulnerable. But the child also learns, to a greater or lesser extent, that his or her needs will not always be met. This teaches the child to deal with feelings of discontent. In a healthy environment, the child learns that it is acceptable to reach out again and ask for comfort or intimacy, even if the child is disappointed in the reaction. There is sufficient trust that the child is likely to succeed the next time.

If the child experiences mainly rejection, he or she will learn that it is dangerous to be vulnerable and will build a wall around his or her emotions, as it were, and an attitude of invulnerability will appear. Presenting him- or herself as invulnerable becomes the way to ensure that others cannot harm the child.

The ability to be vulnerable, is essential to permit intimacy, to be truly touched. And at the same time, vulnerability is connected with fear. The fear of rejection. Both vulnerability and invulnerability are a reaction to the fear of rejection. Where a person's vulnerability is about a need that others *do* them no harm, invulnerability is its distortion: the need to trust that others *cannot* harm them (Veenbaas et al., 2007; Weisfelt, 1996).

Intimacy plays an important role in loss in comforting and being comforted. To comfort someone, one must have the ability to come close. And to receive comfort, it is essential to allow proximity and intimacy as well as be open about deep emotions and longing. There is extra pressure when people who have isolated themselves, and are hard to connect with, are required to take part in this intimacy.

Intimacy in the Partner Relationship

The way in which people experience intimacy is based on a large collection of experiences, from early childhood as well as from the rest of their lives. New experiences are continually being added and people build a complex concept of (and verdict on) how they relate to and move through intimacy.

The sum total of these experiences helps make decisions such as to how vulnerable or invulnerable someone wants to be in a situation and what he or she does and does not want to let others see during contact.

In the partner relationship, this applies to both partners. Each brings to the table their own history, family, habits, and ways of dealing with vulnerability and invulnerability. To touch each other on the boundary demands that both partners are open and curious, that they see and accept the other person for who they are. And that's not easy. People are inclined to project their ideal image of a mate or their longing onto their partner in their search for someone who will satisfy their needs. Conflict arises when the partner does not meet this image or need.

If partners are prepared to explore their own themes in their personal development, growth in intimacy may arise. This intimacy is needed to deal with setbacks, losses, and major events that will inevitably cross their paths, together. Intimacy also offers the proximity and the space that allows each to see the needs of the other in dealing with loss, even though those needs may be completely different from their own. Both partners do not always have the same needs and cannot always share everything in their grieving process. They often need their own space as well as to be together. Each may need to be comforted in a different way. And each may deal with their pain differently. It helps when there is sufficient mutual trust so that one's space needs do not increase the distance between the two.

Sexuality

Intimacy is about the longing to be touched on one's boundaries; sexuality is about the longing to dissolve those boundaries. To fuse and become one. Intimacy and sexuality have much in common and are, at the same time, very different. In general, sexuality comes after intimacy. When two people touch each other's boundaries intensely and it gives them enjoyment, they want to touch each other even more intensely. Past all boundaries. That is when the boundaries are dissolved and sexuality is experienced. They satisfy their longing for fusion. Then comes the inevitable moment when both withdraw slightly and each becomes aware of their own boundaries once again.

Of course, sexuality can also exist without intimacy. It can then become a Game. We spell Game with a capital 'G' because we are referring here to the term *Game* that was introduced by Eric Berne in his book *Games People Play*.

> **Definition:** The term *Game* is described in a book written by the Canadian psychiatrist E. Berne (2016). Games (with a capital 'G' to emphasize that they are different to child's play or party games) are social interactions that are detrimental to those involved. These

patterns of behavior lead to the same (nasty) outcome time and again. And although most people are well aware of the pattern, they continue to repeat it.

If sexuality becomes a Game, it will have consequences for the way the partners experience sexuality in their relationship. Sexuality can, for instance, be used as leverage to get something done from the other or impose their will. Or it can be used to bind someone or build confidence. Sometimes people damage each other. Examples are abuse of power by sexual abuse or incest. In the context of this book, we will not elaborate on this subject. When guiding clients however, this subject could come up. Painful experiences in relation to sexuality also often lead to loss of safety and sometimes even to loss of a secure childhood or loss of the ability to experience intimacy.

Intimacy, Sexuality, and Grief

To grieve and long to be touched, cuddled, and made love to all at the same time can be very confusing. The agonizing pain, the grief, the longing for the person that is no longer there, seems such a different emotion to the longing for intimacy and sexuality. Most people, especially if they have lost a partner with whom they had a sexual relationship, find this to be a difficult topic to discuss. There is sometimes shame, or fear of the reaction of the family or those around them. But there can also be guilt.

Intimacy in the Working Relationship

It appears that intimacy is very important in a working relationship. To truly bond is an important condition to work together and to attain work goals. Intimacy in the working relationship can be defined as colleagues asking each other for feedback and being able to ask for support and help, daring each other to be vulnerable and letting others see when they are having doubts. This intimacy is essential to mutual trust. It allows employees to be close to each other when there is tension, pressure, or stress, or when mistakes are made, when (intense) experiences in their home life impact work, when there are goodbyes to be said, and when there is a celebration. As in one's personal life, intimacy cannot be taken for granted in the workplace.

Changes in organizations often cause a lot of 'bother' (Swieringa & Jansen, 2005) and can be painful, even traumatic. In each case, the result will be a grief reaction (Kets de Vries & Balazs, 1997). The extent to which (leaders in) organizations are able to effectively pay attention to the (consequences of the) losses that these changes entail, largely determines the extent to which employees can once again experience the intimacy that is necessary to work together successfully.

Intimacy and trust can come under high pressure due to the quantity and frequency of changes and the way in which these are guided or managed. It then becomes more difficult to talk about expectations, to learn from each other's mistakes, to feel comfortable, and to commit to the goals of the team or the organization. The things that apply to organizations and managers also apply to training and educational settings, where lecturers and fellow students can establish themselves as secure bases, and to club life, music, sports, faith, charities, and so on.

Counseling: Two Sides of the Coin on the Theme 'Intimacy and Sexuality'

When a counselor and his or her client work together on the client's question, they build a relationship. During the first phase there is a welcoming and a (psychological) contract is formed. Then the relationship develops. Intimacy grows between the client and his or her counselor. As we have read in this chapter, the intimacy allows someone to be touched. Sometimes the touch will be physical (within the professional boundaries of integrity and as acceptable to both parties), but other times it will also be emotional and cognitive. The counselor connects on an intimate level and addresses themes and topics that are bound to cause tension in the client. Or the client may find them (too) painful, or may not have enough faith that the counselor will stay close by when things become difficult, or (very) emotional.

Avoiding intimacy (see Figure 4.1) may stem from fear of being hurt or disappointed, or not having learned how to experience intimacy during youth. But losing a loved one can also lead to avoidance, especially if there was an intimate connection.

By making a connection and becoming intimate, the person takes a(n) (unconscious) risk that a goodbye will follow. Only by accepting that the

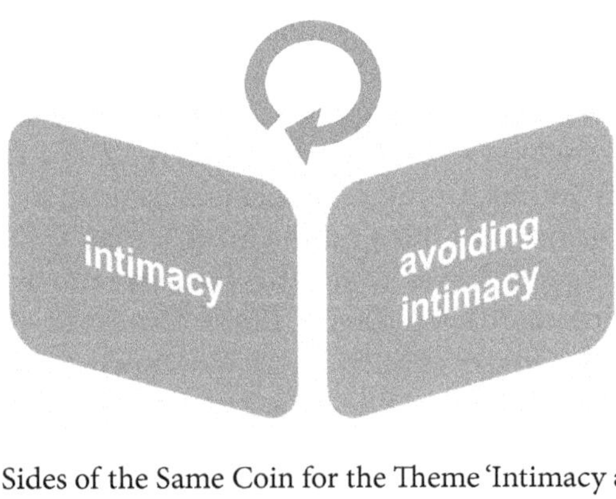

Figure 4.1 Both Sides of the Same Coin for the Theme 'Intimacy and Sexuality'

future loss is inevitable does intimacy become possible. Usually one is unaware of the risk. But after a major loss, when clients feel that they cannot go on, it is important to attend to this. The focus then lies in learning how to connect and be intimate all over again. The working relationship between the counselor and the client is important practice material for this.

For counselors, it is of the utmost importance to learn about their own dynamics in intimacy so that they will remain aware of their own tension, fear, needs, and longings pertaining to intimacy and can put this knowledge to work in the relationship with the client.

Dialogue

Amanda, from the case study at the beginning of this chapter, comes for her first session with her counselor, Robyn.

Robyn: You must be Amanda! Welcome!
Amanda: Thank you. And thank you for making time for me so quickly.
Robyn: What can I do for you?
Amanda: Well, I would actually like to be in a relationship for a change. I am quite sick of being on my own.
Robyn: That's a clear question. And what made you decide to knock on my door and do something about it, right now?
Amanda: On the one hand, I like being alone. I am quite happy by myself and I have clear ideas about what I do and don't want in life. So, I have been proclaiming to be happy single for a long time. But to be perfectly honest, I am not happy at all. During the recent holidays for instance, I felt really grim. I was invited to celebrate Christmas with a good friend and her family, but I cancelled that. I could not deal with seeing all the cheerfulness and coziness. A sudden urge made me send you the email, but now I am actually glad I am here.
Robyn: So, if I understand correctly, you had a sudden urge to send me an email to ask for help, but you being discontent with the situation, started some time ago.
Amanda: Yes, that's correct.
Robyn: What else can you tell me about your discontentment with the situation?
Amanda: Slowly but surely, all my friends are having children and those who don't have any yet, are in a relationship. Everybody has someone. I have a nice house and everything I want. I go on vacation often and see my friends on many occasions, but quite often, I feel lonely.
Robyn: And what do your friends say about that?
Amanda: I don't really know. We never talk about things like that. I always try to have a good time with them and tell them fun things about my life.

I also ask them about theirs but I never really talk about very personal things. I don't think they would be that interested. They know me as someone who never worries about things.

Robyn: And how does it make you feel that they only know this side of you?

Amanda: Well, I have never really thought about that. I think that I am fine with it. Otherwise they will only stick their noses into my business and talk about me.

Robyn: Is that important to you, that they don't talk about you and mind their own business?

Amanda: Not really important . . . I just don't like it when someone sticks their nose into my business, thinks all kinds of things about me and pities me or something.

Robyn: So, you like it when people don't interfere too much in your life and don't pity you.

Amanda: Yes, exactly.

Robyn: Does that also mean that you like to keep people at a distance?

Amanda: What do you mean by that?

Robyn: Each person shows a part of themselves to the outside world and keeps a part to themselves. Usually you are not aware of this. It stems from what you have learned and what you have experienced. When you first meet someone, you show very little of yourself but show more and more as you get to know the other better. It becomes more intimate. You could say, the more you dare show yourself and the other does the same, the more intimacy increases. The word 'dare' already gives away that it can be quite nerve-wracking or even scary to do. And it could make you decide to show less of yourself. To make it less nerve-racking. Can you relate to that?

Amanda: What I can relate to is that I get claustrophobic really quickly when someone comes close. When someone tells me really personal things, it makes me nervous. I try to get away as quickly as possible. I will go and get coffee, or go to the bathroom or so.

Robyn: So, you get claustrophobic when someone comes closer and you get nervous when someone tells you something personal. Would it be okay to explore that further?

Amanda: Yes, I guess so.

Robyn: Who were you with the last time it happened?

Amanda: With my friend Taylor.

Robyn: Would it be okay if I was your friend Taylor for a bit?

Amanda: Sure, go ahead!

Robyn: Would you mind standing up? I am going to stand here and ask you to stand opposite me at a distance that feels comfortable.

Amanda: Okay. (Chooses to stand at a distance of about 13 feet.)

Robyn: Is this okay for you?

Amanda: Yes, it feels fine.
Robyn: (Takes a step nearer Amanda.) I am glad you are here!
Amanda: My head understands that this does not make any sense, but I feel really embarrassed all of a sudden.
Robyn: What does it feel like?
Amanda: As though I have a knot in my stomach. I feel so nervous. This is intense!
Robyn: What do you want to do?
Amanda: Take a step back!
Robyn: Go ahead.
Amanda: (Takes a step back.) There! That's better!
Robyn: This is something you are very familiar with, is it not?
Amanda: Yes, that's exactly how it always goes, but I never realized it until now. That is very upsetting. I want so much for it to be different.
Robyn: I would like to work with you on bringing more intimacy into your life. I think that it could be an important step towards having a loving relationship.

Questions for Self-Reflection

- Who do you allow to get really close and who do you not allow close? What makes it different?
- How do you deal with emotional, intellectual, and physical distance and proximity?
- How does your birth family/own family/team/department/class/group deal with their emotions? How does this affect (the way) you (function)?
- How do you deal with giving and receiving feedback? And how does your birth family/own family/school/work deal with it? How does this affect (the way) you (function)?

Exercises

Exercise—Intimacy and Proximity

As a counselor, it is important to be able to attune your own need for proximity and the degree to which it is easy or hard for you to that of the client. It is our relationship with intimacy that has us always gauging whether or not to allow someone to come closer and in which form. Physical proximity can be clearly felt, even without actually touching someone. It is also important that your client become aware of his or her own reactions and dynamics concerning physical intimacy and proximity to be able to do the work required to solve the problem. At what distance from someone else does the client feel comfortable, and how is he or she inclined to react to this? Is the client comfortable there? Does the client feel like he or she belongs? In order to be able to use this technique for a client, we need to have insight into the way we deal with distance and proximity ourselves.

Instruction: Make groups of two (A and B). A stands still and B stands first on the left, then behind, then on the right, and lastly in front of A (facing each other so that you can look each other in the eye). In each successive position, B takes the time to feel what it is like in that place. Which distance feels okay, and which inner motion does his body want to make? Is B comfortable in that position? Share your thoughts and feelings briefly and then switch roles.

Practice in different groups of two. Also, be sure to practice with men and women.

Variation:

> Ask A to be the client and to find a place in the room to stand. B then, as the counselor, moves through the space and regularly asks from where he or she is standing at that moment, how it feels to A. May B come closer? Vary in distance and proximity, combining this with standing in front of, behind, and on both sides of A.

Variation:

> Is A able to close his or her eyes as B moves through the room and varies in distance and proximity? Ask about the difference between this and the previous experience with eyes open.

What happens to A if B varies not only distance and proximity but also body position and posture? B can turn towards or turn away, walk towards A or move away. Look A in the eye or look away. B can make him- or herself large or very small. B can sit or lie on the floor or spread his or her arms to invite A to come closer. Which dynamic does B observe in A? Ask what A recognizes, what it reminds A of.

Are you able to hug each other afterward? Think back to the hug and make a note of how much physical contact there was: just shoulders, shoulders and chest, stomach contact? Discuss together:

- What did you notice about yourself?
- What were the differences between the different people, with men and with women?
- What was it like for you to do these exercises?

- What is your experience on the balance between giving and receiving intimacy, on an emotional and physical level?
- Which elements do you recognize as coming from your own background?

Exercise—Proximity/Making (Eye) Contact

This exercise is aimed at making contact with someone without words, in order to experience how this feels to you and to the other, when there is (eye) contact accompanied by complete attention and conversely how it feels when there is (eye) contact without any attention being paid to the other person.

Instruction: Divide into groups of two and sit on two chairs facing each other. Sit as closely together as possible with the knees almost touching. You should be able to look each other in the eye.

- Decide together who is A and who is B.
- Sit quietly for a while without words or touch.
- Then make eye contact and be fully present in the moment.
- Notice how it feels to be completely present and connected with another person. Notice what happens at the level of your attention, feelings, and bodily sense.
- Next, disconnect from each other. Avoid contact, by letting your mind wander, think of other things. Be absent. (N.B.: if you are even just thinking about the exercise instead of doing it, you are already and immediately absent.)
- Notice how this makes you feel.
- A reconnects with B and is completely present, but B remains aloof and disconnected.
- Notice how this feels.
- And then B reconnects with A and when B is truly present, A disconnects.
- Notice how that feels to you.
- Then A reconnects again and both A and B are, once again, fully present.
- Finally, both end the connection. You have now completed the exercise.

Discuss with each other afterwards:

- What is it like to connect in this way, by only using eye contact and not saying anything?

- What did you notice about yourself?
- What did it feel like when you disconnected yourself?
- What did it feel like when the other person disconnected from you? What did you notice about yourself?
- What did you learn from this that you plan to use in your own practice?

Exercise—Drawing the System of Origin

An important aspect of counseling is helping the client to identify the presence of role confusion in his or her past. Take unsafe or avoidant forms of attachment and unhealthy forms of parent-child relationships and bonds into consideration such as parentification and triangulation. These are all unconscious 'decisions' at a child's level. A family constellation can help make such role confusion visible for the client. As it is less likely that there is a whole group of representatives available when giving individual counseling, a 'free' drawing of the system of origin will suffice.

In addition to the 'linguistic' forms of counseling (asking questions, interpreting answers) and the body-oriented methods (exercise, dancing, body-work, constellations), artistic methods offer an additional input when counseling by addressing the unconscious and creative side of the client. The value of artistic methods in counseling is mainly the appeal to work forms other than the conscious, linguistic abilities of the client and that they appeal to the imagination. Making art and expressing oneself creatively turns out to be a deep human need. People are, despite the fact that they are biological beings, not adapted in advance to their environment at birth. People need to adapt the environment to themselves in order to survive. This adapting of the environment that is offered has been taking shape in artistic expressions since the beginning of time and throughout all cultures. In this process of adaptation, of shaping the environment to make it suitable for living, the process of creating has also been the basis of all aesthetic design. In addition, works of art are objects that are not only, or possibly not at all, characterized by their usefulness, when applied. Art is characterized in particular by the fact that it appeals as a creation. This also evokes an aesthetic response in the onlooker. The counselor's task in a creative counseling process is therefore to help the client become aware of their own aesthetic response to what they have created (Levine in Neimeyer & Thompson, 2014).

This creative process consists of several steps:

1. The first step, as in any type of counseling, is to clarify the question or problem with which the client is struggling. It is helpful to discover how the client handled comparable situations in the past and what the client

expects from the counseling. The counselor is to assume that the client has creative resources available, even if these seem unattainable under the given circumstances of the loss.

After that has been made clear, the actual creative content is shaped by using several different work methods such as drawing, painting, or sculpture. Whatever work method appeals to the client is appropriate. The client's skills and the possible functional restrictions posed by certain methods should be considered. Everyone can draw on a functionally sufficient level. Work forms such as sculpting, embroidery, quilting and so forth, however, demand a higher skill level and are more suited to clients with some background in these art forms. During the creative process the client needs to appeal to his or her own imagination. This evokes a mood change during counseling. There is utmost concentration on the artwork and at the same time a moment of relaxation as the problem disappears into the background because the imagination takes over.

(N.B.: 'functionally sufficient' means that the 'artwork' does not have to be 'beautiful.' The aesthetic response to the end product is not a matter of being moved by the beauty of it, but that the artwork touches the observer and tells its own story.)

2. On completion of the artwork, it is time for the aesthetic analysis, on the one hand, to uncover the client's response to his own artwork and, on the other hand, to examine what it was like for the client to go through the creative process. Because the counselor was witness to the creation of the artwork, the counselor can also recognize and acknowledge what the effect of tapping into creative resources was on the visible behavior of the client. Be sure that analyzing the artwork is about the message that is given by this process as an answer to the question that was introduced at the beginning of the session.
3. After the analysis, it is possible to explore what the client got out of it and what he or she will take away into life outside of counseling. As is the case with many other work methods, most insights come in between sessions, which will allow them to do their work on an even deeper level.

This exercise consists of the work method 'drawing,' for which coloring pencils, crayons, and so on can be used. The specific question that the client has brought to the table can be used to build this exercise, but for the initial drawing, the issue is more generic. Ask the client to draw his family of origin on a sheet of paper, where:

1. Everyone is included in the drawing and is given a place on the paper, regardless of whether they are (still) alive, deceased, were stillborn, or entered the world by miscarriage.

2. The spacing between the drawn figures, their position on the paper, the pose they are drawn in, and the direction they are facing in relation to the others are important and need to feel emotionally correct for the client.
3. The figures do not have to resemble the actual members of the client's system, but should be pointed out or marked so that they are recognizable to the counselor.
4. The client is given the freedom to use any color he or she is attracted to. Also, give the client the choice of whether or not to represent the members of the system figuratively or symbolically.

The counselor should take note of the client's actions and demeanor while drawing. Also, the counselor should take note of the client's pose, timing of drawing, intensity, and, if possible, facial expression, and so forth. When the client has finished drawing, or when the previously specified time is up, talk to the client about the drawing and try to include the following questions:

- Do you want to share your drawing with me?
- What was it like for you to make this drawing?
- Did you have any difficult moments while drawing?
- Which parts were easy (or easier) to draw and which were hard(er)?
- Where are you in the drawing?
- Who are the other figures in the drawing?
- Did you draw everybody (use the genogram to check whether it is complete)?
- What does their place in the drawing mean to you? What does their place, their pose, and the direction they are facing in relation to the others and in particular in relation to you, mean to you?
- Do the colors mean anything to you? If so, what?
- What do you see in the drawing?
- Do you recognize anything in the drawing that has to do with your question?
- What change would you like to see in the relationships in the system?

Instruction: Figure out which is your own place in your system of origin by making a drawing. Make your own drawing and position yourself as the pivotal figure. Make sure you include all the members of your system of origin.

Divide into groups of three (A is the counselor, B is the client, and C is the observer) and take turns counseling each other using the sample questions that refer to this theme. Use the client's drawing to get an idea of the system of origin. Evaluate briefly after each session and then switch roles.

Exercise—Constellation Using Mats (Additional Exercise)

In addition to the constellation exercise using mats to explore the system of origin in Chapter 3, this constellation can also be used to uncover role confusion in the system. The preparation and execution of the exercise is identical to the Reaching Out and Withdrawing in Attachment Strategies exercise in Chapter 3. In this additional exercise, however, it is important to look at the 'order' in the system. The order should be as follows:

1. children should stand in order of age, side by side from eldest (left) to youngest (right);
2. parents should stand side by side, the man on the right and the woman on the left; and
3. parents and children should stand opposite and facing each other.

Additional questions may be asked when the initial constellation does not reflect the systemic principles of order, that is, when the client is apparently not standing in his or her 'own' place:

- What physical feelings does the client have when standing in his or her own place in the initial constellation?
- What does it feel like to learn that the place is not correct according to the systemic principles of order?
- What need arises as the client stands there?
- What did the client want for the parent(s)?
- What did the client need from the parent(s)?
- What burden has the client been carrying that was not properly theirs nor meant for them?
- How heavy was it to carry this burden?
- Whose burden is it ultimately?
- What is needed to give the burden back?

Instruction: Divide into groups of three (A is the counselor, B is the client, and C is the observer) and take turns counseling each other on the possible role confusion within the system of origin by putting down the mats. Bring the whole system of origin into focus. Use the additional questions to help you with the exercise described above. Evaluate briefly after each session and then switch roles.

5

SEPARATION AND LOSS

A Case Study

When Robert was only a toddler, his little brother drowned. He did not remember much from that time, except for the image of that tiny little body in that huge ambulance that was etched into his memory. While his parents were overcome with grief, he went to school, played with friends, and played football in the streets. When his mother cried, he would sit beside her quietly and sometimes place his little hand on her arm. And when his father had difficulty getting through the day, Robert would put his favorite music on for him. He grew up to become a friendly, quiet man. He never spoke about his brother, but he visited his parents on a weekly basis. After college, he took a job as an ambulance paramedic. It was an intense job. He saw a lot, but handled it well and always stayed calm. His colleagues always sought him out to blow off steam after a particularly intense shift. His superiors were very pleased with him. On one particular night, his ambulance was called to the scene of a car accident. A young family had lost control over the car and hit a tree. After a quick assessment, he focused his attention on the young mother who was trapped in the car and unconscious. It took enormous effort to stabilize her. Once she was ready for transport, he looked around at the scene. A little boy caught his eye. He was also lying on a stretcher. He could not recall what happened next. His colleagues did not notice any change. Apparently, he finished the job on automatic pilot. But that night, he could not sleep. And that continued during the nights that followed. He became short-tempered at work. His reactions were blunt and abrupt. His colleagues did not understand, but left him alone. His work became sloppier. He overlooked wounds and gave his colleagues at the casualty ward incorrect information. At one time, it was even his fault that a woman went into shock. After several performance appraisals and eventually a reprimand, the hospital board decided to fire him. He tried to raise an objection, but quickly resigned himself to their decision. Too tired to put up a fight, he spent his days in bed. He hardly ate and stopped taking care of himself. His general practitioner suspected depression and referred him to a counselor. Six months later, he stood at the grave of his little brother for the first time. His eyes slowly read his name as the tears poured down his cheeks. My dearest little brother, he whispered, how I have missed you.

Without Goodbyes, No Hellos

Each contact, each encounter, each relationship will end at one time or another. Sometimes after a few minutes, once in a while after eighty years, but eventually there is always an end. That is inevitable.

In Chapter 3, we extensively discussed the theme of attachment. The attachment theory of the English psychiatrist John Bowlby forms an important basis for understanding what attachment is and how attachment can develop. Within Bowlby's theory, separation and separation anxiety play an important role. The second part of his trilogy on attachment and loss is completely devoted to these two themes (1988b).

According to Bowlby, we speak of separation when the attachment figure, usually the mother or the father, is (temporarily) unavailable. Examples like when the mother briefly leaves the room, does not directly come when the child cries, or when a father does not look up from his book when the child asks for something are minor incidents. A father who does not visit his child after the divorce, a mother who dies, a caregiver who finds another job, or a mother who is regularly away from home due to psychological problems are examples of major incidents.

The presence of attachment figures mainly relates to their direct accessibility, even more than to their physical, bodily presence. The term 'absence' refers to the inaccessibility of the attachment figures. Yet accessibility on its own is not enough. Children also need their bonding figures to respond appropriately to their needs. The responsiveness to the signals that children give and the appropriate reaction to the children are essential for reassurance and for their sense of security and safety. Only when attachment figures are accessible and effectively responsive when a child reaches out can they be considered truly available.

> **Tip:** In the following, the 'availability' of attachment figures will refer to them being both accessible and appropriately responsive to the needs of the child.

This combination is essential. When attachment figures, for example, remain emotionally inaccessible, but are physically present, this still means they are unavailable for the child.

Bowlby assumes that the young child develops models about the 'external world' and about the 'internal world.' He calls these models working models. Based on these working models, the child interprets events and creates expectations and predictions about the follow-up and reactions from others. Within the working model of the 'outside world' there is an important role for the attachment figures: who and where they are and how they will respond to the needs of the child. In the model of the 'inner world' the awareness of how 'desired' or 'undesirable' the child considers him- or herself to be in the eyes of his attachment figures is central. On the basis of these two models the child constructs their expectations and predictions about how available attachment figures will be and how available they will be when the child reaches out for support. Based on these expectations and predictions, the feeling of (un)certainty is then determined by the availability of the attachment figures and the possible fear that the attachment figures will make themselves unavailable to a greater or lesser extent. This perception, the expectation of whether or not the attachment figures are available, lies at the basis of the child's later tendency to respond with fear to potentially threatening events during his life.

Bowlby elaborates on this, using three assumptions:

1. When confident that their attachment figures are available to them, people are much less susceptible to fear.
2. The confidence in the availability of attachment figures, or the lack thereof, slowly builds up during a child's younger years and then remains virtually unchanged for the rest of the child's life.
3. The various expectations that children develop about the availability of their attachment figures are fairly accurate representations of actual experiences from their childhood.

Anger is a very common reaction in children to the threat of or actual separation from attachment figures. Anger and its behavioral expression are actually an appropriate response when a child tries to stand up for itself when its needs are threatened. Whether the child's anger will achieve what it has set out to do, which is to persuade the attachment figure to stay, is debatable. In other words, on a transactional level, anger is not very effective in this situation. The parent may feel pressured by the anger, and then perhaps become less inclined to give in. Or the parent may be frightened by the child's vehemence and shut down. Anger can also serve to mask the (separation) fear. Parents are often inclined to respond to the anger and not see the underlying fear of the separation. Children learn through experience which behavior evokes which response. When attachment figures show the behavior desired by the child, the child will show this behavior more often in an attempt to have the attachment figure repeat the desired response the next time. In this way, children learn to suppress and mask anger in an attempt to 'manipulate' the attachment figure. Incidentally, 'the desired response' is not always the action that the parent (attachment figure) also thinks is most desirable. For example, if the child notices that anger causes a parent to react angrily, which is also a form of attention, the child may subconsciously draw the conclusion that being angry draws attention and that negative attention is better than no attention.

From the first separation experiences and from the experience of the availability of attachment figures, the child's ability to deal with separation takes form. When a child learns that separation may cause fear, but that it will be comforted or taken care of, the child builds inner confidence so that it can deal with departure. It learns that separation is followed by new contact. Being able to say goodbye also brings the opportunity to make new connections again. Every farewell is a new beginning.

Separation and loss are inextricably linked to the human desire for contact. There is the longing for that which has been lost, to end the separation and, if possible, to make the loss undone. At the same time, stemming from the deeply human need for permanent and continuous connection, there is a desire for new relationships, for new contact, new connection, and attachment. These may feel like conflicting desires. Sometimes, there are feelings of guilt towards that which has been lost, as if it or they were being replaced. The discomfort that arises from this conflict between desires and needs leaves us feeling confused and emotionally paralyzed. This is normal. It is something to be endured after loss.

Rituals for Loss and Saying Goodbye

Rituals mark a rite of passage, a transition. In this respect, rituals are important for all themes on the Transition Cycle. In our society, we have numerous institutionalized rituals, for example around birth, marriage, and funerals. Rituals also play an important role in public holidays, birthdays, or traditional celebrations such as Eid al-Fitr, Yom Kippur, Easter, Thanksgiving, Christmas, and New Year's. Rituals can be culturally determined. For example, in many cultures there are rituals around becoming adults, such as the Hindu upanayana, the Catholic confirmation, and the Jewish Bar or Bat Mitzvah. Some African tribes send young men lion hunting to prove their courage and masculinity. And many more such examples can be found.

However, not all personal transitions or losses have formal rituals. There are many personal events in which there is departure and loss, but for which there is no special place or consideration. For events like bankruptcy, a broken relationship, or a pregnancy that ends in an early miscarriage, there are no rituals. Other examples are schooling that was never completed, or an accident that caused disability.

A ritual marks the transition. There is a conscious goodbye. Only with that can the grief be properly addressed by allowing and experiencing the meaning of this parting. Rituals appear to help people who have suffered loss. They reduce tension and increase confidence. Rituals help to regain a sense of control over a situation that has been disrupted by loss. This 'having a grip' on the situation is important in enabling one to assign meaning to the loss (Baumeister, 1992).

All rituals, including self-created, private rituals, can help even those who claim not to attach meaning to the ritual. Even though there is no evident causal relationship between the action in a ritual and the desired outcome, for the participant in the ritual, the intention with which the ritual is performed proves to be sufficient for experiencing that result (Norton & Gino, 2014).

Sometimes a spontaneous ritual emerges. A woman puts a stone in her garden to commemorate the baby that was in her belly for such a short time. A sign at the entrance of the office is taken down and returned to the founder after a merger. In counseling, a ritual can be created to help mark a farewell. The ritual is given its personal content by the counselor and the client together and shaped into an 'organized collection of symbolic actions,' and thus acquires a form and structure that is appropriate for the situation and the person (Hart, 2003, p. 23). In this way, the ritual can provide a certain degree of 'completed past tense' for the person with the loss.

To design a 'counseling ritual,' a number of steps can be identified:

1. Preparatory phase, in which the counselor explains the design and the intention of the ritual.
2. Reorganization phase, in which the client collects objects with special symbolic meaning—*linking objects* that symbolize a connection.
3. Completion phase, in which the client parts permanently with the collected objects through a farewell ceremony.

4. Cleansing ritual, in which the client distances himself from the moment of parting by a physical or symbolic cleansing.
5. Reunification ritual, in which the client, usually with a joint meal, comes together again with loved ones and relatives.

A ritual consists of more components than just a farewell ceremony. Specifically, the preparation and conclusion of the ritual with loved ones and acquaintances adds therapeutic value to the process as a whole.

Rituals mainly consist of symbolic actions. These actions take place with symbolic objects, that is, objects that have a certain meaning because they refer to something or someone related to the loss. For example, the object might have a resemblance to whom or what was lost. The object is given an emotional meaning by the client. The object can be, for example, a photo or image of the deceased, but it can also be a drawing of a certain period, or an object that represents a certain quality, such as a stone that can stand for someone's hardness. Other symbolic values can be given to something that has belonged to the other person, has been touched by the person, or has been in the vicinity of the other person ('contiguity'). Garments or other belongings of the other person can be used for this.

A ritual takes place within a certain time frame, but the duration can vary per situation. Sometimes it feels good for the client to carry a symbol around for several months. The counselor can ask the client now and then how it feels to carry the object around and if that changes over time. Other times, it's better to give the ritual a controlled structure with an end date. It is important that the counselor and the client coordinate carefully together. The counselor can submit ideas (or can discuss this with colleagues in peer groups) and offer suggestions or proposals. The client indicates what he or she likes and needs. Together they need to make clear agreements on how to move through it.

In this way a ritual (in the narrow sense of the word) begins to take shape. These types of rituals are aimed at a specific theme such as 'the loss,' 'the goodbye,' or 'the grief.' Here are some suggestions for such rituals:

1. Write a letter to the person you are saying goodbye to. For example, use the 'Nine Steps Model' (Van Geelen-Merks & van Wielink, 2015), described in Chapter 5. Read this letter to one or more witnesses. Burn the letter. Round off with the witness(es).
2. Find a stone. Paint a symbol or a scene that reminds you of the person you have to say goodbye to on the stone with solvent-free paint. Put it in a special place in clear view during a specified period of time. On a set day, take the stone back to the place you found it. Return it to nature. On your return, describe to witnesses how it felt. Tell them what touched you, what you left behind.

3. On a pretty piece of paper, write down a message to the person or the object you have lost. Fold it into a paper boat. Put the boat in a river somewhere. Watch the boat float downstream. You can do this ritual together with several people and several boats simultaneously.
4. A client who lost his father at a very young age and who did not really know him as a result thereof, visited old friends and relatives who had known his father during his life. He visited the house his father grew up in as well as his old boss. He then wrote a book about him. When the book was published, he was finally able to say goodbye to the father he had missed so dearly.
5. By making a lifeline of the period during which he was employed at the company, another client was able to ponder all his happy and less happy memories. In his mind he revisited the positions he occupied, the teams he had been a part of, and the departments he had managed. When he had finished, he asked his grown-up children to meet up with him. He told them his story about what he had learned during all those years. His children were touched by his openness. With an official gesture, he handed his lifeline drawing to his youngest son. They then all drank a glass of champagne together. Finally, he was able to start enjoying his well-earned pension.

Counseling the Other Side of Grief and Loss

In this chapter, we take a moment to reflect on the importance of saying goodbye. In their younger years, people develop their own way of dealing with loss and departure. Loss and saying goodbye can cause fear. Fear of abandonment, fear of loneliness, fear of having to fend for yourself and not being able to cope. During counseling, we regularly come across those who subconsciously avoid loss and necessary goodbyes. It may seem that this form of denial in reaction to loss, or permanent missing of something or someone, or the avoidance of saying goodbye, allows someone to pretend that the loss did not happen. Or maybe that it did happen, but it did not mean anything, that the relationship was not important. Or by pretending that there was no goodbye: as if the bond is still complete and unchanged.

It can be very tempting to avoid saying goodbye. In an attempt to stay one step ahead of grief. Part of the process of denying the grief (see Figure 5.1) is thinking that new contact will be made just like that. What actually happens here is that one takes a shortcut on the Transition Cycle in an effort to get to new connection more quickly (Figure 5.2). By skipping parts of the process, one may think that the grief can be avoided. We have all experienced such moments: attempts to unconsciously outrun and outsmart grief.

The same happens in organizations, for example, when any mention of the former organization is prohibited after changes occur, like reorganizations and

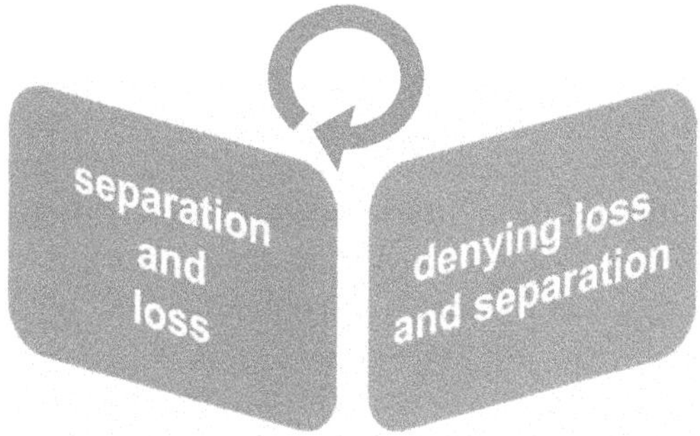

Figure 5.1 Both Sides of the Same Coin for the Theme 'Separation and Loss'

mergers. Employees are expected to connect themselves without any problems to the new organization, the new brand name, or the new logo, or to bond with new colleagues and managers. Organizations often think that they are entitled or obliged to take such a shortcut on the Transition Cycle, out of fear of the 'hassle' that always ensues, or the urge to 'make haste,' or based on the well-known management principles of 'control and monitoring.'

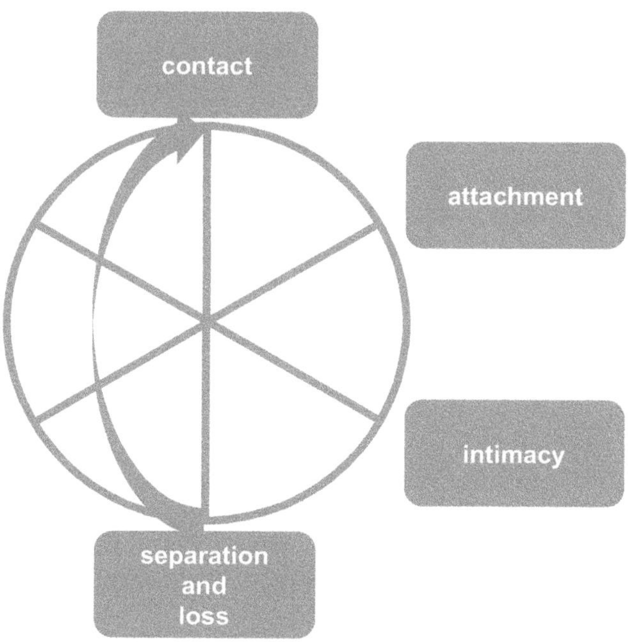

Figure 5.2 Taking a Shortcut on the Transition Cycle

The counselor will encounter different variations, as well as the oscillation from the one side of this theme to the other, in professional practice. For a client who finds it difficult to say goodbye for example, the dynamics will be expressed by having trouble with leaving at the end of a session or the client will be unwilling to end the series of sessions. Clients who deny their loss, often do not seek counseling. When they do come, they will not formulate their question in terms of the loss. Somewhere in their past, they have come to a subconscious conclusion that saying goodbye is too painful or dangerous. If a counselor is able to observe this dynamic and to stay patiently and mindfully present, as a secure base, the client may start to feel safe enough to explore this distressing theme.

Dialogue

This is a dialogue between Robert from the case at the beginning of this chapter and his counselor Jack. They have already had several sessions. Initially they only discussed the situation at work. A lot had happened. It helped Robert to organize his thoughts on everything that had happened. In the beginning, he was mostly angry at his managers, but now he is able to view the situation with a little more distance and is also able to see his role in the outcome.

Jack: Good morning Robert, it is great to see you again.
Robert: Good morning! Well, I would not say 'great' just yet (grins). But it really is good right now.
Jack: How are you doing?
Robert: They are small steps, but I am feeling better. I have been sleeping better lately. I have been mulling over the things that happened during the last months at work less often. It feels good to be able to talk about it. My mind is calmer lately.
Jack: I am glad that it helps you to talk about it. I'd like to go further back in time today. You told me that the first years as a paramedic went very well. Your superiors were pleased with your performance and you got on well with your colleagues. Tell me more about that time.
Robert: Yes, those first years went by without a hitch. I was always able to stay calm, which made me seem stable and confident. That was good for both my patients and my colleagues. I tried to recapture that when it started going wrong, but for some reason or another, I just could not anymore.
Jack: When did it change exactly?
Robert: I can't pinpoint the exact moment. I became more somber, slept badly. I think that started about three years ago.
Jack: About three years ago, you say. Let's go back to that time three years ago. Do you remember what time of year it was? Was it summer or winter, for example?

Robert: (Thinks about it.) It was the beginning of summer. I remember it being very light. Usually I loved it being light, but I was having trouble sleeping then. I would go to sleep very late and wake up early.
Jack: Okay, so it was the beginning of summer that you started having trouble sleeping and you started feeling down. And that was new to you.
Robert: Yes, that's never happened to me before. I'd never had trouble sleeping before that time.
Jack: So that was an obvious change. Could something have possibly happened during that period that caused these complaints?
Robert: It is possible. A lot happens when you work on an ambulance of course.
Jack: I would like you to close your eyes (closes his own eyes first to invite Robert to follow) and in your mind, go back to the months before you started having trouble sleeping. Let any images, sounds, smells, feelings come to mind while you think back to the period before the summer three years ago. Take your time. I am here. (Now Jack opens his eyes again so that he can observe Robert.)
Robert: There are all kinds of thoughts flashing through my head. I am feeling very agitated.
Jack: You feel agitated. It is okay to feel agitated. In the meantime, breathe gently in and out.
Robert: I think that I feel sadness. The agitation now feels more like sadness.
Jack: You now feel sadness. It is okay to feel the sadness. Keep breathing in and out. Do you see any images appearing?
Robert: (Starts breathing deeper, takes his time.) I am arriving at the scene of an accident in which a family is involved. The car is completely wrecked. Especially the woman on the passenger's side is in bad shape. I focus on her. I feel charged, emotional. That is new to me. All of a sudden, I see a little boy. The look in his eyes. I feel afraid. I don't know. As if it affects me deeply. (Opens his eyes and stays still for a while longer.)
Jack: (Waits a while, because he sees that Robert is still thinking about it.)
Robert: Wow, that was quite intense.
Jack: How is it now for you?
Robert: Calmer, but now also confused. I don't quite understand why this apparently still has such an impact on me.
Jack: Events in the present can unconsciously bring you into contact with something that took place long ago. In your youth for example. It is possible that this is also the case in your life story. I would like to look at your lifeline with you next time. At the positive and negative events and periods in your life that you have experienced. I will give you some more detailed information to read about making the lifeline. If you make it at home and bring it next time, we can discuss it.
Robert: I am on it. I can hardly wait!
Jack: See you next time!

Self-Reflection Questions

Self-reflection questions for this theme are:

- Which losses have you suffered in your life, personal and business?
- How do you deal with saying goodbye?
- What themes from your own history do you recognize in how you say goodbye?
- Which losses are in the past and which losses are actually about the future, about unfulfilled wishes and dreams?
- Which desires play a role?

Exercises

Exercise—Lifeline (Addition for the Theme Loss and Saying Goodbye)

In addition to the lifeline exercise described in Chapter 1, approached through the theme 'feeling welcome,' the counselor can once again take a look at the milestones on the lifeline with his client, with the perspective of the theme 'loss and saying goodbye' in mind. Each time the lifeline is revisited, the counselor needs to ask the client the question: which new insights and/or moments have been added since the previous time we looked at this? In addition, as each new theme on the Transition Cycle is explored, the counselor can invite the client to look back again at the moments on the lifeline. Based on the new theme on the Transition Cycle, the client can then analyze the circumstances around the important events and explore what is needed for transformation.

Instruction: Counsel each other in groups of three (A is the counselor, B is the client, and C is the observer), for instance, by using the self-reflection questions relevant to this theme. Use the lifeline drawn during the exercise in Chapter 1.

Additional questions that can also be used with this exercise:

- Which goodbye or which loss is not yet marked on the lifeline? Why is that?
- Which goodbye or loss do you still need to confront? What is it that still needs to be done in order to make this happen?
- Which of your most impactful goodbyes or losses have been raked up in later losses?
- Which goodbye or loss most occupies your mind at this point in time?

Evaluate each turn briefly and then switch roles.

Exercise—Goodbye Letter

Some losses have not yet been consciously confronted by the client. Unexpressed or unfinished issues may still be carry influence. By writing a goodbye letter, the client is given the chance to work this out on paper and attend to issues that need to be put into words. The client writes the letter to something or someone to which he or she is or was attached.

The letter is written using the nine steps method.[1] Experience has taught us that it is effective to follow the nine steps from beginning to end. Allow the client to take their time. The client may feel reluctant to follow some of the steps. Ask the client to make a note of this. The reluctance indicates an underlying cause.

Advise the client to be concrete, to say what they have to say, to write freely. It can be helpful for the client to know that the letter does not actually have to be sent.

The Nine Steps:

1. Blame
   a. What are you angry about?
   b. How angry are you?
   c. What do you blame him/her/it for?
2. Missing
   a. What have you lost (through this change)?
   b. What do you miss about the person or the situation concerned?
   c. How had you imagined it all to be and how is it different from what you had hoped for?
   d. What are you disappointed about?
3. Apologize
   a. What is your share in it all, what did you do?
   b. What would you have liked to have done (differently) and what did you neglect to do?
   c. What are you sorry about, what do you feel guilty about?
4. Thanking
   a. What are you pleased with (afterwards)?
   b. What can the other person thank you for?
5. Giving back/keeping
   a. What are the good things you will take away from knowing the other person or being in the situation? Think for example of certain behaviors, views, preferences or disapproval, norms and values, a certain view of things.

b. Which positive aspects of the other person or situation would you like to keep?
c. What would you like to leave behind, what would you like to give back?

6. Revising beliefs

    a. What beliefs are holding you back? Think of certain sentences you say to yourself or that you used to hear in your youth (e.g., 'stop whining, just do it,' or 'asking for help is a sign of weakness').
    b. How do they sound when you adapt them so as to help instead of to hinder?

7. Forgiveness

    a. What will or can you forgive?
    b. What do you forgive yourself for?

8. What now?

    a. What have you learned?
    b. How are you planning to live with the new understanding and decisions?
    c. What goals are you setting for yourself, or what task are you faced with now?

9. Reconcile

    a. Which ritual fits your goodbye and the step that needs to be taken in your grieving process?
    b. How would you like to mark the change?

> **Instruction:** Write a goodbye letter for a loss you suffered using the nine steps described above.
> In groups of two:
>
> - Read the letter out loud to each other.
> - Tell your partner what touches you in his or her letter.
> - Which step was the hardest to write about? What meaning can you give to this?
> - How has it helped you to write this letter?

Exercise—'What Still Needs to be Said'

To deepen the experience of the previous exercise, express the new insights gained by writing the goodbye letter out loud to the person the letter is addressed to. In the same way that the letter does not have to actually be sent, this conversation does not actually have to take place with said person. The effect on the relationship is the greatest when this is actually possible, but even just saying out loud what needs to be said during the exercise is effective for the client. An empty chair facing the client, on which the person addressed in the goodbye letter is imagined to be sitting, can be used for this purpose. Or the counselor can fill the role of the absent person. Whichever option is chosen depends on the situation and the counselor's intuition.

Ask the client to think about what still needs to be said based on the goodbye letter. Put an empty chair across from the client and ask him or her to imagine that the recipient of the letter is sitting in the chair. Now let the client actually address that person as if he or she were here in the present and let the client say what needs to be said.

Let the client change his or her position by taking a seat in the empty chair. Questions that can be asked:

- How does it feel to be in this place, in the position the other person is in, to receive this message?
- What effect do you think the message will have on the other person?
- How do you think he or she will react?

Ask the client to react in the other person's name to what the client said. The client focuses on the empty chair that he or she just sat on. Let the client change places again and ask him or her to react, as themselves, to what was just said. The above-mentioned questions can be used here too to relate to the position of the client him- or herself. Let the client switch roles until there is 'nothing left to be said.'

In a variation of this exercise, the counselor takes on the role of the other person and reacts in his or her name, based on what comes to mind at that moment.

Instruction: Counsel each other in groups of three (A is the counselor, B is the client, and C is the observer), based on the goodbye letter from the previous section. What still needs to be said by the client? The counselor explains the exercise, puts the chairs in position, and invites the client to address the other person as if they were there.

Evaluate each round and switch roles.

Exercise—Untangling Multiple Losses

When multiple losses occur either simultaneously or in quick succession, it can be very difficult to differentiate between the reactions one had to each of these losses. A client may be overwhelmed by the accumulated grief. It can be helpful to the client to untangle the web of losses and the grief that belongs with each loss. A counselor can help a client gain an overview by disentangling or unbraiding the multiple losses, or to make it more concrete by following the different story lines separately. This does not lessen the total magnitude of the loss, but allows the client to more easily grieve 'in pieces' (Neimeyer, 2016, p. 153).

In order to get a clear view of the bigger picture once again, it can be helpful to begin by identifying the different losses. One could ask the client to draw a separate piece of timeline, with enough room to incorporate the different losses in a short period of time. At first, the primary losses will be identified: who or what is lost? This list of losses can then be entered into a column in a special matrix designed to help unbraid the various losses.

To illustrate: when a child's parents get divorced, that child also has to deal with moving to a different house, followed by the inevitable change of school. It might not be clear which effect each loss has. By naming each loss separately, listing them one at a time and placing the different aspects side by side, the client will gain a much-needed overview and more understanding of each. This will make clear that different losses evoke different reactions and that it makes more sense to look at each experience independently of the others.

The following questions can be asked about the various losses, so as to be able to better distinguish each from the other:

- What good memories do you have before the loss occurred?
- What was your relationship like, what role did you have?
- Who were you in the relationship, how did you behave?
- What are the predominant feelings?
- What would help you deal with this loss now?

By placing the losses horizontally at the top and the questions in a vertical column, a matrix is created. Each cell in the matrix provides an understanding of a specific aspect of the loss, allowing the knot to be disentangled. See the example in Table 5.1.

Table 5.1 Matrix of Loss

	Before the divorce	Before moving house	Previous school
Pleasant memories?	Eating together, goodnight kiss from both parents	My own room	Best friend in the same class
Relationship, role?	Dad helped me with my homework, I helped mom with cooking	Playing with the neighborhood kids	Popular in class

	Before the divorce	Before moving house	Previous school
Behavior?	Making jokes, teasing laughing	Building huts in the forest	Playing football on the playground
Feelings about the loss?	Feeling sad about my parent's sadness, fear of the future	Angry about the loss of my own room, missing the children from the old neighborhood	Feeling insecure about whether I can make new friends
What would help?	When my parents stop hatefully criticizing each other	If I can hang up my posters in my shared bedroom	If I invite new classmates to my birthday party

Instruction: From the lifeline exercises in Chapters 1 and 5, untangle multiple losses that occurred in a short amount of time by making use of a table as illustrated above.

Note

1. Original by Maarten Kouwenhoven, adapted by Jakob van Wielink.

6
GRIEF

A Case Study

Oliver had been feeling restless for quite some time now. He did not sleep well at night and had palpitations. He went to the doctor several times but he could not find much wrong with him except a slightly elevated blood pressure. He was advised to take it easy. Oliver waved away the doctor's suggestion that he could be suffering from burnout. He loved his work. And he was the hub of the team. Colleagues who could not take the pressure often sought him out. He enjoyed his status. They thought of him as the person who could always find a solution. He failed to cut down on his overtime. Only when he collapsed at the coffee machine and was then taken to hospital in an ambulance did he realize that he had pushed himself too hard. Fortunately, they could not find anything physically wrong with him, but this time he decided to go and see a counselor to learn how to handle the pressure at work. At first, during the sessions, he is more concerned about his absence from work. With great conviction, he declares that he is the most experienced employee and that he is indispensable at the moment. His colleagues were not able to handle the work pressure at this time. He feels a huge responsibility towards them. He describes it as a responsibility that sometimes feels like a burden, but says that it is his to carry. Oliver has always worked above and beyond what was needed. The counselor asks him what role the theme 'responsibility' plays in his personal life story. Oliver tells him that he was the eldest child and always helped in his parent´s shop. His mother was sick a lot. She could hardly manage to take care of the five children. His father was entirely focused on the shop. He could use any help available. So, Oliver learned from a young age to tackle anything set in front of him. There was always work to do in the shop. There was no room for being tired or sick. 'You are not a momma's boy, are you?,' his father said whenever he wanted to sit down or felt sad. Swallow your tears and move on. It had become a way of life. 'What tears are you swallowing now?' The counselor's question confuses Oliver momentarily. He is quiet for a while. Then he starts talking. He and his wife have wanted to have children for a very long time. Finally, she became pregnant. He was ecstatic to see her so happy. But after seven weeks she started bleeding. The pregnancy ended in a miscarriage. It crushed her. Oliver could not help but go back to work immediately. Away from the sadness. His own, but also his wife's, intense sadness.

Grief follows goodbye. This makes grief a logical next theme on the Transition Cycle. Anyone who has bonded with something or someone must learn how to live without whomever or whatever has been lost. You could say that grief is about the process of learning to live with what or whom is lost. The course of the process varies per person and per situation. The models and theories in this chapter help one understand what grief is and the factors influencing it.

The Duality of Grief

> *Grief is an intensely personal, contradictory, chaotic and unpredictable internal process. If we are to navigate it, we need to find a way to understand and live with the central paradox: that we must find a way of living with a reality that we don't want to be true.*
>
> (Samuel, 2017, p. xvii)

There are several factors that influence grief in reaction to loss. This is explained in the Two-Track Model of Bereavement (Rubin et al., 2012). In track one, it is important to consider the interaction of biopsychosocial factors that affect physical and mental well-being. In this category Rubin places the more or less visible effects of grief: the feelings people express, behavior such as withdrawing or looking for support, the somatic concerns often reported when someone is grieving or has lost someone. The other track considers the emotional attachment and the relational aspects to who or what was lost as an important part of grief. This track also considers the memories, the frequency of these memories, and whether they are happy or considered a burden. These less visible effects take place inside people's minds and bodies and can be compared with that (largest) part of an iceberg that is submerged. While this is barely noticeable to the outside world, it forms the center of gravity for grief. The Two-Track Model is the first model to introduce the concept of 'continuing bonds' (Klass et al., 2014)

By emphasizing the relational aspect of the loss during the grieving process, whereby different grief reactions can be traced back to different styles of attachment, the Two-Track Model acknowledges the influence of Bowlby's work. The Two-Track Model is not so much a process model or about how people deal with loss as it is a model that draws attention to the various aspects of visible and invisible grief.

Grief Oscillates Between Past, Present, and Future

The Dual Process Model (Stroebe & Schut, 1999, 2010) links the different views on grief with the uncertain course the grieving process takes. The model illustrates the complexity of dealing with loss. A crucial part of this model is that healthy grieving means engaging in a dynamic process of oscillating between loss-oriented and restoration-oriented stressors and coping (see Figure 6.1). On the left side of the model, the loss-oriented side, are stressors that come from focusing on and processing the loss of our loved one and our relationship with that person. On the right-hand side, the

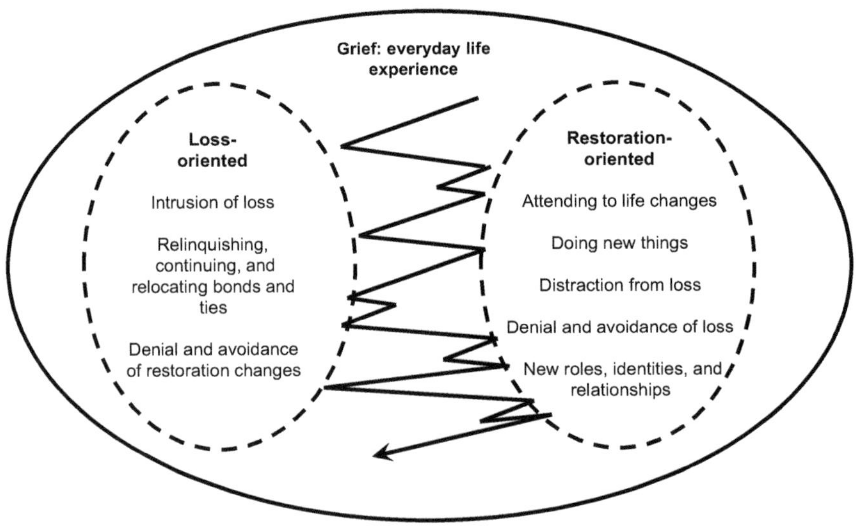

Figure 6.1 Dual Process Model

Source: Stroebe & Schut, 1999, 2010; copied with permission from Taylor & Francis

restoration-oriented side, are aspects that have bearing on doing or having to do new things, moving on, diversion. Grief entails the oscillation between these two orientations. What the oscillation looks like differs from person to person and from moment to moment.

Someone who is loss-oriented focuses on the loss and on what it means to him. He feels emotions, has thoughts, and has physical sensations from the loss. He learns new things about himself, as he is now 'someone dealing with this loss.' He will redefine the relationship with the person or that which is lost: breaking and redefining bonds and attachment. The former is more definite than the latter. Which of the two will be applied depends on the nature of the relationship and the situation in which the loss occurred. Dealing with a loss is also, per definition a, preferably temporary, denial and avoidance of recovery-oriented actions. Incidentally, loss orientation is not always perceived as a choice. It can intrude, uninvited and unwanted by means of, for example, a memory tied to a scent, a song, or an image.

Restoration-oriented or future-oriented actions are part of restoration orientation. This includes everything whereby the client focuses on change, takes new action, and/or seeks distraction form the grief. Work, school, a sports club where everything is still the same as before the loss, offer temporary solace and peace: 'time-off' from the chaos or the pain of the loss. No judgment is passed where loss- or restoration orientation is concerned. One is no better than the other. Also, no solution is offered; there is no final situation to work toward.

The model presents an oscillation in time in which the loss orientation and the restoration orientation appear to be fighting for supremacy. First the loss dominates on the foreground; then the restoration takes over. And then the loss immediately demands our attention again, even before any attempt at restoration activities is made, and so on and so forth.

In reality, these dynamics are even more turbulent: in this duality the situation is not so much a case of either/or, but rather and/and. Loss and restoration happen at the same time, are present simultaneously, turning this duality into a confusing combination for someone to go through. To clarify further, we use the analogy of the computer: although it may look like it, there is no real multitasking when there is only one processor (like the cognitive part of our brain), only of processes that run at high speed alternately in the fore- and background. This creates an illusion of simultaneous and parallel processes. In the Dual Process Model this can be symbolized by overlapping the loss- and restoration orientations (see Figure 6.2). The arrow indicates that there is a relative shift in focus, but that both orientations will almost always be present simultaneously.

By carefully attaching or sewing a treasured past to a future that has been changed and made uncertain by the loss, you might begin to re-weave the

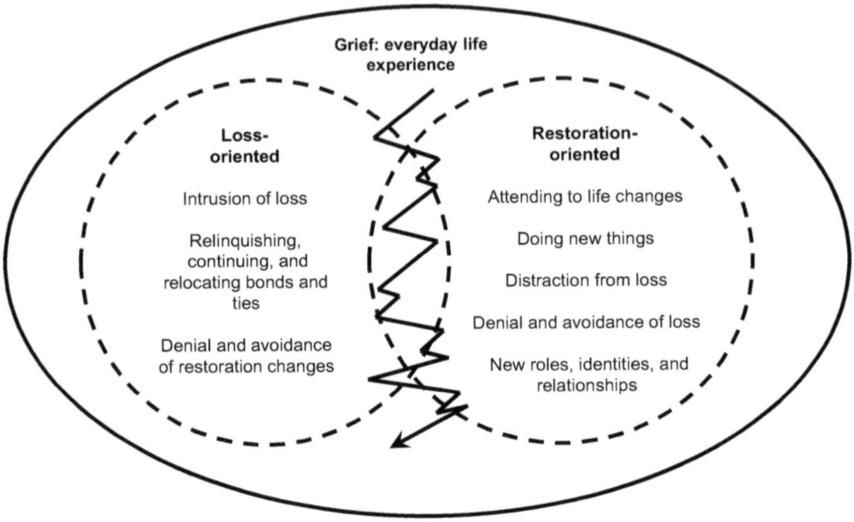

Figure 6.2 Dual Process Model—Overlapping

torn fabric of life (Neimeyer & Thompson, 2014). The oscillation between loss orientation and restoration orientation can metaphorically be seen as the stitching of the surgeon or the sewing of the tailor where the line itself is the thread. The two orientations can be drawn closer together, when the thread is pulled carefully. In this way there could be integration, whereby the torn fabric can be stitched up, even though the scar or seam will always remain visible.

Sometimes one orientation is more pertinent than the other for a longer period of time. The oscillation then seems absent. Usually it eventually starts up by itself again. But sometimes it does not. This could (but does not have to) be cause for concern. When someone is exclusively focused on loss and is unable to move towards a restoration orientation, there is risk of depression or becoming isolated, because it is very hard to connect and have relationships in this orientation. Someone who is only focused on restoration orientation and is unable to move towards the loss orientation may perhaps have difficulty facing the fact that the loss has occurred or acknowledging the meaning of the loss. In the long term, there is a chance that symptoms occur that cannot be directly tied to the loss, such as exhaustion, somatic complaints, or burnout.

Grief as Pileup of Crises

By consciously using the verb 'to grieve,' the emphasis is placed on the fact that grief is not a static condition that is limited to a collection of psychological symptoms or diagnoses. Grief is better described as a developmental process (Neimeyer, 2016). This development process is characterized by working through several crises that present themselves consecutively and overlapping in time. The characteristics of a crisis can be described in the following way: on the one hand, the situation has changed so drastically that the 'old' answers no longer offer a solution. One has to search for new answers in order to deal with the new situation. On the other hand: there are two extremes contained within this crisis, two opposites or polarities from which one has to choose or at least find a balance. Here too, one can recognize the polarity and the oscillation in the effort to find new balance:

1. The first reaction to the loss is an attempt to find balance between reaching out and connection, and withdrawal and isolation. If the person with whom the deepest connection and bonding existed becomes unattainable through loss, then not only is the depth of the loss enormous, but also the one person to whom one would turn in times of such need is gone. In the search for a way out in this period of grief, the dynamic arises between reaching out to someone for support and consolation, risking rejection and withdrawing to be alone with the loss.
2. When the dust from the first crisis has more or less settled, the next crisis to be confronted is security versus insecurity. Stemming from the separation anxiety that can be triggered by the loss, this crisis is characterized by unrest, a high degree of sensitivity and the search for an answer to the questions 'where and how' the lost loved one, the lost object, the lost dream or the lost perspective can be given a place in emotional and social terms. It is about finding space to talk and keep talking about the loss in dialogue with others, especially if some time has passed since the loss occurred. Support and acknowledgement of the loss and the importance to the client of whomever or whatever was lost, are essential here. This is more a reconstruction of the attachment and the continuation of the bond than a release of ties.
3. The last crisis to be dealt with is the meaning of the loss on the one hand and futility on the other, in an attempt to restore a certain level of coherence in one's own life. It is the search for how the loss changes who you are. One's self-image can change after loss. In this crisis one needs to reconcile these different images with each other. There is the question of whether the client feels the freedom to be him- or herself or if the client has to or chooses to play a role, as well as the question of who the client is allowed to become. In this new image of who the client will allow him- or herself to be, even though he or she has not realized it yet, also lies the potential of growth after loss (see Chapter 8). This creates the possibility to grow to a new level in personal development, a level that is reached by confronting the loss and working through the grief. This can motivate

one to reprioritize values and goals and make new choices. That does not necessarily mean that the loss later can or will be seen as something positive. Even though the result is personal growth, the price (the loss) may still be considered (too) high. Even though there is often growth, the counselor may never offer any prospect of this happening in advance, in an effort to console his client. Hopefully however, personal growth can stand side by side with the loss, allowing a deeper sense of compassion with others, sometimes in similar circumstances. This allows a deepening of relationships and connection to others, as many of those having suffered loss have reported, making their lives richer than expected during their initial grief.

Factors Influencing Grief

There are enormous differences in reactions to loss. And all people grieve differently. In this section we will take a look at the various factors that influence grief.

Attachment Styles and Grief

Loss can have very different consequences for different people. What causes these differences? It seems that in particular the attachment style of each person is of influence. Both the attachment style that originates from the family of origin and the style that was developed in the relationship in which the loss occurred. Each goodbye and each loss in the present touches on the very first goodbye and the first loss from the past, the very first time that one reached out as a child to an attachment figure who was unresponsive. The very first separation from the attachment figure, the first attachment dynamic that is made, forms the onset of each following loss reaction. The pain of separation and separation anxiety that the small child felt lie at the base of each loss in later life. This is true even when there is no recollection of the first and oldest separation before the development of language in the brain. Preverbal experiences are recorded somatically.

It is hard enough to deal with a loss when someone is securely attached. Especially when it is an attachment figure that is lost. Even when there is a strong inner representation of the attachment figure and one is securely attached, grief is demanding and difficult. But when someone has an insecure attachment style, the loss has an enormous impact. In the case of a dismissive avoidant attachment style, the loss of an attachment figure can be so overwhelming that the survival strategy one normally falls back on, avoidance and keeping a distance, will no longer suffice. When the avoidance coping no longer works, the person with dismissive avoidant attachment style may be overwhelmed with the emotions always kept at a distance that the person never learned to deal with. For someone with an anxious-preoccupied attachment style, the loss could at the same time mean the end of a dependency relationship, leaving the individual alone without any warning. For someone with a fearful avoidant attachment style, the loss can trigger both extremes of the other insecure attachment styles: the dependence and being overwhelmed by emotions that have always been kept at bay.

Besides the uniqueness of the person suffering the loss, the coping strategies and resilience of that person, there are several more factors that can influence and thus aggravate the grief that someone is dealing with. Several of these conditions are listed below.

Meaning and Nature of the Relationship

One of the most important factors that determine the weight of the grief is the meaning and nature of the relationship. That does not mean however that the grief is only more intense if the relationship was 'good,' or if the meaning of the relationship was already clear in advance. It is however the intensity of the grief that retrospectively can be seen as a yardstick for the nature or quality of the relationship.

Sometimes the intensity of the grief comes as a surprise, if it is greater than expected. Even people that could not tolerate each other (anymore) in life, such as ex-partners, or children with a disrupted relationship with their parents, can be overwhelmed by the intensity of the grief on losing that person. In addition to the meaning of the (original) relationship, there is also the irrevocable part of the loss. This loss ends all chances of restoring the disrupted relationship or of dealing with any unfinished business.

Although there is no recipe for grieving correctly, people often perceive their environment through their personal experience of grief. Because (attachment) relationships differ per individual, the loss will affect each individual differently. In the event of the loss of a loved one, each individual will at first miss the elements of their own relationship with the deceased. If these differences are shared openly, it may result in a shared loss experience carried by a group, even though each has their different experience. This can prevent someone from becoming isolated because they feel that they are the only ones grieving in this way.

The Social Network

Social support is very important in dealing with grief, and lack of support through a social network heightens the risk of solidified grief. A social network basically consists of everyone from each system that the client is a member of. This includes both one's own family as well as one's family of origin, but also friends, (sports) clubs, and work. Although the client has to do the grief work themselves, support from those around them is indispensable.

If the loss has also taken place in one's inner circle, especially if the loved one was an attachment figure, matters are complicated further.

Social media can also be considered part of the social environment. Not all contacts on social media are personal friends or acquaintances. And yet we share personal events. More and more often, this includes our losses. It gives the opportunity to reach a great number of people and elicit reactions.

Reactions do not always feel supportive however. Because there is not much personal interaction in the communication, it becomes more about the layout and the wording of the message, sometimes accompanied by emojis. The interpretation of the message can be complicated because it mostly lacks the non-verbal aspects (intonation, body language, facial expression). It seems to be easier on social media to give negative and judgmental reactions. This makes it risky to use social media around loss and grief. Depending on the chosen medium, the support of a large group, even when the members are not physically close, can, however, be of great value.

Another aspect of social media is that the profile of someone who is deceased cannot always be removed. Sometimes the relatives do not have the passwords, but more often, they are happy to leave the profiles to create a feeling of closeness. On special days such as birthdays or the anniversary of passing, memorial messages can then be posted. People who are linked to the profile see such updates and not everyone appreciates such a side-effect. To unfriend a deceased acquaintance is perhaps too big a step for many people. Another (unintended) effect may be that the profile pops up as a proposed person to befriend. Many people find this a bit creepy.

Nature and (Special) Circumstances Regarding Loss

Major losses are in itself already experiences that can possibly shake human existence to its foundations. Sometimes there are also special circumstances that make the loss even more difficult to deal with.

Natural Expectation of Loss Based on Age

Everyone knows that they are going to die one day, even though not everyone thinks about it all the time. It is natural to expect that people die when they are old. Natural loss can be expected, and is more concurrent with our world view, which can help the grieving process. However, when loss does not meet this natural expectation, it can shake a person's world view and fill them with uncertainty.

When a child loses its parents, or a colleague or friend dies young, it does not fit in with the view of a fair and just world. The loss is then not only about someone one cares for, but perhaps also about losing faith in the predictability of life. This can aggravate the grieving process and weigh down the ability to deal with the loss.

The loss of a child is the biggest fear of (almost all) parents. The harshness of the grief cannot be explained by simply linking it with the attachment style of the parents. As described earlier, children in a healthy family situation cannot be secure bases or attachment figures for their parents as parents conversely can be for their children. Bowlby therefore suggests that in addition to the behavioral system of proximity and security-seeking that the child evokes towards the attachment figure, there is also a behavioral system in which the attachment figure takes on the role of care provider. This behavioral system in parents is activated in response to the child reaching out. The caregiving behavioral system is the inverse of the proximity-seeking behavioral system, and has a different purpose: to protect another person, to ensure the survival of that person and not to protect oneself. The reward for the parent lies in the deep feelings of gratitude and fulfillment when the child grows up in a healthy manner. These are important and meaningful elements for the psychological identity of the parent. The grief of the parent who loses a child is therefore not based on the original separation fear from the attachment figure, but on a reflection of this in the activation of the care provider behavioral system without the child being able to receive this care. For parents, this is often accompanied by a deep sense of guilt, failure, and shortcoming towards the child.

> *I was unable to separate my longing for a child from the holy vow, the costly oath to do my utmost to protect that child, once born, if necessary with my own life. That child came, I have done my utmost to protect it as it grew up and when it was just out of my hands, it is killed in the evil outside world. I can find many arguments to rationalize my failure (Tonio was an adult, he lived in his own place, he carried the responsibility for his own safety), but that does not release me from the shame of my own shortcomings. I have never lain on a psychiatrist's couch, but if such a person had asked me, as you now have: 'Where does that shame come from?' I would have answered as follows. I have often seen my own father fail as a father. And by that I don't mean that, due to a lack of authority, he was unable to end a noisy pillow fight his children were having. No, I am aiming at situations in which he endangered his offspring through disgraceful irresponsibility. . . . I protected my brother and sister as well as possible, and was ashamed of the man who should have actually protected the children. . . . I am saying, things could have been handled better. If I then were to become a father myself, I vowed that I would take a slightly different approach. And for twenty years, I managed to keep my vow. In the meantime, the old shame lay in wait patiently, ready to lash out at me with a horsewhip in case I fail at fatherhood.*
>
> (A.F. Th. van der Heijden, father of Tonio and writer of the requiem novel with the same name, in an interview with Coen Verbaak)[1]

The parents may feel that they have failed in their parenting, failed to protect the child. Even if in reality they cannot be blamed for anything (Kosminsky & Jordan, 2016).

Hidden, Invisible, or Disenfranchised Grief

Grief is often not acknowledged when the (meaning of the) relationship is invisible or not open or when events cannot be made public. The loss remains hidden. Saying goodbye is made difficult or even impossible and can result in solidified grief. The term *disenfranchised grief* with reference to such losses was introduced by Kenneth Doka (Doka, 1989).

Hidden or invisible grief can relate to tangible, but also to intangible, loss. Tangible hidden losses are often suffered when the circumstances cannot be made known to the public, when they are forbidden (in certain circles) or stigmatized, happen secretly, or give rise to shame. Examples are when an extramarital partner passes away, a cosmetic surgery intervention is unsuccessful, when there is a miscarriage or abortion, when there are losses suffered by children that go unnoticed by adults, or when losses are suffered by parents of disabled children.

A special form of hidden or invisible grief concerns the loss of (domestic) animals (Lommers & Van Amsterdam, 1992). Animals can have great meaning to their owners; the bond between humans and animals is often a special one. For many people, an animal is part of the family, sometimes even a replacement or substitute for a relationship. Although animals are often dependent on people for their care, animals can still function as a secure base for their owners through their faithful attitude. Often human traits are assigned to their animals, and according to the owners, there is mutual understanding. Then when an animal dies or goes missing, the human may feel a great sense of loss leaving a deep emptiness. People do not always understand what it feels like to lose a pet. The loss of an animal and the emotions it gives rise to in children evokes empathy and endearment. Many still remember the first time they lost a pet. Often this is also the first time that children experience loss up close. For adults, however, the loss of an animal can be far-reaching and unfortunately there is often little empathy. This too can be called hidden or disenfranchised grief.

Examples of intangible losses are losses such as the loss of youth, ideals, dreams, or faith/trust. Hidden, intangible grief can be to remain childless when it is not your choice.

Twenty percent of the Dutch adult population is childless. In the UK and USA these statistics are much the same. For a long time, people thought that those people had consciously made that choice. But this is not true. Eighty per cent of those who are childless have more or less ended up that way, according to researcher Renske Keizer (26) of Erasmus University Rotterdam. She recently obtained her doctorate on this subject. Only ten percent of those who are childless have really deliberately chosen not to have children. The other ten percent knew at a young age that they would not physically be able to have children.

(Van Lookeren Campagne, 2010)

Sometimes it is not possible to have children, even though that person wants to start a family. Sometimes someone discovers too late that he or she would like to have children, but it turns out to be no longer possible because of his or her advanced age. This proves to be a difficult subject to talk about. When others around them are pregnant and are rightly looking forward to becoming parents or when friends or siblings are already having children, this loss can be very painful. An unplanned of even unwanted pregnancy, while possibly also an invisible loss for the pregnant woman, can lead to a great level of incomprehension by the woman who cannot have children.

Also (or perhaps precisely) in the case of disenfranchised grief, the counselor can play an important role as a witness to the story that had to remain hidden and needs to be heard. Together the meaning of the relationship with that which is lost is investigated and where necessary goodbyes are finalized.

Loss by Unnatural Causes

Death by unnatural causes such as accidents, suicide, violence, and violent crime can aggravate grief. The loss is almost always unexpected and caused by an external intervention. The idea may arise that, if it had just happened differently, the loss might have been prevented. Many surviving relatives find it difficult to accept that. This means that in case of loss through unnatural causes, it will be difficult to give meaning and the sense of meaninglessness may continue to prevail.

1. Loss by suicide
   Suicide can be a devastating experience for family and friends, evoking feelings of guilt, shame, and inadequacy and sometimes anger and helplessness. In some cases, there has been a long preliminary process of treatments and admissions. In other cases, somebody steps out of life totally unexpectedly. The fact that the deceased himself had a hand in their own death and chose to put an end to their life can be extremely confronting for relatives and friends. For example, they may find it difficult to grasp that the relationship they had with the deceased was not sufficient reason for them to carry on living. Or they blame themselves for not having picked up on the signals. Or they are angry that the deceased has not tried harder to talk about their situation or solve their

problems. Looking back, doubts can also arise about their relationship with the deceased. A complex palette of feelings and thoughts can arise and it can interfere deeply with their self-image. Suicide is still considered taboo in our society. This can lead to secrecy and isolation and can aggravate grief.

2. Loss through accident or violence
   The loss of a loved one through violence is a particularly shocking experience. When someone is killed in an accident or is victim of a violent crime, not only is it inconsistent with the natural expectation of dying from old age, in most cases there is someone who is at fault or a perpetrator. Feelings of anger and guilt can then play a major role and may be aimed towards the person who is to blame. But sometimes people involved also blame themselves for the situation, which makes them feel guilty ('If only I had . . .').
   When an accident is caused by recklessness or 'own fault,' the anger can be aimed at the deceased themselves. The processing of grief can thus be extra complicated.
   A possible legal aftermath can either prevent someone from grieving, as well as the opposite: old feelings and emotions can come back again.
3. Loss when someone goes missing
   A disappearance brings a lot of uncertainty. When someone has gone missing, this results in a huge conflict in the first task of grief: to accept the reality that another person is really dead. There is no confirmation of the death of the missing person and there can remain hope that he will return. The grieving and thus the processing of the loss cannot commence as long as there is still hope for return.
   In addition to the emotional impact of someone who has gone missing, there are also practical problems. If there is no death certificate, and the settlement of financial and legal matters cannot take place. Only after a certain amount of time the missing person can formally be declared dead. By requesting this declaration, however, the surviving relatives may get the feeling that they are betraying their loved one and are guilty of his death. It is precisely the combination of emotional and practical problems that makes such a loss so hard to bear.
4. Not being able to say goodbye
   A loss breaks the relationship between the deceased and the next of kin. If the latter did not have the opportunity to say goodbye, this complicates the grieving process. It is important for the next of kin to be able to say goodbye. Here, unspoken items can be discussed or unfinished business can be concluded. This may be important for both the one who is dying and the person staying behind.

When the loss is unexpected, for example through an accident or crime, it is still important to be able to say goodbye to the physical body (or remains) of the deceased. Otherwise, the first task of grief, acknowledging the loss, becomes problematic for the next of kin.

It becomes much more difficult when the goodbye has to take place after an accident in which there is serious mutilation. Viewing the remains can have a huge (long-term) impact, making it difficult to decide which is worse: the intruding image or not saying goodbye. In that case, it is important to find a middle road and find a way to use identifying characteristics so that the survivor can still positively identify the deceased and make sure that there is no chance of misunderstanding or mistaken identity.

How Different Groups Grieve Differently

We can roughly say that women grieve differently than men and children grieve differently than adults. In this section, we shed light on the differences. In each group, there are aspects that can affect grief.

Difference Between Men and Women

Women grieve differently than men. Of course, we generalize if we put it this way. And we are quick to stereotype. Yet it is possible to make a distinction between a 'male' and a 'female' way of grieving (Delfos, 2008). To be clear: men can grieve in a feminine way and women can grieve in a masculine way. Grief is and remains a personal and individual process.

Throughout the world, in all cultures, male and female are considered two polarities, two opposites. Just like night and day or light and dark. A well-known form is the sign Yin and Yang. The images that exist about 'the masculine' and 'the feminine' are ancient and stored in what the psychiatrist C.G. Jung called the collective memory. It is this memory that we draw from when making a list of male and female characteristics. These lists are generally pretty universal. In short, the masculine can be described as outward orientation (on the outside world), focused, creative, enterprising, competitive, giving, focused on 'Becoming' instead of 'Being.' The feminine can be described as receptive, caring, accepting, focused on preservation, security, inner knowing, connected with others, 'Being' instead of 'Becoming.'

As we have said before, men and women have both the masculine and the feminine in them. But in general, it can be said that there are differences in upbringing at home, at school, and sports clubs in the approach of boys and girls. And those differences in approach originate from the described archetypes.

The 'feminine' or 'masculine' ways of grieving differ in the way in which the loss is dealt with. The female is inclined to seek contact, is more vulnerable, can be comforted, is inclined to look for the deeper meaning of events, focuses on creating a home, security, lets the pain and the grief out. The male focuses more on what needs to be done, arranges the things that need to be arranged, keeps an overview, determines what the next step is, makes decisions.

The linking of styles to men or women is not important in itself. When a client recognizes his or her own coping style in a counseling situation, and a view has been given of the other coping styles, linking this can be helpful. Especially if it helps partners in a relationship who have a shared loss to see that their own way of grieving or their needs do not necessarily match those of the partner. That men and women can grieve differently does not mean that the one 'grieves less' than the other, or that the loss therefore means 'less' to that person. The effort it takes to share the loss, each having different coping styles, in order to find acknowledgement and solace with and from each other, can put pressure on the relationship. The shared loss may be given a unique personal meaning by each person and therefore will be different, but neither is less significant even though each has a different coping style. Being aware of this can help both in taking up enough space to deal with the loss in their own way and at the same time also be there for the other person.

It can be helpful if there are role models available of the same gender, so that they can function as examples of other coping styles from which to learn. Men therefore need men to allow themselves to grieve (Van Lent, 2016).

Grief in Children and Young People

Admittedly, children do grieve differently than adults, but more important than the differences, is the insight that children really do grieve (Fiddelaers-Jaspers, 2010, 2014; Stichting Jonge Helden, 2016; Spuij, 2017). In the past, children were, and sometimes still are, often kept away from loss because it is assumed that 'they will not understand' or 'should not have to be confronted with the pain.' At present, the prevailing belief is that children benefit more from openness about what is happening during and after loss. Even if young children do not yet have the cognitive skills to understand what the loss entails, or whether the missing is definite or not, children benefit from honesty.

Children already experience several types of loss on their own. Consider, for example, the very first inevitable loss, the loss of the safety and security of the womb at birth; the losses when the attachment figure leaves the room, or leaves the child at nursery or school; the loss of the breast when they are weaned from nursing, or a cuddly toy or loss within the family due to divorce or death.

An important difference between the way children and adults grieve is that children grieve 'in smaller segments,' as it were. Children can be grappling with the loss one moment and the next moment they are fully involved again in their game. Fortunately, children can go back and forth, because grieving and growing up is a burdensome combination. Children are constantly learning and developing, thereby also gaining a new awareness of the loss and acquiring new skills to deal with it. This also means that the loss can return later in life, because in every new phase of life the permanently missing of a meaningful other will have new consequences. Grief takes place in a social context for children too. It is essential that there is support available in the immediate vicinity, preferably within the family. The parents, brothers, and sisters are usually closest. But a child can also receive support from its grandparents, uncles, aunts, cousins, teachers, neighbors, sports coaches, and so on. When the loss takes place in one's own family or family of origin, and the other family members are also grieving, combining care for the child with their own grief is a big challenge for caregivers. If there is also a separation, out-of-home placement, adoption, or foster family involved, then that is already a loss situation in itself. When another loss is stacked on top of that, the load is increased further, and at the same time the environment is not ideal for providing support.

Very young children, aged up to three years, lack the cognitive notion to grasp what 'loss' is. Children at this age, however, are very sensitive to moods and emotions in the environment, especially within their own family. They are also perfectly capable of feeling the emotional absence of a parent in grief, although they cannot grasp this on a cognitive level. Children cannot be fooled when it comes to attention and care. The emotional unavailability of a parent will therefore affect the child, who is still fully dependent. Even unborn children, in the womb, can experience effects of a mother's grieving (Noten, 2015).

Grief in children of this age can manifest itself in other behavior, such as changes in sleeping and eating habits, more crying, unrest, but also in withdrawing or clinging. Children at this age can also go looking for who or what was lost, or continue to wait for their return, because they do not understand what the loss entails. It is often visible in their play how they process the loss and what they absorb of their parents' grief. Finally, it is not uncommon that in the case of a death in the family, very young children indicate having contact with the deceased.

In children from age three to six there is already a realization of a difference between life and death. They are however still unable to grasp the finality of a loss through death. At this age, children often ask many practical questions about how, what, and why. For parents these questions can come across as very direct, especially when they are about the memorial service, the cremation, or funeral, or about how matters concerning the divorce are arranged. Questions about where someone is when he is dead will challenge opinions and beliefs a parent has about whether there is anything after death. For many adults this causes tension between their own convictions and what they want to tell the child at this age.

Children between three and six years old combine an apparent practicality with childlike, magical thinking. The child is able to establish a relationship between what it has, or has not done, with the loss. For a child, this relationship can seem very logical and obvious and this can lead to guilt and behavior modification. For parents/caregivers there is a chance here to talk about the loss with the child.

In children between the ages of six to nine years, realization dawns that a loss due to death is irreversible or that the other parent will never come and live at home again after a divorce. The finality of the loss becomes clear, but the consequences for the future will not yet be clear. At this age, children can understand that they are vulnerable. They become aware that this loss means that other people they love can leave or even die. Parents cannot protect them from this realization. Parents can, however, enter into a conversation with these children about what this means.

Children aged nine to twelve now know that everything that lives can also die. These children are less dependent and therefore often have the tendency to demand less attention. They do not want to appear 'childish,' especially if there are also older children around. Yet especially at this age children struggle with the same uncertainties younger children have, only they have less childlike frankness to ask questions about this.

Teenagers realize fully that loss is inevitable and omnipresent. Teenagers generally try to keep emotional loss at a distance, but if there is a confrontation with loss, it hits them very hard.

All children want their parent(s) to be happy, sometimes only on an unconscious level. Children can make extreme adjustments in their own behavior to accommodate this, without parents explicitly asking for it. However, if inappropriate behavior in the child, such as taking over care of the parent(s), persists for too long and children are not thanked and discharged from their new role, this will disrupt their development. These systemic effects of role confusion are also described in Chapter 4, on the theme 'sharing intimacy' on the Transition Cycle.

Grief in Young Adults

In the phase of 'no longer being a child' but also 'not yet adult,' the phase of adolescence or young adulthood, new experiences await: even more than before, young adults are to maintain their own relationships and are confronted with their own roles and responsibilities in dealing with the loss of another person. The parents are not always involved in the friendships that they have entered into, so the initiative to go to a funeral, for example, lies with the young adults themselves. The expectations they have of themselves, as well as those of society about the 'adult' role when supporting others who have suffered loss will confront young adults with their own life experiences.

Grief in Adults

Implicitly, adults are often the 'standard group' when one speaks and writes about grief. On the one hand, 'everything' applies to them, on the other hand we run the risk that we no longer specifically recognize them as a group. However, adults also have their specific and individual needs when dealing with grief. Their life experience does not necessarily enable them to handle loss at all. An adult who loses a parent, even if it answers to the natural expectation of age, also loses a (potential) secure base and is confronted with their own childhood. Themes of the Transition Cycle will turn up again.

Grief in the Elderly

Just as with adults, there is a misconception that older people are better able to deal with loss because of their lengthy life experience. But one cannot get used to loss, although one gets to know oneself better and better in loss situations and one may be less surprised or overwhelmed by them. As people grow older though, they run a greater risk of losing more and more loved ones and acquaintances. The chance of losing their life partner also increases. The fact that these losses fall within the expectation of loss due to age does not detract from their significance or from their weight.

The piling up of successive losses is not without consequence. It reduces the carrying capacity, certainly in combination with isolation resulting from the decreasing social environment and due to decreasing mobility. And all the while, the burden grows with each loss.

With increasing age, we get closer to death. This awareness can cause a sense of meaninglessness, on one hand, because of the ever-growing realization that control of the situation diminishes and, on the other hand, because of the limited possibility to revise one's goals in life.

The Grief of the Intellectually Challenged

One may be tempted, due to a certain lack of cognitive abilities, to make a comparison with children, but people with mental challenges have a different view of the world through their life experience and physical development. They do however have the same trouble with the notion of what loss is and with the definitive nature of something being permanently missing, and are in that aspect comparable to children. Depending on the nature and burden of the mental challenge, people may have access to language in varying degrees. The less use that can be made of language, the more important it becomes to involve someone physically in everything that has to do with the goodbye. The balance between emotional development and intellectual development also plays an important role in the question of to what extent someone can be involved and supported when suffering a loss. The grief reactions given from social-emotional development can be very different than what would be expected on the basis of cognitive development (Meeusen-van de Kerkhof et al., 2001).

Due to the large variation in the degree of mental challenges, the expression of grief often has many different forms. There are also often delayed grief reactions. It is helpful to be able to participate in and be involved in farewell rituals, as well as to be supported by family and other caregivers (Heyvaert et al., 2012).

The Grief of People With Acquired Brain Injury

A special group consists of people with acquired brain injury (ABI), which could be caused by a brain hemorrhage, tumor, accident, or excessive alcohol consumption. The limitations of this disorder can have two sides: one visible and the other invisible. Enclosed in that physically invisible side, there can also be an intellectual disability. As a result, the way grief is expressed and the way in which the loss is dealt with may seem incongruent with the visible age. This may complicate the connection with the need for support of someone with ABI.

What makes this group special is that those with ABI have their own personal loss situation. There is always a life before and a life after the injury. If there is an active memory of how it was prior to the injury, then the restrictions posed by ABI make them conscious of their loss. The visible part of the loss often consists of loss of function and sometimes loss of feeling in the paralyzed parts of the body. The invisible losses often involve a combination of losses of cognitive functions, which can also manifest themselves in communicative limitations, behavioral changes, and emotional consequences. These often seemingly invisible effects (as seen from the outside) can lead to hidden—disenfranchised—grief.

In ABI patients there is loss of cognitive functions, such as problems with short- and long-term memory, resulting in information no longer being stored or memorized. This can sometimes cause problems with recognizing other people's faces. In addition, there are problems with attention and concentration or keeping things in perspective, which makes the carrying out of daily activities problematic. Communication and language also suffer from the loss of cognitive functions, so that, apart from the behavioral and emotional changes that can also affect the original character, people with ABI run an increased risk of social isolation.

Anticipatory Grief

Anticipatory grief can occur when people can see the loss coming. In situations where the parting and the loss have become unavoidable, such as when someone in a reorganization fears redundancy or dismissal or is told that he or she will be made redundant in the near future. Or when someone is facing an operation where part of the physical functionality will be lost, if a loved one is terminally ill, or treatment has been stopped, grief reactions can already occur before the imminent loss. That does not mean, however, that this anticipatory grief is only focused on the actual loss and should be seen as 'preliminary work.' On the contrary, after the loss, grief can change its form and it is impossible to predict how the person will react to the loss, despite the anticipatory grief.

The Grief of the Terminally Ill Themselves

Counseling a terminally ill client is a very special form of counseling, as this is someone who is confronted with anticipation of the loss of his or her life.

When someone is terminally ill, they are confronted, on the one hand, with the finiteness of their own life and, on the other hand, with reactions from their environment. Sometimes there is tension around the illness, when someone decides they do not want treatment anymore while those in their environment keep urging them to try everything. In the remaining phase of life, the themes of the Transition Cycle come into the picture profoundly, looking back on (the meaning of) the life lived on the one hand and on the other hand looking ahead at the time remaining, what is (and still is) of significance and what can be left behind.

The Grief of Young People With a Short Life Expectancy

Another special form of an impending end of life is when young people have a short life expectancy. The combination of the finiteness of life with the loss that discounts the expectation of naturally dying of old age makes the burden heavier for the person and their environment. The meaning of a short life is often difficult to interpret in terms of goals achieved, making it much more problematic to attribute meaning to it.

In the Netherlands, the six-year-old terminally ill Tijn visited a radio show called *Serious Request* in 2016. He came with his father to the Glass

House (the location where the show was being broadcasted) to paint nails for charity.

Tijn's ambition was to raise a few hundred euros, while everyone else was challenged, in turn, to get three others to have their fingernails painted.

> *The reason will make you feel a little sad, but there is a silver lining. Tijn is six years old and in May we were told that he has brain stem cancer (DIPG), and this is his last Serious Request, because his life expectancy is less than a year. Yet we felt it was important to help children who can't even turn six. Now we have decided together to challenge three people to have their fingernails painted and then donate 1 euro. If you do not want to have them painted you donate 10 euros.*[2]

The personal story and his altruism touched so many people that his charity drive with the hashtag #heelhollandlakt (all in Holland are painting fingernails) took off. Tijn's campaign yielded 2.5 million euros. Tijn's initiative even turned around the downward trend in *Serious Request*'s revenues.

Additional Aspects in Grief

Grief can be influenced by many factors. Some of them may be more difficult to recognize at first. These concern older losses or hidden losses. This section highlights aspects that can (unexpectedly) place an even heavier burden on grief.

Cumulative Loss

Grief can be aggravated if several losses occur simultaneously or in succession. But other factors can also aggravate grief, such as the loss of income when the breadwinner dies, or uncertainty about work (job retention) when someone is unable to (come to) work because of grief.

Losses can also have an effect over time if the original loss has the effect that future events will no longer occur. For example, in case of loss of a child, the parent will no longer see the child grow up, graduate, develop a relationship, or become a parent (and they will not become a grandparent through this child). These effects, secondary losses, are often not immediately conceivable and sometimes occur later in life, so that the original loss, though from a different perspective, is touched on again.

If losses follow each other in time without the losses being integrated into the life (-story), there is an 'accumulation' of losses (Noten, 2015). However, if multiple losses occur at more or less the same time, there may also be a risk that the losses will be 'braided' together (Neimeyer & Thompson, 2014; Neimeyer, 2016). For the client it can then be unclear which loss has evoked which grief response(s).

Delayed Grief

Sometimes grief comes much later (Ankersmid, 2015a). This brings the great challenge with it to recognize it as such at that later time. Due to all sorts of circumstances, it can happen that someone cannot cope with the loss at the time it takes place. This can happen, for example, when a child loses a parent at a young age and either does not realize the effect of the loss, or does not have the space to grieve. Subsequent (loss) experiences often evoke grief from the previous loss. The earlier strategy of coping with the loss, namely, suppressing it, often does not work anymore. Grieving for the new loss brings back the grief for the old loss. A seemingly joyful event can also trigger old loss, such as becoming a mother or a grandmother, in which case the impact of having grown up without a mother might suddenly dawn on a woman.

Transgenerational Grief

When exploring the attachment style of the client, the counselor always looks into the family of origin. In the exercise with the genogram in Chapter 2, attention is also given to the origin of the parents. It is precisely in those previous generations that the roots of attachment are passed on. The (attachment) history of the parents and ancestors is of great importance. Unconsciously, messages from the parents' families are passed on to the children, messages that their parents have in turn received from their parents. Profound losses in previous generations often leave their mark on later generations. Secrets from previous generations can also be passed on. The same applies to guilt and shame. Even though no one can personally do anything about it and is in no way responsible for it, such themes can have a big impact because of the loyalty ties with the larger system of origin.

When making a genogram, it makes sense to map out the grandparents as well as the parents. When details are missing, or the client does not know the (first) names, dates of birth or death, there is perhaps a deeper knowledge of a time when something happened in previous generations that has affected the client's parents and their families. Themes such as emigration, war, crisis, oppression, secret relationships, illegitimate children, being on the 'wrong' side of the war, or being betrayed have a much wider effect than merely on those who have experienced it first-hand.

The attachment styles of children, especially in their insecure forms, also appear to have a generational aspect. Children respond to their attachment figures, usually the mother. The behavior of the attachment figure in response to the child reaching out is the determining factor. The behavior of the attachment figure cannot be seen apart from their experiences during their own childhood. It is not so much the factual events that appear to be of influence, but rather the inner experience of the attachment figure during these events.

For example, when the mother has had to deal with abuse of any kind in her own childhood, it is not so much the abuse itself, but the way she deals with it that affects the contact she has with her child. She determines (consciously or unconsciously) which form of secure and reliable availability that she can offer her child. Developmental psychologist Mary Main calls the ability that women seem to have to still be responsive and available to their child, even when they have an insecure attachment style after a difficult youth of their own, 'acquired secure attachment' (Kosminsky & Jordan, 2016).

Continuing Bonds

A lasting connection despite loss, stemming from the view that grief does not have to 'go away,' can be very helpful. Although the relationship ends in physical form, the bond does continue to exist, but merely changes shape. These *continuing bonds* (Klass et al., 2014), in a classical sense are about contact with a deceased loved one that continues in a certain way. For example, the deceased is still seen or heard, or possessions are kept (external continuing bonds). This external form can, however, also lead to a certain degree of dependence on 'appearances' or objects. With this, external continuing bonds, especially in combination with an anxious-obsessive or avoidant attachment style, pose the risk of solidified grief (Yu et al., 2016).

Internal continuing bonds exist when a permanent presence or influence is felt. People integrate inspiring aspects of the other in their own lives, in their own personality. In this way the relationship does not end, but it changes from a physical form into a more symbolic continuation. The relationship can also grow within the person who has suffered the loss as he develops and grows. The need for internalization is greatest when grief is most intense. It is however irrelevant how long ago the loss occurred. The time elapsed since the goodbye or the loss is irrelevant; the point is to allow the grief (Russac et al., 2002). This internal form of continuing bonds in particular is felt by people to be extremely supportive. In this way, on a psychological level, there can still be an attachment figure present (Kosminsky & Jordan, 2016).

The internal form of continuing bonds is essentially about the internalization of secure bases. This means that the continuing bonds should be placed in a context broader than merely a permanent connection with a deceased person because secure bases can take on different forms. In this way, someone can also derive support from the permanent connection with a homeland one has left behind, a previous organization or a terminated relationship. This internal support works positively in the ability to deal with the loss, to make new connections and may even offer enough support to be a secure base for others.

Continuing bonds, the permanent connections, directly oppose the ideas of Freud, which are based on the definitive letting go of the lost love object (decathexis). These two approaches can be viewed as two extremes in the views on grief, giving rise to contradictions that seem difficult to combine in counseling. The proven positive influence of internal continuing bonds when dealing with loss seems to contradict the grief work described by Freud. Yet that grief work covers more than just finally letting go. Consciously saying goodbye is part of the work when dealing with grief and contributes to the conscious transformation of the relationship towards continuing bonds.

Continuing bonds offer support to remember and commemorate. The environment can be of great influence. If the person concerned feels little support or permission from the environment, it can be difficult to cherish any permanent connection. When, for whatever reason, there is a taboo on the relationship, the continuing bond and its positive effect come under pressure. This occurs, for example, when a new intimate relationship considers the memory of the previous relationship as too threatening, or the employer does not want to hear the old company name anymore after the reorganization. The space to allow the development of continuing bonds and to internalize secure bases also provides room for 'growth after loss.' This space comes from the theme of 'giving meaning' on the Transition Cycle, the subject of the next chapter. Giving meaning is also the theme that enables people to 'complete the circle' and to open up to new contact, in which the continuous bond is integrated and interwoven with life as it continues.

Counseling: The Other Side of Grief

The other side of the theme 'grief' is characterized by 'no longer feeling, resistance' (see Figure 6.3). Unconfronted grief wells up again at other times. Usually at times when there are other setbacks. There is an important relationship between burnout, depression and illness on the one hand and the avoidance of grief on the other (Leader, 2008). The tricky thing is that at such

Figure 6.3 Both Sides of the Same Coin for the Theme 'Grief'

a moment one has long lost sight of the original loss. As a result, the avoided grief is sometimes no longer recognized as grief.

A counselor needs to pay attention to the themes of loss that are hidden behind the question. Solidified grief can create a vicious cycle, a downward spiral of emotional distancing, withdrawal from contact and a sense of meaninglessness. The spiral gets tighter and people become completely stuck. By working through the themes of the Transition Cycle, one broadens one's mind and identity (Kohlrieser et al., 2012, p. 61). By completing the circle, growth takes place (see also Chapter 8). In this way, the cycle is a spiral that moves upwards. Resistance can be an obstacle to growth in counseling. As a protective mechanism it is used to keep pain out. Resistance has a negative effect on a social level because others will give up their attempts to come close. It is all too human to leave someone alone who 'does not want to be helped.' The dilemma here lies precisely in the determination of whether 'wanting' is correct. Resistance alone is not enough to determine that the other does not want to be helped; it is quite possible that the other person does not know how to seek help. It is up to the counselor to make this distinction and, in his or her role as a secure base, to explore the resistance with the client.

Using the Dual Process Model, it becomes apparent that both sides, both the loss orientation and the restoration orientation, are necessary for grieving. The balance can vary per individual. The same applies to the duality within the themes of the Transition Cycle. The counselor also pays attention to this during counseling, consciously and critically considering his or her own preferences per theme.

Dialogue

Oliver from the case study at the beginning of this chapter has already seen his counselor Ethan several times.

Ethan: Good morning, Oliver. It is good to see you again.
Oliver: Thank you.
Ethan: How have you been, since the last time you were here?
Oliver: I have had ups and downs. The past week it actually went quite well. I have been gradually working more hours at a time. My colleagues are really great. They are reacting really well. It is nice to be back again. Only Harry who works in the financial department. That's a really unpleasant guy. He came into the office uninvited last Thursday. It really winds me up when he does that. I lay awake all Thursday night and just could not go on Friday. I was exhausted.
Ethan: What got you so wound up? What happened?

Oliver: Harry is just a really weird guy. I don't like him. He just walks around and then all of a sudden he will say: 'Hey, so you finally decided to come to work again! Did they get sick of you at home?' He then sniggers a bit and leaves. So irritating!
Ethan: What do you find most irritating?
Oliver: That he makes it sound as if I am sitting at home for fun. As if I am having fun working four-hour days. It makes me so mad. I would like to punch the guy in the nose!
Ethan: I see that it really upsets you. Amazing that one sentence can cause so much turmoil.
Oliver: I just don't understand why he would say such a thing.
Ethan: Unfortunately, he is not here right now so that we can ask him about it. Instead, we could explore why you are so affected by it. What do you think about that?
Oliver: Yes, well maybe that's a good idea. I am not prepared to spend another sleepless night because of that man.
Ethan: We will return to the moment that Harry walked into the office. Are you able to think back to the situation?
Oliver: Oh certainly, I have done that quite a few times in the past few days. (Smiling slightly.)
Ethan: Okay, what happened to you when he walked in?
Oliver: I remember looking up from my computer and I saw him coming in. It is quite a large space and I sit near the back. He was scouting the room
Ethan: So, you saw him come in. And how did your body react?
Oliver: I wasn't paying much attention to my body. But thinking back, I immediately feel the tension again.
Ethan: And where do you feel this tension?
Oliver: Mostly in the vicinity of my stomach.
Ethan: Do you have that often? Is that a familiar feeling to you?
Oliver: Um, I never really pay attention to such things. But I am familiar with it, so I feel like that more often. And I suppose you want to know when? I will have to think about that . . . I am not really sure.
Ethan: So, you have had this feeling before, but you are not sure in which situation. We will go back to Thursday then. Do you remember exactly what it was that Harry said? (Stands up and walks over to the flip chart board.)
Oliver: He said: 'Hey, so you finally decided to come to work again! Did they get sick of you at home?' Something like that.
Ethan: (Writes the sentence on the board.) So, this was literally what Harry said?
Oliver: Yes, that's right.
Ethan: And which messages were you also hearing him say, even though he didn't actually say them?

Oliver: You are lazy. You are cutting corners. You are sitting at home for fun.
Ethan: (Writing this all down on the board.) And what else?
Oliver: You are always exaggerating. A sissy. A quitter.
Ethan: (Continues to write everything down.) And what else does it sound like he's saying?
Oliver: That I am useless. That my wife Izzy does not want me either. That I am worthless.
Ethan: Those are quite a few messages. Are there any more?
Oliver: That I am no good.
Ethan: I will add that one too. It is quite a list. How does it feel to look at everything written here?
Oliver: Intense. Painful. (Suddenly overcome by emotion.) Sometimes I just don't see the point of it all anymore. I feel so worthless.
Ethan: (Is quiet for a while, in close proximity, without doing anything.) Yes, that is very painful.
Oliver: (Blows his nose.) Harry knows exactly which buttons to push.
Ethan: Well yes, that's one way of putting it. Harry is probably not even aware of the effect his comments have on you.
Oliver: No, I don't think so either. He is really not such a bad guy.
Ethan: Unintentionally he puts his finger on your sore spot: your old pain. In the present, something old is touched on. Harry's remark is just hitting it dead center. What old pain could it be, do you think?
Oliver: Well, last time we were talking about my father. I suspect it has something to do with him. He also used to give me that worthless feeling. That it was never good enough, no matter how hard I worked.
Ethan: And why was that so painful for you?
Oliver: That he never noticed how hard I tried. He always had some remark to make. He just didn't see that I was trying my hardest for him, for a pat on the head.
Ethan: What did you miss in the contact with your father?
Oliver: (Stares straight ahead, then tears fill his eyes.) I wanted him so badly to come and see the hut I built. That he would come in and sit with me and that he would be impressed by the stairs I had built myself to get into it. I had even built a chair for him. But I never dared ask.
Ethan: (Waits and stays close by.) I would love to have seen you sitting in that hut. It must have been a beautiful hut!
Oliver: Yes, it was a mighty beautiful hut! Really well built.
Ethan: And how painful for the little boy you once were. I can hear the intense longing in your voice as you tell your story. For a father who was proud of his son.
Oliver: Yes, I never had a father like that. I had never considered that this would be such a big thing. But now I feel how much it hurts when I think about it.
Ethan: Back then, you weren't able to allow yourself to feel the longing and the pain. You did what you could to grow up after that and I believe you

succeeded pretty well. But now it is time to reflect on what you missed and who you are missing. That is called grieving.

Oliver: (Laughing.) Oh, so that's grieving! Well that's just great!

Ethan: (Laughs with him.) Yes, well, it sure is! See you next time, then we will happily continue grieving!

Self-Reflection Questions

- How do you react to loss? What happens inside your body, what happens inside your head?
- Were there periods during which you spent a lot of time on loss, or rather no time at all? What caused these differences?
- How do you express your emotions and thoughts when something is lost?
- Looking back on your life/career/education, which losses have you not yet grieved over, for example, by 'carrying on with life' or by suppressing your feelings and thoughts? How does this influence your life/career/education?
- Which grief that originated when you were growing up influences your life/job/education at the present time? What is it like for you when someone asks about it?

Exercises

Exercise—Lifeline (Addition With the Theme 'Grief')

To build further on the lifeline exercises in Chapters 1 and 5, the counselor can take another look at the milestones on the lifeline from the viewpoint of the theme 'grief.'

Instruction: Counsel each other in groups of three (A is the counselor, B is the client, and C is the observer), for example, by using the self-reflection questions relevant to this theme. Use the lifeline drawn during the exercise in Chapter 1 that you worked out further in Chapter 5.

Additional questions that can be used for this exercise include the following:

- Which goodbyes and which losses did you grieve over at that moment? Which goodbyes and losses did you not grieve? What was the reason that you did not grieve?
- Which goodbye or loss have you yet to grieve? Is there anything else that you need in order to do so?

Evaluate each turn briefly and then switch roles.

Exercise—Returning the Burden

This exercise (Veenbaas & Goudswaard, 2011) is helpful when the client carries a burden or responsibility that actually is not his or hers to carry. Subconsciously, he or she may have always taken his mother's misery into account by not burdening her with his own need for attention. Or maybe the client was held responsible for the safety of a younger brother, causing the client not to experience the freedom to explore with friends. Perhaps the client subconsciously felt guilty over war crimes committed during the war by a grandfather. Or is the client still frugal, since his or her father once declared bankruptcy? The client symbolically returns the burden to whom the burden belongs.

Instruction: Counsel each other in groups of three (A is the counselor, B is the client, and C represents whom the burden is returned to; when working with a client individually, the counselor can place him- or herself in the position of C, using a dedicated mat on the floor or an empty chair).

- A asks B what burdens him or her.
- B takes time for inner exploration and to feel.
- A supports by being present and eventually asking questions guiding B to a deeper level.
- When B has made contact with his or her burden, A asks B to pick up a stone (or any other object with some mass) and to imagine the stone representing the burden symbolically.
- A asks B for whom this burden was carried.
- C positions him- or herself opposite B and represents the one for whom B carried the burden.
- B connects to C, carrying the weight of the stone.
- B takes the time to internally observe what happens in this moment.
- B then returns the burden to C. B can then speak the following sentences: 'I carry your burden, I carry your . . . I lovingly carried it for you all this time, but it is not mine. So it is not mine to carry either. It is yours and it is yours to carry. I hereby return it to you.'

Evaluate each turn and then switch roles.

Exercise—Travel Report

Life is like a journey and on that journey, when grief arrives, it can feel like an unplanned, unexpected, and unwanted survival trip—a survival trip that someone was not prepared for. It is precisely for this reason that it is of value to have the client write a travel report about this survival trip, to look back, to reflect on where they are now and to have a preview of where they want to end up and how to get there; it is a report about trial and error, learning, growing, and discovering who the client is and what the client considers important and dreams about.

> **Instruction:** Write your own travel report about a loss that you have suffered.
>
> With a peer, share your travel reports by reading it to each other. Then discuss together:
>
> - What touches you in the other person's travel report?
> - What inspires you?

Exercise—Loss-Boxes and Loss-Cupboards

One of the creative work methods around the duality of grief, about allowing the loss in or temporarily storing it away, consists of making loss-boxes (Fiddelaers-Jaspers, 2006; Krawchuk in Neimeyer, 2016) or loss-cupboards (Fiddelaers-Jaspers, 2006; Wouters, 2010; Harris in Neimeyer, 2016). Both methods make it possible to create a (little) treasure chest in your own personal style by decorating a box or a small chest according to your own taste and needs. This creative process immediately offers a possibility to work with the loss on another layer of consciousness, because the choices for the decoration of the boxes or chests have just as much meaning as what is put in afterwards. To make it even more intriguing, it is possible, for example, to decorate both the inside and the outside. The boxes and chest have a lid and can be closed, in order to be able to (temporarily) store and lock away what is kept inside. The decoration of the inside can also be stored (temporarily) and hidden from view. In this way it is possible to make a distinction between the way in which someone presents themselves in their grief to the outside world and what someone wishes to keep to themselves.

The loss-boxes can also be used as worry-boxes, depending on the needs and situation of the client. In this, the losses or the worries can be given a place, both in a metaphorical sense and in a physical tangible sense by writing the losses or worries on paper. After decorating the loss-boxes, there is room to discuss the choices for the decorations. Then the client can name the losses or concerns they have, write them down and store them in the box. The facilitator is there to support in the process of making the losses explicit, both locatable and ambiguous losses. By writing the losses on paper and storing these pieces of paper in the loss-box, the client gets the opportunity to take the losses out of the box later and further explore them. The strength of the work method lies in being able to close the box, so that the loss can be stored away. At another moment in time the box can be opened voluntarily to further deal with the loss. This gives the client more control over dealing with the loss.

This exercise is also suitable for a group. The creative process provides a special atmosphere in the group. By sharing the losses, a broader recognition and acknowledgement ensues.

A variation of this exercise is the loss-cupboard or -chest, in which tangible objects that are connected to the loss are collected, stored away and taken out when desired. Here, too, the goal is mainly to regain greater control at those times when the client is about to confront the loss and the potentially stormy emotions that go with it. The loss-cupboard can also be a small box or chest just like the loss-box, but may also be large enough to put a number of objects in it. The loss-cupboard can also be a real cupboard with different drawers, where losses each get their own place. Thus, the client not only has the choice of whether and when he or she wants to be occupied by loss, but also, by choosing which drawer gets opened, with which (specific aspect of the) loss the client wants to occupy him- or herself each time. The loss-cupboard can, just like the loss-boxes, in a metaphorical sense, contain objects that are connected to the losses of the client. However, there is added value when tangible objects such as photographs, music, letters, and jewelry that have an emotional value are placed in the loss-cupboard. In this way, the objects that give an emotional reaction to the loss can be taken out and put away again. Thus, there can be a form of emotion regulation through the timing of making contact with the objects concerned.

Sometimes people do not change parts of their personal space after the loss of a loved one. Rooms or entire houses are, as it were, frozen in time, leaving objects and clothing belonging to the loved ones untouched. This may indicate solidified grief, especially if the objects remain scattered throughout the whole house. In this way, it appears on the outside as if nothing has been changed by the loss. Because the objects are open and exposed in the home, it is not possible to choose when someone wants access to the objects. They always catch the eye and there is no way to regulate being confronted with the emotional reactions to seeing the objects. The timing of the moment in which the need to clear up or store objects is always a very personal one. The counselor should always explore when someone indicates that he or she is experiencing problems in dealing with the loss. The counselor can then, for example, suggest bringing the objects together in a cupboard or room. In this way, a person can make their own choice to go inside, so that they are not confronted all of the time with the objects that focus attention on loss and physical absence.

Instruction: Make your own loss-box or chest. Name the aspects of one or more losses on your lifeline, write them on little pieces of paper or find symbols for these aspects, and place them in the loss-box.

Counsel each other in a group of three (A is the counselor, B is the client, and C is the observer). You can make use of the following questions if you wish:

- What was it like for the client to make the loss-box?
- What was difficult?
- What choices did the client make for the decoration?
- Which choices for the decoration were easy (easier) and which were hard(er)?
- What is the difference between the inside and the outside?
- What does the decoration say about the client, what does it mean to the client?
- Which losses or which aspects of losses are given a place inside the loss-box?
- How does it feel to close the box?
- What would it be like for the client to open the loss-box?
- At which moments will the client open the loss-box?
- What would the client need to open and then close the box again?

Evaluate each turn and then switch roles.

Exercise—Beauty and Consolation: Art in Grief

In addition to the creative methods in which someone who is grieving creates something to express the goodbye, the loss, it is also possible to use the expression of existing works of art: paintings, images, poems, texts, songs, music, sound, visual art, dance, motion, film, theatre, and so on. All forms of expression, classical or popular, that can appeal to multiple layers of meaning or symbolism, are suitable to bring the unpronounceable, the unspeakable, of a loss closer and to share this with others. Art can therefore also serve as a secure base.

Ask the client to select an artwork of their own choice that has emotional value for them and is supportive in grief. Share with the client in the experience of the artwork, by looking together or listening, and ask what it is that makes this artwork so special for the client. Examine how this work of art is supportive of the way the client deals with the loss:

- What did you choose?
- Shall we listen to/look at this together?

- What speaks to you in this work of art?
- How does it appeal to you?
- In which way do you feel that it gives you support/comfort?

> **Instruction:** Pick your own artwork. Counsel each other in a group of three (A is the counselor, B is the client, and C is the observer). You can make use of the above-mentioned questions if you wish.
> Evaluate briefly and switch roles so that everyone gets a turn.

Exercise—Unfolding the Image

The unpronounceable, the unspeakable, of a loss sometimes leaves us, literally or figuratively, speechless, without words. Sometimes the memory of the loss is too intense, the images are so intrusive, that it is not possible to talk about it directly. In order to give the client the space to keep the images of the memory at a distance and thus keep the emotions somewhat manageable in counseling, the technique of 'image-unfolding' can offer a solution. The literal image of the memory is replaced by a symbolic image and the questions of the counselor are therefore about the symbolic image instead of the actual memory. The questions relate to the client's experiences and sensations with the symbolic image, in which it also relates to the client's experiences and sensations with the actual loss.

Preparation and first steps:

- I would like to do an exercise with you, in which we will not discuss the event that took place in which the loss itself occurred, but in which you create an image in your mind that can symbolize the loss.
- Please sit upright in your chair, put your feet together on the floor, and put your hands in your lap.
- If possible, would you please close your eyes with me? Or else focus your eyes on a point on the floor.
- Now focus your thoughts on how the loss feels in your body. Which image, or object, comes to mind?

Image-unfolding questions:

- What shape does it have?
- Does it have another shape as well?
- Where in your body do you feel the shape?
- What is it like to feel the shape there?
- How big or how small is it?

- How much space does it take up?
- How heavy or how light does it weigh?
- How dark or light is it?
- Does it give light? Is it standing in the light or in the dark?
- How hot or how cold is it?
- What would the structure feel like if you were to touch it? Would it be rough or smooth? How rough or smooth is it really?
- Can you move the form? Can the form move itself?
- What happens when the form moves?
- How well do you know this shape?
- Does this shape feel familiar or strange to you?
- How safe or scared does this shape make you feel?
- What does this shape mean to you?
- What happens when you focus your attention on the shape?
- . . .

Instruction: Counsel each other in groups of three (A is the counselor, B is the client, and C is the observer), by using the questions above.

Discuss briefly after each turn and switch roles so that everyone has a turn.

Notes

1. From the magazine *Vrij Nederland*, The Republic of Letters and Fine Arts: http://blogs.vn.nl/boeken/schrijver/we-konden-niet-kapotter/#, consulted on 29 May 2016.
2. See nrc.nl, How Tijn (6) gives Serious Request a boost with #hollandispainting, consulted on 15 January 2017, on www.nrc.nl/nieuws/2016/12/22/ongeneeslijk-zieke-tijn-haalt-duizenden-euros-op-via-heelhollandlakt-a1537906.

7

MEANING RECONSTRUCTION

A Case Study

Aisha no longer feels like she belongs in the organization after the merger. She tells that they are still in the same building, but there is a different logo on the front of the building. She is required to answer the phone using a different company name. The atmosphere as it was with her colleagues has changed now that new colleagues have joined from the other organization. Aisha no longer feels 'at home' in her organization. She says that she has been kept up to date through newsletters that were sent around during the reorganization. And there were several informative meetings. All changes were explained during these meetings and the new colleagues were welcomed in a festive manner. Aisha herself however is not feeling so festive. Although she has tried to get over it, her gloomy feelings continue. After a few months she contacts the organization's social worker. In answer to the question Which goodbye in her past does this merger remind her of? Aisha is silent for a moment searching for the words. The two can't be compared of course, she says hesitantly. Then she tells the story about how she left her home country with her mother when she was a little girl to be reunited with her father who was already living and working in the USA. Her mother was completely happy to be back together with her husband. But Aisha lost her familiar surroundings and all her friends.

Only now that she is thinking about it does she realize how much impact this move had and she feels how much she misses her native country. She realizes that she is mainly focused on adapting and integrating in the USA. She wants to fit in with the people around her as much as possible. By allowing herself to become aware of what she has had to leave behind, she can make room for her 'being different.' For the first time, she talks to her mother about the past. Only now she hears that it was difficult for her mother too, what she misses. She makes more and more room for her native country in her life. She adds new colors in her house, different furniture; she learns to cook traditional dishes and listens to music with the sound of her native country. Her colleagues notice that Aisha has changed. She is more cheerful, laughs louder, and wears colorful clothing. And above all, they are now regularly surprised by delicious Asian snacks. Aisha: 'I could not imagine ever going back. I am an American. I love this country. And I am happy with what my native country has given me. I don't have to choose. It is a part of who I am.'

Grieving Takes Place in a Social Context

Dealing with grief takes an emotional, physical, cognitive, and spiritual effort. Giving meaning to a loss, that is often perceived to be completely senseless and thereby meaningless, requires the client to combine all those efforts in revisiting and revaluating past events on his lifeline in order to try and piece the shattered parts together again somehow. The terms (making) *sense* and (giving) *meaning* may each evoke a different emotional response, we make no distinction between the two. In this context they have the same significance.

Rewriting the Story of Your Life

The American psychologist Robert Neimeyer often uses the concept of giving meaning in relation to grief. He calls it reconstruction of the meaning of what is lost (2005, 2006, 2016; Neimeyer & Thompson, 2014). This means that the life story has to be rewritten, a story that takes an unexpected turn because of a loss. The story continues, after a change of plot, without the person or thing that is lost. It is also possible, however, that the life before the loss will also be viewed in a different light. The life story is then rewritten and revised, as events from the past, memories, are interpreted differently, their emotional state being changed. After all, people are narrative beings. This narrative process of reconstructing and revaluing is a social process: the story is rewritten in the interaction with others with whom there is an intimate connection.

We will never know. . . . We can never say with certainty, but. . . . With this assumption, twenty years later, there is finally a plausible explanation for the circumstances surrounding his death. His life is given shape in the form of a story. And a story, no matter how dramatic, is always easier to bear than the incomprehensible or unknown.

(Van Dijk, 2017)

This narrativity (the ability to construct a fitting story) makes it possible to heal: healing in the sense of being able to integrate the loss, so that life can be lived without fundamental obstacles on a daily level.

Rewriting the story is also an attempt to put the loss in the context of one's own lifecycle. The reality of putting events in a new perspective is hard. A loss challenges someone to revisit the events from his past and to interpret them again, starting from the very beginning. Events that had seemed established facts before then. The loss not only changes the future someone counted on, leaving the future open and unknown, it also forces reorientation of the past, before the new world that has been turned upside down by the loss can be explored. In the Dual Process Model, the interaction between the loss orientation, the past, and the restoration orientation, the future, is clearly illustrated.

Rewriting the life story contributes to taking back control (even when it is an illusion), of having a grip on the situation, even though the loss itself is fundamentally beyond our control (Baumeister, 1992). Neimeyer (2014, 2016) distinguishes between the event story, the loss itself and the backstory, the story about the events that preceded the loss. In constantly retelling and reshaping the backstory, the client can discover aspects, however small, that he or she can control. Regaining some grip can help to rebuild the self-esteem and personal values. This is especially important when these have been challenged by the loss. For example, someone may feel guilty because they have not done enough to turn the situation around, or because they did not say everything that needed to be said, or someone feels insecure and left alone. Not only does self-esteem come under pressure in that situation, but personal goals in life may have become unclear.

The telling of the backstory irrevocably always leads back to the moment the loss occurred. By reshaping the backstory, however, the event story can be integrated into the overall story and a coherent narrative is formulated. Where the event story initially forms an unforeseen break in the life story, the challenge lies in connecting the stories in a certain way. This does not have to be seamless, the break line or scar may remain visible. It is about making the entire life story your own, and experiencing a certain degree of continuity, despite the break in the story.

The different layers and levels of life stories can be seen as collections of everyday events, 'micro-narratives,' which take place within an overarching life story: the 'macro-narrative.' The overarching macro-narrative forms part of the identity and consolidates our self-understanding. However, experiencing loss undermines perceived certainties and thereby question these narratives. Nevertheless, it is good when people can continue to integrate the ever-changing micro-narratives into a macro-narrative, causing it to change too.

> *The belief that it is possible to create a good life is primarily undermined when confronted with a category of questions that are at best only partly solvable based on rational knowledge and professional expertise. These are the 'slow' questions that are internally connected with experiences of finiteness, uncontrollability and powerlessness.*
>
> (Kunneman, 2009, p. 17)

That is a difficult task, partly because one is confronted with complex or unanswerable questions.

By reconstructing the personal life story, reworking the past, and refiguring the future, it is possible to find new meaning after loss. There is no (or no longer any) guarantee that things make sense or have meaning. And meaning cannot be rediscovered or found just like that. And however difficult it sometimes is for others close by, meaning cannot be imposed from the outside in, certainly not with clichés. Dealing with loss and change requires an active process of meaning reconstruction. It is about trying to gain a sense of control over one's life again, after the recurrent question: 'Why is this happening to me?' It requires a re-examination of goals, to give life (new) direction once again. Often foundational personal values have to be reconsidered in light of the loss and the question is then: 'What is (still) important to me now?' These values are important because they contribute to new goals in life. The loss can have a negative effect on the self-esteem, especially if there is guilt or shame. Acknowledgment can be found in staying actively engaged in getting one's own life back on course. This means that what is lost can then be placed in a (broader) context.

> *When we experience an accident or a disaster, or when we are confronted with a serious illness, we are in the first instance a victim. The main issue is the feeling of helplessness. Something happened to us, something was done to us—'out of the blue' and we are left speechless. The book of events is always open halfway through, but it does make a difference whether there is a sense of beginning and end, a framework, page numbers, an ISBN, a cover with a title. It feels different when the book has fallen apart and the pages have no page numbers and are scattered all over the place. As a victim, you stand with the page on which the present is written in your hands without a context to put it in, without a reason, without a future. A fragment, a scrap of text without a script. And actually, you tend to look for the nearest paper shredder, but you do not know where to start looking. Chaos. So, there is only one thing left and that is to search for the other pages, reading them, looking for fragments*

you recognise, restoring your memory, reconstructing chronology. But one thing is certain, it will never be the same story again.

(Bohlmeijer, 2012, pp. 82–83)

And so, the writing of the life story continues.

Internal and External Meaning

There are two paths that can be followed towards meaning reconstruction: an inner path and an outer path. There is intrinsic meaning when people address sources within themselves that lead to answers to questions about purpose and meaning. They can apply their skills to bring convictions and opinions in line with the reality of the loss (see van Wielink & Wilhelm, 2011). These are called coping skills: the ways people have learned to cope, ways in which they deal with emotions, tension, and stress. But also, ways of communicating, tackling or avoiding and seeking or securing social support (Fiddelaers-Jaspers & van Wielink, 2015). Coping skills are important to help find the strength within themselves to deal with the loss. To experience this power inside can in itself already be beneficial and therefore significant. Re-shaping the relationship that has been broken by the loss, in which the memories live on, is an important part in completing the 'grief work' (Worden, 1991).

External meaning reconstruction means that people look outside themselves for something to give meaning to a loss. One could look in a church, a religion, or a community. The question here is whether someone is able to connect with a system that is larger than themselves, in order to be able to give meaning using the values that apply within that system. People can find support in finding meaning, in religion, beliefs, and philosophies. It also happens though that people are no longer able to reconcile the experiences of loss with the values and the false sense of security offered by such systems. Faith in a good God, for example, can be seriously undermined when people are confronted with evil in the form of loss. Important in external meaning reconstruction is therefore not only the extent to which someone can connect with the external system, but also the extent to which the system meets the person's needs. When dependency on the system results, this will limit the person's options to choose a direction or take control. They can then lose control. As a result, their ability to find meaning will diminish (Baumeister, 1992).

Positive and Negative Meaning Reconstruction

When discussing the Dual Process Model, the two polarities were explained: the loss orientation and the restoration orientation. Grief oscillates between these two poles. Meaning reconstruction could also be seen as oscillation between the two poles of positive and negative meaning attribution that can take place during both the loss- as well as the restoration orientation.

Meaning reconstruction is an active process. Meaning cannot be found in advance and cannot always be found at that moment one is seeking it. Meaning often needs to be derived from events that in themselves are void of meaning. That is not always possible. The Dual Process Model shows that dealing with loss is not as clear-cut as older models suggested. The model illustrates a loss orientation and a restoration orientation. Each orientation can further have either a positive or a negative outcome, linked to the options the client has to find meaning. On the side of positive meaning reconstruction of the loss orientation there are happy memories of that which was lost, finding support from concerned others, the positive interpretation of events, and the positive revision of goals. There is certainly room for joy, which can come as a surprise to someone who is grieving. Sometimes these positive feelings give rise to guilt and/or shame.

Negative meaning making around loss orientation often manifests itself in the form of worrying, 'what-if' thoughts, and oftentimes feelings of guilt and shame about the circumstances of the loss or the relationship prior to the loss. This is what gives the loss its physical, emotional, mental, and spiritual burden. There is a risk of finding a negative explanation for events and an inability to find new goals in life or to adapt to existing goals. On the side of the restoration orientation, in addition to positive meaning making, there is also a negative side. These two sides are mirrors of the positive and negative meaning making on the side of loss orientation, where happy memories and positive interpretations contribute to meaning in a positive sense whereas worrying and negative interpretations contribute to a negative sense.

Meaning reconstruction, whether in the positive or negative sense during loss- and restoration orientation allows the client to get a better grasp on the situation in a way. It makes no difference whether the outcome is negative or positive. In this way four possible situations are created, each with their own inner dynamics (see Table 7.1). This causes tension with the outside world, which often only sees the two possible situations—that of the loss or that

Table 7.1 Matrix of Meaning Reconstruction

	Loss orientation	Restoration orientation
Positive meaning reconstruction	Joyful memories, lasting connection, it was meant to be, the loved one is in a better place now.	Feeling the freedom for hobby, new job, relationship, new opportunities made possible by extra money, taking a step up on the career ladder.
Negative meaning reconstruction	Worrying, what-if thoughts, feelings of guilt or shame, negative meaning reconstruction.	Feeling guilty about taking new steps, constant worrying.

of the restoration orientation. This is especially the case when the outside world is focused on leaving the loss behind them and aims their attention on restorative activities. This will result in lack of understanding for the person who derives positive meaning from the loss, or gives negative meaning to the resumption of restoration-oriented activities.

Counseling: The Other Side of Meaning Reconstruction

The other side of meaning reconstruction is to feel a 'sense of meaninglessness,' or 'bear a grudge' (see Figure 7.1). This is mostly expressed when it is difficult 'to accept' or undertake restorative activities.

The desire to be whole, an eminently human and universal affair, makes people want to write the plot of their story themselves, despite everything. That wholeness is the incentive to always search for the meaning of life. Giving meaning is something that cannot be commanded. It can only be discovered when you purposefully go looking for it. Based on the conviction that life is inherently meaningful, it is up to everyone to formulate answers to life's questions. This journey of discovery cannot be engineered (Frankl, 2004), but the person with a broken story cannot escape the journey: 'In the same way that you have to confront grief, you also "have" to give meaning to life events, however difficult this may be. To give meaning to a loss is not the same as saying that a loss has been meaningful or that you accept the loss' (Fiddelaers-Jaspers & Noten, 2015, p. 53).

Clients who come to see a counselor with feelings of meaninglessness and resentment about a loss do not generally feel that they have a choice to search for meaning. This is often difficult for their environment to deal with. They may experience that others are withdrawing a little from contact. The same applies for the counselor. You may want your client to feel more positive and find meaning again. The pitfall here may be that the counselor wants

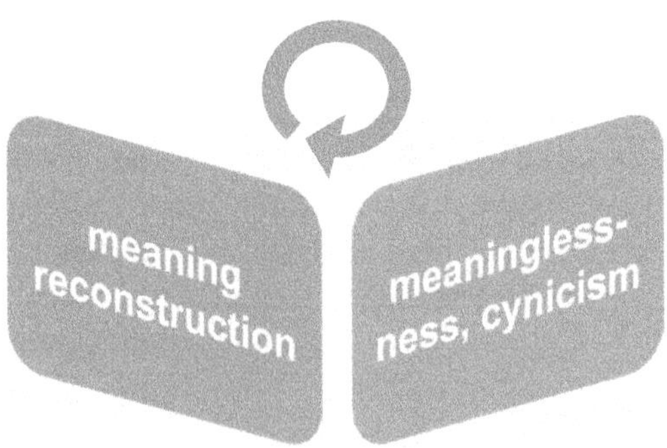

Figure 7.1 Both Sides of the Same Coin for the Theme 'Meaning Reconstruction'

to convince the client that there is real meaning to be discovered and that there will be light again. In general, this is not helpful to the client. The feelings of meaninglessness and senselessness are the client's reality. It will make the client feel very misunderstood and unseen if the counselor is always trying to convince them to see reality differently. It is then advised to let go of the topic of sense-making in the first instance and explore the other themes of the cycle. In this way, space can be created to re-examine the theme of meaning reconstruction at a later moment. For example, explore together with the client how the relationship with the person lost came in to being. How was that? How did it go? Are there any photos? What was nice and what was difficult? What are the good memories? In this way, the counselor takes the client along on the path to reconstruct his or her story.

Dialogue

Aisha has been to see her counselor Hannah several times now.

Hannah: Hi Aisha, it is good to see you again.
Aisha: Hi Hannah, I brought you something. I was trying out recipes this past weekend and I think you will like these biscuits I made.
Hannah: Why thank you, how sweet of you to bring me some.
Aisha: I was at my mother's this past weekend and she told me that in our culture, it is custom to bring food when going somewhere on a visit. So, I thought, I will bring biscuits.
Hannah: So, you visited your mother this past weekend. How was that?
Aisha: During our previous conversation we had agreed that I would have a conversation with my mother about the time before our move to this country. I told you then that I didn't know if my mother would be open to it, because we normally never talk about such things. But it so happened that my father was away this weekend because an aunt of his had passed away and he went to the funeral. So, my mother invited me over. And straight away I thought: this is my chance.
Hannah: Aha, so your father wasn't home. You were alone with your mother.
Aisha: Yes, and that was pretty special, because my father is almost always around when I go and visit. That was also the first thing my mother said to me when I arrived, that she was pleased to be alone with me for a change. That made it so memorable. Before the move, my mother and I were always together, without my father. After the move, everything changed, because the relationships shifted. My mother was more focused on my father and she was taking English classes. I had to go to school and also had to take extra English classes. We saw each other a lot less during that time and my father was around most of the time.

Hannah: Did you manage to talk to her about that?
Aisha: Yes, it was very touching to hear that she was so homesick at first. She told me how often she thought back to our old house and of the family that stayed behind. We talked about everyone and she even had photos of them. Photos I had never seen before. We looked at them together and we both cried. For the first time ever. It is weird that crying together can make you happy. And my mother told me about things they used to do and dishes she and my aunts used to cook. Using all kinds of ingredients that weren't available in this country. And how upsetting that was to her. But that she quickly learned from the group of women she got acquainted with to cook local dishes.
Hannah: It sounds like your mother was also happy to be able to talk to you about these things.
Aisha: Yes, it was really wonderful. It felt so very special. We should have done this a long time ago. We cooked all kinds of things that she remembered from the old days. We drove to another town, where they had more choice in foreign vegetables and a certain type of goat meat. I have never seen her like that before. She became so lively.
Hannah: Did you also talk about the reason why your parents decided to come here?
Aisha: I knew of course that my father had a job here and that we were only able to follow him once he had arranged everything. My mother was looking forward to living in the new country, because my father was so positive about what it was like here and about all the opportunities it offered. It took a few years before we could emigrate. It was a more difficult transition than my mother had expected. But she didn't want anybody to know just how hard it was for her. I think that is why she never spoke about it.
Hannah: What was it like for you to hear this?
Aisha: It makes me very sad to hear that she was so desperately miserable and didn't tell me.
Hannah: So, you are sad for your mother. And what does it mean to you personally and to the little girl you used to be?
Aisha: I think it would have been nice if I had known. I felt very lonely then. I thought that I would ruin things for my parents if I was sad. Because I thought that they were so happy about the move. So, I put on a brave face and tried to fit in as much as possible.
Hannah: And looking back, what did the move mean to you as a person?
Aisha: (Sighing deeply.) What did the move mean to me as a person? That is a good question. On the one hand the move cost me a great deal. I felt lonely and different from the rest for a long time, all the while trying hard to fit in. But on the other hand, I was given the opportunity to get a good education in this country and to find a good job. That would probably have gone very

differently in my home country. It is much more traditional over there and most of the girls stay at home. So, I am very grateful for that. And now, after having spoken to my mother, I feel closer to our country now. (Sighing deeply.)
Hannah: What advantage do you feel that it could have for you that you feel a little closer to your country?
Aisha: I can join the best of two worlds together. I come from there and am rooted here. I believe that is the advantage.
Hannah: In which way is it different to when we first started this process?
Aisha: In the beginning I thought that I would have to choose between one world or the other. But now I realize that I am all of it. That gives me so much room.

Self-Reflection Questions

- Which meaning do you assign to profound events in your life?
- Are you inclined to search for meaning inside or outside yourself? How do you go about that?
- What does your work, education, organization, or institution mean to you? Have you noticed any changes, and if so, what are they?
- What is the balance like between your work/education and other meaningful relationships and activities?
- Do you feel sufficiently inspired by your job/education, your contact with colleagues/peers/fellow students/friends, and so forth?
- Are you able to be an inspiration for others as much as you'd like? How do you do that?

Exercises

Exercises—Meaning Reconstruction

Instruction: Counsel each other in groups of three (A is the counselor, B is the client, and C is the observer), using the self-reflection questions relevant to this theme. Evaluate each turn and then switch roles.

Exercises—Backstory and Event Story

When a client comes to see a counselor, there is always the challenge to connect the back story to the event story. The client's question always relates to the difficulty they are having with the disconnection from the continuity of the life story. It is then necessary to explore the event story as well as the back story in an attempt to integrate the loss in the ongoing life story. Asking the following questions may be helpful:

- What is the story of your life before the loss?
- What is the story of the loss?
- Which break occurred in your life story through the loss?
- How was the story of your life changed by the loss?

Instruction: Counsel each other in groups of three (A is the counselor, B is the client, and C is the observer), by inquiring into the back story and the event story of the loss. Use the questions relevant to this exercise. Evaluate each turn and then switch roles.

Exercise—Virtual Dream Story

This exercise (Neimeyer, 2014) combines the creative element of writing with a focused assignment to process a number of predefined elements of the story. To promote the creative aspect and working on a deeper level, the counselor imposes a strict time limit in advance, about 7–8 minutes. This gives the consciousness little opportunity to be critical, because someone immediately has to start composing a story where all elements are given a place. At an unconscious level, various choices are made, which the counselor can examine together with the client after the writing has been done.

The writing assignment given by the supervisor to the client has a broad subject field: 'write a story where all of the following elements are incorporated.' These elements can be chosen by the counselor from a number of relevant concepts from the fixed sets of categories (see Table 7.2).

The writing assignment must incorporate only one of the reasons from the table above relevant to the issue the client is dealing with. The assignment may also incorporate two situations/scenes, two figures/characters, and two symbolic objects. The counselor keeps an eye on the time as the client writes.

When the client has finished writing, or when the time is up and the client has finished the sentence he or she was writing, the counselor can ask the client to read the story out loud. Then the counselor asks the client to read the story out loud once more. By literally giving the story a voice, both counselor and client are themselves witness to the story. The story, which the client, on a certain level, is now hearing for the first time, resonates on several levels.

The counselor and client can then together explore what the story means for the loss. You can use the following questions for counseling:

- What was it like to write the story?
- What was it like to read the story?
- How did your body and mind react?
- What difference was there between reading the first and the second time?

Table 7.2 Categories With the Ingredients for a Story

Reason	Situations/scenes	Figures/characters	Symbolic objects
A great loss	A heavy storm	A wise woman	A red rose
An old loss	An angry sea	A mysterious stranger	A burning fire
A traumatic loss	A long journey	A booming voice	An old map
A serious illness	A secret room	A stifled sob	An ambulance
A lost dream	A cool stream	A shining angel	A strange mask
A lost goal	An unearthly light	A white pigeon	An empty bed
The search for a new goal	A deep gorge	A talking animal	A closed door
Seeking support	A dark cave	A whispering snake	A wooden coffin
...	An empty house	A wrinkled old man or woman	A nude sculpture
	A sunrise	A song overheard by chance	A treasure chest
	A sunset	A strong man	An old key
	...	A weeping child	A dusty mirror
		...	...

Source: Neimeyer (2014); copied with permission from Taylor & Francis

- What choices did you make to determine the main character/narrator?
- From what perspective is the story told?
- What does this mean to you?

Instruction: Write your own Virtual Dream Story, using the guidelines in the exercise above. Be sure to choose the elements from Table 7.2 in advance. In a group setting: make sure everyone uses the same elements.

- A reason;
- Two situations/scenes;
- Two figures/characters; and
- Two symbolic objects.

These elements must appear in the story, with the content being your own choice. Limit the time to write to a maximum of 8 minutes. Keep an eye on the time and then finish off your sentence after 8 minutes.

Counsel each other in groups of three (A is the counselor, B is the client, and C is the observer), as described in the exercise above.

- The client reads the story to the counselor.
- The client reads the story to the counselor once again.
- The counselor asks the client the questions that go with the exercise.

Evaluate and switch roles, so that each gets a turn.

Exercise—Virtual Dream Story (Intensified Version)

In the exercise to write the Virtual Dream Story, one can add an empathic or experience-oriented layer by placing two empty chairs opposite the chair in which the client is sitting. The counselor first asks the client:

- Which element from the story can you connect with the most?
- Which element from the story can you connect with the least?

Ask the client to visualize the element on one of the chairs and the element on the other. When the client sits on one of the chairs, let him identify with the element of the story that is visualized on that chair.

Then ask the client to first sit on the chair with the element with which he or she can least connect, and attempt to identify with it. The client then may speak out loudly, on behalf of the element from the story that was visualized in the chair where the client is currently sitting, to the element that is being visualized in the other empty chair. What will the element with which the client could least connect with in the story tell the element with which the client could connect most in the story? From the client's difficulty in connecting to the element in question, we know that this element symbolizes a need. The client can be made aware of this need by identifying with the position of the relevant element.

Tip: It is important that the client actually speaks to the other element personally and in the first person singular as if the other element were there in the present. In other words, not 'I think I would then say something like . . ., because . . .,' but rather 'I . . . you, because. . . .' This strengthens the connection when identifying with the element.

After that, the client can change position, sit in the other chair, and identify with the element with which he or she was able to connect most in the story. What is it like for this element to hear from this position what was said to it? How does this element relate to the other from this position? This exercise in changing position can be repeated several times, whereby the counselor continues to explore the relationship between what is said by the elements and what it means for the client in the light of the question with which the client is working. When addressed *as* the client, the client sits in his or her own chair.

A Case Study

Aisha, the client from the case study at the beginning of this chapter, wrote her Virtual Dream Story using the reason 'a big loss' (see Table 7.2). Beforehand she had indicated that she wasn't such a writer and doubted whether she would manage to put something on paper. Still, during the 8 minutes of writing, she concentrated on her story and at the end she looked up from her paper in amazement, when she realized that she had apparently written two pages effortlessly. The situations she had been given for her story were 'an empty house' and 'a rising sun.' The characters were 'an old woman' and 'a talking animal.' The symbolic objects were 'a closed door' and 'a dusty mirror.' Hesitantly Aisha read her story for the first time. The second time, reading went smoother and she could emphasize what she considered to be important. Aisha could connect the most with the closed door, she said afterwards, and the least with the rising sun. Uneasily she sat on the chair opposite hers to identify with the rising sun in that position. She managed to close her eyes and she sighed deeply. The words came slowly: 'I don't want to rise up, like the sun. . . . There is nothing that is worth shining my light on. There is nothing that should be heated by me. . . . And "closed door," you are doing well. You are closed nice and tight. Reliable. I appreciate that in you.' In the other chair, as a 'closed door,' it seemed easier for her to identify with the symbol. The words came quickly: 'Yes, I feel firm. I am fine.' Then she fell silent. And continued: 'and something wants to get out. . . . I thought I was supposed to keep something out, but there is something inside that wants to get out. That wants to stand in the light.' She fell silent again. Back in the chair as 'rising sun' she could say: 'Come out. It is safe, you can come out; I will shine my light on you and warm you.' Back in her own chair Aisha looked back with astonishment on her own words: 'I didn't expect this. . . . I now notice that I am holding something inside, instead of protecting myself against something from the outside.'

Instruction: Counsel each other in groups of three (A is the counselor, B is the client, and C is the observer) as described in the exercise above, based on the Virtual Dream Stories exercise from the previous section. Evaluate each turn briefly and then switch roles.

Exercise—Chapters of Our Lives

When rewriting the story of our life, reinterpreting the back story, it can help to actually see our life story as a book with chapters and to give each chapter a name (Neimeyer, 2014).

Ask the client, with the help of the lifeline if necessary, to name the chapters in his or her life story. Let the client make a table of contents for the 'book of my life' with chapter titles that are descriptive of the period in question.

The client can be given this assignment as homework or can be given time during the session. If this exercise takes place during counseling, it will require about 10 minutes to compile the table of contents. Afterwards the counselor can discuss the chapters with the client using the following questions:

- How did you allocate your chapters? Were they chronological or did you choose another classification? What was your choice based on?
- How did you arrive at this choice for the chapters? How did you determine their limitations?
- When does the story begin? What kind of foreword about where you come from, your family of origin, your parent's relationship, could still possibly be added?
- Where does the story end? How would the story be allowed to continue?
- Looking at how your life story has developed, has this happened gradually or suddenly? If you continue to develop along this path, where will you stand in five to fifteen years?
- Who is the author of your life story? Are there any important co-writers that deserve to be mentioned, who share a part of the honor or the blame for how the story is unfolding?
- What would the story sound/look like if told/written by your father, mother, or older self?
- Who is the most important target audience for your book? Who would appreciate it the most and who would want to change or rewrite it?
- Is there another, deeper layer in your story, a silent story that is not seen or heard by the reader? What would (possibly) be the cost for you personally or for your relationships, if you kept a part of it quiet? What would your life look like if this layer were more integrated in your life story?

- What title would you like to give your book? Which illustration/picture would you want to place on the cover?
- What genre would the book with your life story be?
- What common thread runs through your life story? Do you also recognize other threads and do they strengthen the main thread? How would your life story unfold if those other threads were given more attention and emphasis?

Instruction: Write your own chapter titles for your life story. Keep an eye on the time.

Counsel each other in groups of three (A is the counselor, B is the client, and C is the observer), using the exercises in this chapter and using the questions as described above. Evaluate each turn and then switch roles.

8

RESILIENCE—COPING, TRAUMA, AND THE BRAIN

A Case Study

Peter lost his father suddenly. During a bike ride with friends, his father was hit by a car as he was turning a dangerous bend of the course. He died instantly. Peter immediately took a month off from work. He wanted to take time for this enormous loss. Together with his mother and his brothers, Peter arranged the funeral. In order to prepare for what would come next, he asked his doctor what he could expect from the grieving process and how he could get through it as well as possible. It helped him to know what could happen. In addition, he asked for the report the police had made of the accident. He visited the site of the accident and consulted a traffic expert. Together with the traffic expert he submitted a request to the district to adjust the dangerous bend and at the same time place a memorial there to commemorate his father. When he went back to work after a month, he still felt the emptiness and grief for his father, but it gave him comfort and strength to know that he had done what he could. Now, about ten years later Peter decides to move. He is going to the other side of the country, to his mother's birthplace. She is moving along with him. For her, he has found a nice nursing home on the edge of a beautiful forest. Although Peter was initially looking forward to the upcoming move, he has been feeling increasingly gloomy as the date of departure approaches. He does not understand why. This has been a dream for so long. Only when he talks to a counselor recommended by his doctor, it becomes clear to him. The memorial, the place that has kept his father alive in a certain way, has to be left behind when he moves away from the city. It is as if he is losing his father a second time. It is like saying goodbye all over again.

Background

The themes of the Transition Cycle were discussed in the previous chapters. They are themes that interact and that, upon exploration, give more insight into how people deal with attachment, bonding, separation, and loss. Resilience, the ability to deal with major events, is essential. In this chapter, we zoom in on the concept of resilience. We see the role the brain and the body play and how the reaction to loss and Potentially Traumatic Experiences are influenced by it.

Coping

People react in many different ways when having to deal with loss. The manner in which someone reacts depends partly on the nature and severity of the loss and the situation surrounding it. On the other hand, people respond in their own specific way. The ability to deal with problematic situations is called coping. In order to establish preferred behavior with respect to coping, the Utrecht Coping List (UCL) is often used in the Netherlands (Schreurs et al., 1993), in which seven styles of coping[1] are defined. These styles are very different from each other and in principle are applied by every person (whether effectively or not), depending on the situation. The four most common styles can be positioned as shown in Table 8.1.

1. Active problem solving
   Active problem solving is a rational approach to addressing the loss. Because the fight mechanism is at work here, the behavior focuses on problem-solving. Someone with this coping strategy will view the problem quietly from all angles, put things in workable order, and then work in a goal-oriented and confident manner to solve it.

Table 8.1 The Four Most Common Coping Styles

Coping styles	Rational	Emotional
Fight mechanism	Active problem solving	Seeking social support
Flight mechanism	Avoiding/watching and waiting	Seeking diversion

2. Seeking social support
   Looking for social support is an emotional approach to dealing with the loss. Here too the fight mechanism is at work. Seeking consolation, compassion, and help, the person immediately and readily shares the loss with others and then they jointly tackle consequences of the loss.
3. Avoiding and watching-and-waiting
   Avoiding and watching-and-waiting is a rational approach and is one of the flight mechanisms. It is not aimed at confronting the loss but at avoiding it. Let the matter run its course, get out of the way and wait and see what happens.
4. Seeking diversion
   Seeking diversion is an emotional approach and the flight mechanism is in place here. There is refusal to let the loss fully occupy time and thought or to worry constantly. The flight is an attempt to avoid (the effects of) the loss.

Depending on their personal background, people have certain preferred behaviors when dealing with loss. In theory, everyone can use each of the above coping styles. In practice, a person's background and the nature and weight of the experience of the loss determine which coping style they have at their disposal at that moment. When dealing with loss, all four styles can be applied and can alternate in time. Whether a particular coping style is effective or not depends on the situation in which a person finds themselves. For example, the social environment may require a certain coping style (e.g., when there are children to be cared for) or the circumstance might affect the coping style. Ultimately, only the person concerned can judge whether their coping style is effective or ineffective at that specific time. This also does not mean that this particular style is appropriate or effective during the entire period of grief; it is only designed to cope with that specific moment in time.

In case of loss, there is a situation that cannot be undone. Whether coping is an effective mechanism for solving a problem or not depends on the perception of the situation. For example, as long as someone is not yet ready to acknowledge the loss, an active coping style will not work. People choose their own coping styles. It makes no sense to talk about a coping style that does not suit the moment or the person. However, it is possible to offer a different perspective by also offering the other styles of coping in relation to ways of dealing with the loss.

Trauma

As described earlier, all people have resilience, which is the ability to recover or to bounce back after serious setbacks. This resilience is used when confronting loss. Yet some have more difficulty in dealing with a loss than others. Does one person then have more resilience than the other? Does someone, because of the amount of resilience they have, always react to loss in the same way? Why are there different reactions to 'the same type of' loss? Is one loss 'bigger,' 'heavier,' or 'more traumatic' than the other?

These questions are not easily answered. Mutual comparisons between losses are in any case not helpful. Grief as a reaction to a loss is as unique as the individual who suffers the loss and as unique as the relationship that is broken by the loss. In this way, two people cannot suffer the same loss, not even if the two have lost the same person. They will always suffer according to their unique relationship with that person and their unique personality, their own personal, unique, loss. Manu Keirse (2015) calls this appropriately the 'fingerprint' of loss and grief.

Tip: This chapter emphasizes that resilience is a strength that people can access, not only during, but even before a profound event.

Still, resilience will often only become visible in the face of adversity. The worst type of adversity is called 'trauma': an event that is perceived as shocking, leading to psychological and emotional wounding, in a situation that requires more resilience than the person is able to muster at that time. It is a situation for which a person is not prepared, nor has the capacity to deal with. Whether or not experiences are traumatic or traumatizing depends on the nature and circumstances of the shocking event, and it appears to be determined primarily by the way in which the event is experienced and perceived.

For a long time, it has been assumed that all people respond to loss in a certain similar way. For this, let us say, 'average' way of grieving, models have been developed, of which the Kübler-Ross phase model is probably the best known. Differences in grief reactions did not lead to adjustment of the models, but to the conclusion that some people grieved 'in the right way' and other people 'in the wrong way.' To put it bluntly: if someone did not follow the curve of Kübler-Ross, then something was wrong with that person. At most, someone was allowed more or less time to go through the relevant phases, but the content of the phases and their order was not up for discussion for a long time. In order to make people grieve in 'the right way,' the techniques that were developed were usually based on the 'grief work' as described by Freud. All theories of grief work always included the visible expression of emotions.

Research (Bonanno, 2010; Bonanno et al., 2011) on grief shows that reality is more complicated and cannot be illustrated by a single curve. There is no 'average' way of grieving and therefore there is no 'right' or 'wrong' way.

Bonanno makes a distinction between four patterns that people seem to follow depending on the severity of the complaints suffered during grief. This adds more nuance and widens the norm of 'normal' grief reactions. That does not mean that the behavior is desirable. Because of the descriptive nature of the patterns, the advantage of this model is that there is no 'mold' that everyone has to 'fit.'

In their research, Bonanno et al. use the definition of loss events in the broadest sense. Not only the death of a loved one, but all possible profound events that lead to loss are considered. Bonanno had already noticed that people can respond differently to 'similar' events. The word 'similar' has been put between scare quotes deliberately because it refers to the so-called 'objective' events, while people in their subjective experience can each experience an event differently. Care must be taken when comparing 'objective' events, because factors always play a role that lead to a different, subjective experience for those involved. To illustrate: when a man dies, his loved ones and relatives lose the same person, but the loss can be seen from different relationships, from different perspectives depending on roles. His wife loses her partner, her husband. His children lose their father. His parents lose a child, his siblings a brother, and so on. The children also each lose a different father, depending on the meaning of the specific relationship they had with him. On the other hand, based on comparable subjective reactions, it cannot be concluded that different events are comparable. For example, the loss of a job or work can be so profound for someone that their grief reaction is similar to someone's grief reaction to the loss of a loved one. That does not mean that the loss of a job or work is considered as severe as the loss of a loved one. Even if this person agrees that the loss of a loved one is much worse than the loss of their job, the grief reactions can still be just as intense. This can be very confusing for this person and/or for their environment.

Something that is traumatic to one, may not traumatize another person even though the event was actually traumatic. Bonanno overcomes this dilemma by adopting the concept of PTE: Potentially Traumatic Experiences. He uses the word *potential* because the event does not have the same effect on every person, without detracting from traumatizing characteristics of the event. Bonanno uses PTE as a collective name for all types of losses. The word *trauma* or *traumatizing* after a major event should be used with great care, especially when you are in the role of counselor. Every person who has experienced a major event will benefit from recognition. Everyone is entitled to their own perception of an experience.

If people feel that they are insufficiently acknowledged by their environment or by professional caregivers in how profound the experience was for them, they will often get stuck in continuously seeking recognition. For example, by telling the story over and over again in exactly the same way. Or by comparing with others. Or by looking for supporters. This can result in a dynamic in which one's own 'being right' is set off against the other 'being wrong.' This 'competition of suffering' makes it more difficult to deal with the actual loss, since the energy and the attention is focused on other things

An important point in Bonanno's view is that not the event, but only the perception, behavior, and complaints of the client decide whether there is trauma or not. Counselors, relatives, and loved ones cannot determine 'from the outside' for someone else whether an event is or should be traumatic or traumatizing. A client cannot be put in the 'victim' box by others. Incidentally, someone does not have the 'free choice' to suffer from a PTE: trauma leaves traces in the body at a neurological level (Van der Kolk, 2015). The body stores traumatic experiences in its own way, has its own memory and its own form of wisdom (Ogden & Fisher, 2015). We will elaborate on this later in the chapter.

The research shows four different patterns in the courses of grief reactions over time. During a period of two years, there is a category that gradually shows recovery after an initial disruption in daily function. A second category shows delayed grief, in which daily function becomes more disrupted as time passes. A third category displays chronic grief, showing undiminishing high levels of disruption. A final category is characterized by resilience in which people seem to adapt to the change effortlessly.

This final category seems special. It is the largest category, from which we can conclude that most people that experience a PTE are able to handle this without too many disruptions of daily functioning. It is noteworthy because this group never received any special attention in the traditional approaches to grief. There are two reasons for this. Firstly these people, because of the lack of complaints, were never seen by therapists and researchers. Secondly, these people were, in the past, classified under the denominator of 'absent' or 'delayed' grief or 'denial' because of the absence of the expected grief complaints. The question is how these people manage to adapt to a life in which a PTE has occurred without too many complaints. Apparently, these people have the ability to 'bounce back' after adversity. It is less easy to determine what exactly is at the source of this resilience.

Resilience

The term *resilience* is mostly applicable in the face of adversity. Without adversity, without challenge, there seems to be no reason to show resilient behavior. And yet people are innately resilient. Seen from a preventative point of view, it is not only interesting but also important to know beforehand who will and will not respond to adversity with resilience. In this manner, high-risk groups can be identified and counseling can be offered to strengthen resilience. What is this resilience made of?

Emily Werner (2005) conducted a longitudinal study on the development of children on Hawaii. During three decades, she followed children into adulthood. Two-thirds of these children started their lives under favorable economic and social conditions. One-third was faced with very adverse conditions. However, one-third of these children in adverse situations became successfully functioning adults. Werner discovered several distinctive elements:

- Healthy attachment to an important caregiver, such as a parent, teacher, or someone who was available in the role of some kind of mentor.
- The ability to step into the world by their own strength and conditions. These children were independent, not afraid to explore, and had a positive attitude to their social setting.
- Although these children did not have different kinds of or more talent than those who were less successful, these children made better use of their talents and were achievement oriented.
- Possibly the most important element was that these children each had a high internal locus of control and looked to themselves, not to their environment, for success. They believed that one can impact one's own destiny and that events result primarily from one's own behavior.

These elements correspond to what Bowlby calls secure attachment to secure bases that on the one hand provide care and on the other hand challenge a person to explore. From that basis, the children are validated in their self-reliance.

> *Resilience comes from deep within us and from support outside us. It comes from gratitude for what's good in our lives and from leaning in to the suck. It comes from analyzing how we process grief and from simply accepting that grief. Sometimes we have less control than we think. Other times we have more. I learned that when life pulls you under, you can kick against the bottom, break the surface, and breathe again.*
>
> (Sandberg, 2017)

The ability, then, to give meaning to events, from self-reliance and a positive self-image, ensures positive outcomes. From this perspective, resilience is something that people can develop during their lives (Portzky, 2015). Yet genetic predisposition also plays an important role. The separation between predisposition (nature) and upbringing (nurture) is not so much a question of either-or, but rather of and-and. On the one hand, everyone gets a combination of genes from their parents, but on the other hand, they are generally the same parents from whom they receive their upbringing. Moreover, at birth there are stress genes that work like on-off switches. When faced with a threat, the switches will turn on; they will switch off when there is safety and support. Here, safe attachment plays an important role. When attachment figures are sufficiently and reliably available, by being present and responsive to the child's needs, the stress genes will not have to be permanently 'on.' And when there is skin-to-skin contact between a parent and a baby, the baby produces the hormone oxytocin. It increases feelings of calmness and security and suppresses anxiety. It contributes positively to resilience.

Resilience is a stable personality trait. If people are considered resilient before a PTE, they also tend to behave resiliently after the PTE. If, however they have low resilience after a PTE, they also tend to have had a lower level of resilience before the PTE. That does not mean that resilience cannot be learned or increased. It can. Children having faced adversity at a young age can become more resilient later in life.

Whether an event is considered traumatic or not depends not only on what happened, but also on the resilience of the person concerned.

> *While silence keeps us dumbfounded, the path out of it is paved with words, carefully assembled, piece by piece, until the whole story can be revealed. . . . Silence reinforces the godforsaken isolation of trauma. . . . Feeling listened to and understood changes our physiology; being able to articulate a complex feeling, and having our feelings recognized, lights up our limbic brain and creates an 'aha moment.' In contrast, being met by silence and incomprehension kills the spirit. Or, as John Bowlby so memorably put it: 'what cannot be spoken to the [m]other, cannot be told to the self.'*
>
> (Van der Kolk, 2015, p. 232)

Bonanno (2010; Bonanno et al., 2011) confirmed this theory: the perception of the event and how it is dealt with on the basis of resilience is what determines whether a PTE is seen as a threat. The reaction to a PTE determines whether there is trauma, not the PTE itself.

The Brain—Perspectives From Head Office

Riet Fiddelaers-Jaspers (2011a) calls the brain 'the head office,' or in other words, 'the boardroom.' It is the place of human control, the place where the brain is found: the head. The place where people are supposed to make rational considerations, the place of thought. The place that is so often referred to in contrast to the heart, which symbolizes the place where feelings are housed. Or in contrast with the gut, another emotional center in the body, the place where butterflies flutter when in love.

The brain is currently receiving plenty of attention. On one side of the spectrum, scientists such as Dick Swaab (2011) and Victor Lamme (2010) have reduced the human being to little more than its brain. For example, they argue on the basis of brain scans that free will and free choice are illusions. The question is whether brain activity that is visible on scans, before people become aware of it, actually indicates that 'the brain' has already made a choice beyond the person and their own preference. On the other side of the spectrum, for example, the psychologist Douwe Draaisma (2011) and philosophers such as Daan Evers and Niels van Miltenburg (2011) defend human existence as being more than just neurological activity. They argue that such brain scans offer no insight into the content of the choice or decision in a given situation, so that people still have a certain space in which to retain freedom of choice.

In the context of this book, our main focus is on the role of the brain in dealing with loss. People turn out to be real loss-avoiders. The brain seems to keep possible painful experiences at bay. Human intuition is attuned in such a way that, despite our rational capacities, comparable situations of gain and loss are judged differently. An expected loss has two-and-a-half times more impact than an expected gain (Kahneman & Tversky, 1979, Kahneman, 2012). As a result, people shy away from risks, try to avoid loss, and regularly procrastinate when there is a goodbye to be said.

Evolutionary psychology explains this as survival behavior (Portzky, 2015). The wiring in the brain is aimed at avoiding risks and pain in order to allow humankind to continue to exist as a species. The 'alarm center' in the brain continuously monitors whether there is danger. When this part of the brain detects a possible threat, stress hormones such as adrenalin and insulin are released to prepare for a 'fight-or-flight reaction.' These hormones cause an accelerated heartbeat so more blood is pumped to the muscles, which results in an increased state of physical readiness. Everything is done to initiate the most optimal fight-or-flight reaction in the body. In addition, there is also a learning process in the brain itself, influenced by the stress hormone glucocorticoid. Due to the increased emotional state, this hormone ensures that the event is better recorded in the memory. This allows people to remember this event later. From a survival perspective, this is a good thing, because it might help a person to avoid or prevent the threatening situation from occurring next time. A disadvantage of this, however, is that this memory can be triggered at a later stage by a situation that only resembles the original real threat. If the event is perceived as threatening to one's own survival, or traumatizing in another way, then the person may be reliving the original trauma.

This increased state of readiness must of course be curbed again. This task is performed by another stress hormone called cortisol, that has a cushioning effect on the nervous system. Unfortunately, cortisol appears to have a toxic effect on our nerves during prolonged release: it damages the nerve ends (dendrites), causing failing connections between nerve cells thereby losing the ability to transmit information. When the stress of the perceived threat persists for too long, or when there is stress due to too many threatening situations next to or after each other, this results in a self-reinforcing negative effect. Under the influence of the stress hormones, the events are better remembered and tension starts to build up in the body. In addition, more situations are perceived as threatening, which puts a further strain on the body. As a result, resilience, the ability to deal with the threatening situations, is decreased as nerves become damaged and their ability to exchange information becomes more limited.

The development of the brain lags behind humanity's current phase of development. People no longer live in caves, nor do they hunt mammoths. The brain consists of three interacting parts (see Figure 8.1), which have evolved yet kept their original functions (MacLean, 1990).

1. The reptilian brain, the brainstem, or *hindbrain*, consists of the pons and the end of the spinal cord (Medulla Oblongata) and controls the body's vital functions such as breathing, body temperature, heart rate, and blood pressure.
2. The mammalian brain, the limbic system, or *midbrain*, consists of the thalamus, hippocampus, amygdala, and the hypothalamus and is responsible for coordination and motor function, reflexes in reaction to sight or sound, and the reflexive, unconscious linking of sensory information to emotion.

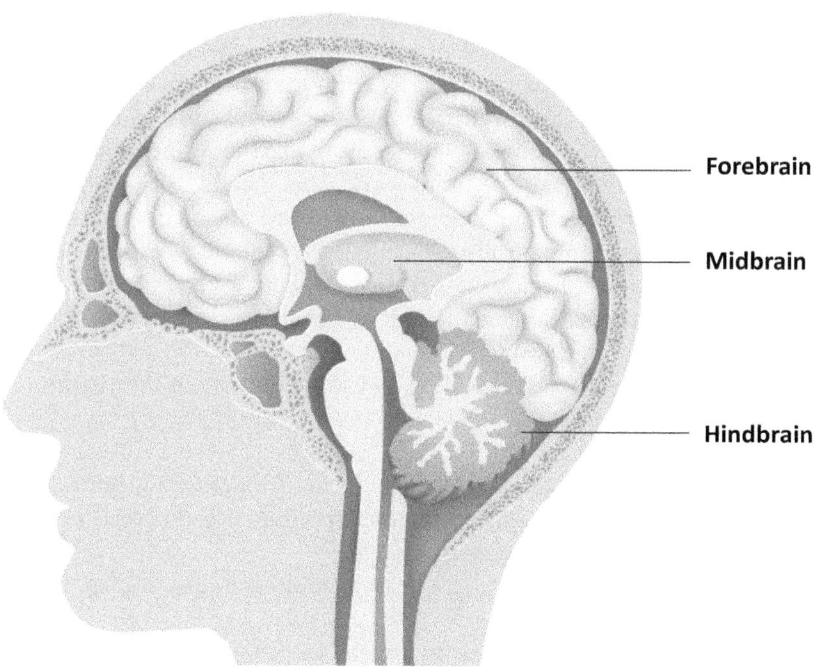

Figure 8.1 Human Internal Brain Anatomy

Source: Teguh Mujiono

3. The neocortex, or *forebrain*, is the largest and most recently evolved part of the brain, with the cerebral cortex and lobes. These are responsible for the cognitive processes, such as logical reasoning, analysis, understanding coherence, making decisions, and planning. It is also the place where conscious and unconscious memories are stored. Conscious emotion regulation takes place here after the reflexive response of the amygdala. In this way it also steers social behavior and impulse control.

Because the brain is divided into three sections, people have the capacity to respond to events in unique ways. Sometimes the reptilian brain reacts even before a situation has entered the consciousness. At that moment, a stimulus from outside the neocortex has not yet reached it and yet we have already responded. When events are perceived to be threatening, people do not even have the time to engage their consciousness. The operating system and the hardware of the brain can be compared to that of an early computer—once state-of-the-art, they are now somewhat outdated. The upgrades of the brain are not quite in line with the further development. Many physical threats are a thing of the past. For physical survival, people no longer have a need for the instincts and motives that date from prehistoric times. For emotional survival, however, people still have to deal with a body that is consciously and unconsciously controlled by a (semi-)autonomous outdated 'computer.'

When children are born, their primitive brain is already present and the mammalian brain develops very rapidly from that moment on. The human brain develops at a much slower pace after the baby is born. A human baby has all the brain cells (neurons) it will need, but it is the connections between these cells that really make the brain work. This means that a baby mainly reacts based on reflexes and feelings outside of its own consciousness. Because verbal development also starts later, the somatic experiences will be stored outside the consciousness (called implicit or preverbal memories). There will be no words available to describe or understand these experiences (Kosminsky & Jordan, 2016).

Small children learn survival skills in a world in which they cannot live without being cared for.

> *Neurological development, it is clear, occurs in the context of our relationships with others, from our earliest caregivers to the people with whom we form close connections as adults.*
>
> (Kosminsky & Jordan, 2016, p. 30)

The experiences stored in their brain lead to certain 'programs' being created. These programs will steer them toward new situations when the brain recognizes in them older similar situations. Situations that recall memories of an earlier threatening event will, mainly unconsciously, activate parts of a survival program, even if someone is not consciously aware or understands what is happening.

> *Early attachment relationships shape an infant's neurobiology and set the course for his or her biopsychological self (Shore, 1996, 2009). Mediated by the greater social environment, this bidirectional, dyadic process directly influences the final wiring of our brains and organizes (or disorganizes) our future social and emotional coping capacities.*
>
> (Lipton & Fosha, 2011, p. 255)

Adults, of course, do not depend on others as they did when they were small. New strategies can be developed from experiential and conscious learning that better match a new situation. This helps integrate loss in their lives. (See also the theme of meaning reconstruction on the Transition Cycle in the section on grief in a social context from Chapter 7.) Kohlrieser et al. (2012) describe the ability to focus 'the mind's eye' of the brain by consciously steering your attention. By focusing the mind's eye, it is possible to access resilience after experiences of loss (see the previous section) and to experience growth after loss (see the next section).

It is important to understand that the above-mentioned stress hormones are transported in the bloodstream throughout the body, while thoughts are passed along by electric signals in the nervous system. The stress hormones are activated by an unconscious part of the brain. Therefore, they always arrive sooner than signals sent by the conscious brain. By that time the stress hormones are already in the bloodstream. That is why one can feel tense before being aware of it and without realizing what is causing it. So, it is not the situation causing it, but rather the part of the brain that is responsible for survival, the part that will protect no matter what. The bloodstream is a slower path than the nervous system, but it starts working sooner and continues to work longer. As a rule, a helpful thought on a conscious level will always lag behind. Counting to ten would not be bad advice in this case. The fear or the anger must first be cleared out of the bloodstream, as it were, before response on a conscious level can take place. The prehistoric fight-or-flight reaction was valuable for survival and thus for evolution. Through this mechanism, humans were alerted to danger before they were consciously aware of it. In modern society, however, the disadvantages often outweigh the benefits. In social interaction, a well-thought-out reaction often has a better effect, especially when the activated nervous system reacts as though a situation is threatening when in fact no threat is intended.

Fortunately, people also have a capacity called 'neuroplasticity': the ability of the brain to adapt. On one hand, this is the ability to learn new skills and to become sufficiently efficient through exercise so that they can be carried out without too much conscious effort. For example, cycling and driving a car are some of these skills, but also juggling, meditating or consciously studying certain beliefs and helpful thoughts. Also, the brain has the ability to allow certain areas of the brain to take over the functions of other brain areas, for example, after a part of the brain has been damaged. Neuroplasticity also makes it possible to repair neuronal damage, such as caused by too much of the stress hormone cortisol. Nerve endings, or dendrites, can grow again and connections between neurons, the number of which determines the speed of the exchange of information and the power of memories, can increase. For this last form of recovery, it is essential to first reduce the general stress level, because otherwise all measures will be useless. Also, it is important to pay attention to nourishment, food, and drink: no alcoholic beverages or drugs, even though these may seem to offer solace in avoidance-focused coping. Furthermore, it is important to undertake sufficient recovery-oriented activities, to ensure that pleasure is experienced. And finally, it is important to train the brain and the body: stimulate your brain with cognitive games, memory exercises, or reading a good book and engage in physical exercise to build a fit body. Certain (muscle) strength training works well because the human body will try to restore the depletion of muscle cells during the training by building extra tissue to be better equipped the next time the body is put under strain (positive use of the evolutionary fight-or-flight response). The brain also benefits from an increase in neuronal connections, aimed at better coping of the (muscular) motor challenges (Portzky, 2015).

As their brain and nervous system develops, babies and children must 'practice' to discover what reactions are appropriate and what are inappropriate. This is not just about learning what behavior leads to fulfilling their (life) needs, but also about having to learn how to deal with social interaction. That 'learning' consists of a complex balance between 'fighting,' 'fleeing,' and 'freezing.' They cannot flee from every unwanted reaction and they cannot fight each time. They will also have to learn to experience discomfort and it is the task of the attachment figures to offer the right balance of care and challenge and to monitor this balance. This balance between too many or too few stimuli has a direct effect on the development of the brain of the child. Both an excess of stimuli, high arousal, and too little stimulation, low arousal, appears to be detrimental to the cell structure, the development of and connections between nerve cells (neurons). This disruption in the development of the brain in childhood also has effects later in life because basic skills for personal and social interaction such as emotion regulation, dealing with stress, and locus of control will not have been developed (sufficiently). Attachment problems in childhood and in adulthood therefore not only have a behavioral component but also a neurological component. The success of counseling loss and grief is therefore directly related to the degree of neuroplasticity that the counseling helps build (Kosminsky & Jordan, 2016).

Stress in itself is not always a bad thing. It is a natural reaction of the body to prepare it for action. Too much stress that lasts for too long is bad for the body through its neurohormonal effect, but only for someone who believes that stress is bad for you. People with a positive attitude towards stress do not appear to be at risk of cardiovascular disease at all even when subjected to high levels of stress. Our brain produces not only the hormones adrenaline and cortisol during stress, it also produces oxytocin (also produced when there is physical contact). This oxytocin ensures that people want to turn to others when they have stress to share their concerns. Those who act on this hormone-based need are also safeguarded from cardiovascular disease at high stress levels (McGonigal, 2016). Neuroplasticity enables people to change their convictions and thus their attitudes towards stress, thereby combatting the adverse effects.

This success in counseling actual trauma depends on the extent to which the counselor is sufficiently able to be reliably present. Only then can the over-aroused nervous system relax sufficiently in the security provided to share the story in dialogue. Before that, the brain is not able to produce a coherent story or to answer the questions of the counselor. The counselor will only be able to use the verbal entrance (through language) when the body and the brain feel that it is sufficiently safe to do so. Body-oriented practices such as mindfulness and yoga offer such opportunities (Van der Kolk, 2015; Ogden & Fisher, 2015).

Growth After Loss

When counselors look back with their clients on negative and painful events, they often discover that something positive has emerged from the loss—that life has been enriched, that there is a new perspective that would not have existed had it not been for the loss. It is called 'post-traumatic growth' by Calhoun and Tedeschi (1889–1990, 1996, 1998). They developed the Post-Traumatic Growth Inventory (PTGI), a self-report scale for assessing post-traumatic growth, focusing on positive scores in the following areas: appreciation of life, relationships with others, new possibilities in life, personal strength, and spiritual change, elements that can also be found in the restoration orientation of the Dual Process Model.

In the context of this book, we prefer to call it 'growth after loss.' After all, this is growth that may result from the search for how to adapt to the new reality after having suffered a loss. The growth is not a direct result of the loss itself. The loss remains a loss, including all the questions and discomfort it brings with it. When people recognize and name growth, the loss has not suddenly become a fairy tale: people will still point out the negative and positive aspects of it. Growth can become visible in several different ways. People who indicate that they have grown after loss do not necessarily experience growth in all areas of life. Some do not experience any growth at all, or do not name it as such. Growth after loss is a consequence of the way in which someone finds an answer for the loss, in their search for meaning (Cozijnsen & van Wielink, 2012).

Dealing with loss can be considerably hindered by a negative approach. For example, relatives clamping onto a court case after a violent crime.

> *Noteworthy in Van Denderen's research [Mariette van Denderen, of the University of Groningen, followed 330 survivors of murder for four years, financed by 'Fonds Slachtofferhulp,' which is a victim aid fund in the Netherlands] is that relatives who clamp onto the lawsuit against the perpetrators, struggle with complex grief processing for a long time. . . . Surviving relatives can remain so angry at the Public Prosecutor's Office and the perpetrator's lawyer, that they will continue to try to have the perpetrator punished more and more severely. . . . The feeling of anger or revenge does not go away.*
>
> (Schildkamp, 2017)

These relatives appear to struggle with (complex) grief symptoms for a substantially longer period of time (Van Denderen, 2017). Other examples of a negative approach are to (continue to) seek out conflict with doctors or hospitals after (presumed) medical failures, or continuously blaming a school when a child takes his own life after bullying. There are relatives who use their energy positively by providing information in schools, for example if someone is killed in a drug case (Van Denderen, 2017). Kohlrieser speaks in this case about turning loss into inspiration (Kohlrieser, 2015). This creates, paradoxically, the possibility that the loss becomes a secure base. The loss itself is indirectly meaningful; it is mainly about the how it has shaped people in a positive way. This possible growth may for example consist of an increased ability to deal with setbacks. Although the loss touched on the vulnerable self, there was also a stronger self-confidence. The growth may also consist of appreciation or increased gratitude towards life or towards that which is lost. Often spiritual or existential growth is also experienced. Life has 'more value.' Issues that were previously perceived as important can be placed in a different, broader perspective. Growth after loss is often not limited to the person grieving, but can also be expressed in increased connection with others.

Adults who integrate negative events into their life stories in a positive way and can tell how events have contributed to their personal growth experience a significantly improved well-being, more than those who are less positive (Lilgendahl & McAdams, 2011). A crucial condition to make this possible, is being able to experience openness and intimacy. It makes learning possible. In this context, Carol Dweck uses 'growth mindset' as opposed to a 'fixed mindset' (Dweck, 2017).

The counselor who is able to stay present by listening with all their being and staying completely focused, can make an important contribution to the level of intimacy in which life events are shared (Calhoun & Tedeschi, 2001). More recent research shows that it is important for growth after loss that people can share their own experiences with others. The emotional experience of sharing one's own story and hearing the other's experiences have an essential added value, which is much greater than that imparted by hearing a story about a third party or reading experiences of others in books (Vough & Barker Caza, 2017). This is important for the counselor for two reasons. On the one hand, the counselor may invite the client to find secure bases in his or her surroundings with which to share his or her story. It can also be particularly beneficial when the client invites a person to come to a session with whom, for example, a farewell letter, or elements of the lifeline, can be shared. In this way, the effect of sharing also grows outside the therapeutic environment. After all, there is then an extra witness who will travel further with the client in his or her (life) story. On the other hand, it is also an invitation to the counselor to introduce his or her own concrete and vulnerable experience into the therapeutic relationship.

Dialogue

Peter has been feeling down for quite some time now. His doctor has referred him to Amelia, a counselor.

Amelia: Good morning. I am Amelia. Welcome!
Peter: Thank you. My name is Peter.
Amelia: Hi Peter, have a seat. What can I do for you?
Peter: I was referred to you by my doctor. I am feeling really miserable and have no energy. Even small tasks cost extra effort. I thought it might be something physical, but the doctor could not find anything. Maybe it is something else then.
Amelia: How long have you been feeling so miserable?
Peter: About a month or two I would say. It seems to be getting worse.
Amelia: Did something happen a month or two ago?
Peter: I have already thought about that, but I really could not say. I don't believe it has.
Amelia: Have there been any changes during the past period?
Peter: No, but I have been very busy with preparations for moving. So, it has been busier than usual?
Amelia: Have you moved recently?
Peter: No, I am moving in six weeks.
Amelia: How are you feeling about moving?
Peter: I am looking forward to it. I have bought a farm, beautifully green with lots of land. I will need to do some remodeling, but I plan to do that

once I am living there. Because otherwise I would have to travel back and forth all the time. It is clear across the country.

Amelia: So, you are looking forward to moving. Are you worried about having to renovate?

Peter: Not at all. I think it will be great to renovate my own house.

Amelia: In what you have told me so far, there are no reasons to explain why you are feeling depressed.

Peter: Exactly. That's what I don't understand either.

Amelia: Let's take a broader look. Sometimes one reacts to something that one is not aware of. Can you tell me anything about your past? Which events had an impact on you?

Peter: I had a happy childhood. My parents stayed together and I did well at school. My university days were more difficult. It took me a long time to graduate.

Amelia: So, you say that you had a happy childhood, but that it took you a long time to graduate. Why was that?

Peter: I got stuck on my graduation thesis. I became overwhelmed with the amount of information and wasn't able to bring any order into it and write a story. I then dropped out for six months and was assigned a tutor. In the end I managed to finish it.

Amelia: How does it make you feel looking back at all this?

Peter: I would have rather not had this experience, but because of it, I have learned that I can ask for help and that I can overcome setbacks. It also helped me after my divorce.

Amelia: Is that the next profound event: your divorce?

Peter: It was profound, but not the next event. First my father died. That was quite devastating.

Amelia: Can you tell me more about it?

Peter: (Is quiet for a while.) Wow, I don't think about it very often anymore, but now . . .

Amelia: What is happening?

Peter: I don't know, I feel like I can't breathe.

Amelia: Just breathe in and out slowly a couple of times. (Breathes emphatically with him a few times.) Does that help?

Peter: Yes, I feel calmer now.

Amelia: How did your father die?

Peter: (Tears filling his eyes.) He was run over. He died instantly.

Amelia: I can see that it affects you, thinking back on it.

Peter: Well . . . I didn't expect that at all . . .

Amelia: Thinking back, what affects you mostly?

Peter: It was so sudden. That morning he left the house completely healthy and that afternoon, he was dead. It was inconceivable. And yet, we had to act immediately. A funeral had to be arranged, we had to call people, authorities.

Amelia: How did you manage?

Peter: At that moment you can move mountains and strangely, it did feel good. During those weeks, I even arranged for a memorial to be placed and that something was done about that dangerous curve in the road.
Amelia: Were there moments in which you could allow yourself to feel your emotions, that you could stop and think about how it affected you?
Peter: To be honest, I hardly cried. That I got so emotional just now, that's something I don't normally do. I thought that I had dealt with it. But now I realize that deep down it still hurts.
Amelia: The next time you come, I would like to explore the loss of your father and how it was for you some more. It seems that it is asking to be attended to. How do you feel about that?
Peter: I didn't expect it to be about this, but it feels right to me. So, yes please!

Self-Reflection Questions

- How do you look back at your profound losses and changes in your (professional and personal) life? How did they shape you? What are you grateful for?
- Have you ever had a burnout or have you ever been overworked? What did you learn from that?

Exercises

Exercise—Coping and Attachment Styles

What coping style does your client adopt and in which specific situations does it show?

- Active problem solving?
- Seeking social support?
- Avoidance and watching-and-waiting?
- Seeking diversion?

Explore together with your client:

- Which examples did your client have in his or her life that made him develop these styles?
- How do these styles help the client deal with the loss?
- What is needed for the client to experiment with other styles?

Instruction: What coping style do you have in which situation? Discuss each other's coping styles in groups of two by making use of the questions above.

Exercise—Inner Separation

The German psychotherapist Franz Ruppert developed a therapy form focused on trauma. Feeling something inside that holds you back in spite of your longing to share intimacy and that prevents you from showing how you feel, or how vulnerable you are, can be symbolized according to Ruppert (2008) as a type of inner separation (see Figure 8.2a). He describes the psyche as splitting up into three parts.

1. The Healthy Self, which is open to the environment and personal emotional perception. This is the part that can reach out to others, ask for and offer support, and accept that things are what they are.
2. The Survival Self, which has the sole function of keeping the trauma out of conscious awareness by any means necessary. It is the gatekeeper and plays an active role in guarding the boundary, making sure that nothing or no one can come near the Wounded Self.
3. The Wounded Self, which holds the pain or trauma experience and unexpressed emotions from the past frozen in time. At that moment, these events and experiences were too threatening and overwhelming (threatened survival), so the Wounded Self froze them inside the subconscious, keeping them underwater, separating body from mind.

Looking at the model from the viewpoint of intimacy and connection, these parts can be represented as different types of hearts (Wentink, 2014) (see Figure 8.2b):

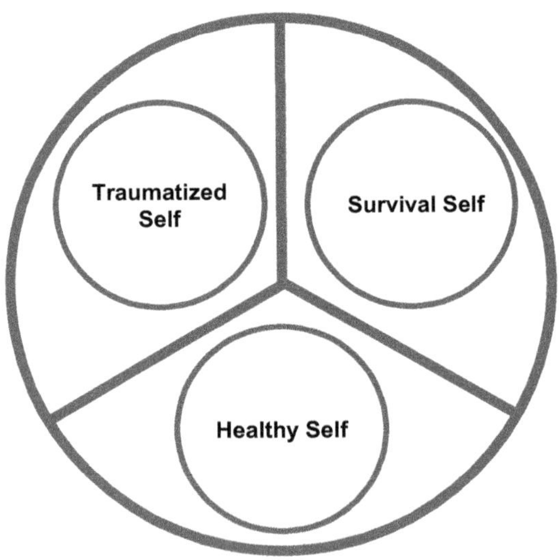

Figure 8.2a Model of Inner Separation

Source: Franz Ruppert, 2008; copied with permission from © Green Balloon Books and Klett-Cotta

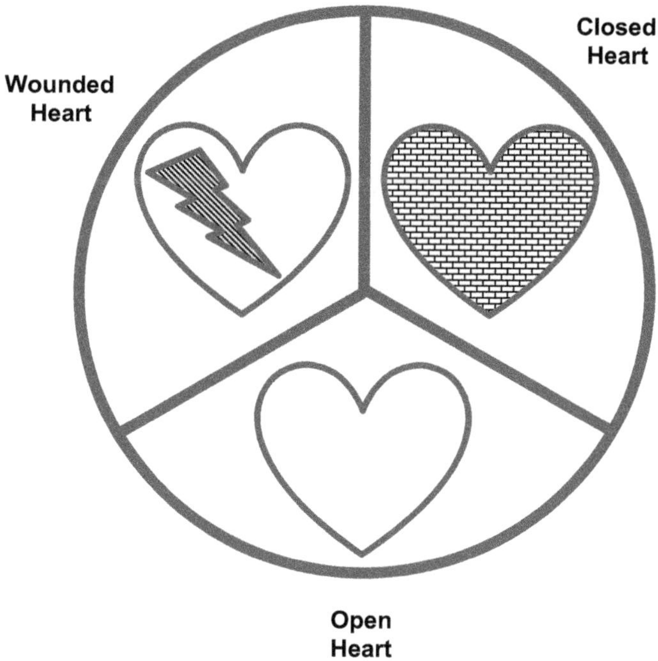

Figure 8.2b Model of Inner Separation

Source: Copied with permission from *Je verlangen—dwaallicht of kompas?: Over verlangens, innerlijke verdeeldheid en vervulling*, by Margriet Wentink, 2014; Eeserveen, The Netherlands: Uitgeverij Mens!

- The Healthy Self is the Open Heart
- The Survival Self is the Closed Heart
- The Wounded Self is the Wounded Heart

The Survival Self has an important task to fulfill. It ensures that the pain is shielded from consciousness. In this way it is possible to keep on living and grow up in painful circumstances. The Survival Self makes it possible to survive. The patterns that were once so helpful and protective, in the now, where these old threats no longer exist, can be a hindrance instead of a help when new situations seem to resemble the old (but are not the same). The reaction patterns that originate in the Survival Self are especially hindering because they have a limited range of possibilities.

Clive, a man who had received many beatings from his father, learned to undergo them passively and not show his emotions. That helped him. Not to prevent the thrashing, but because a show of emotion made his father even angrier. It was Clive's way to prevent a further increase in violence. At a later age however, this pattern became a stumbling block for him in his job, when he was expected to explain his views while under pressure. Each time Clive felt agitated, he would just become quiet and he would withdraw. Only when he started exploring his Survival Self did the pain come out that he had pushed away as a child. By grieving for the loss that he suffered as a child, he not only learned to recognize this pain but also started to experience events in the present differently. In this way, Clive started to learn that it is possible to react in other ways than he had always done before when drawing from the limited pattern he had developed as a child.

The more secure the attachment, the stronger the Healthy Self. From the perspective of the Healthy Self, the client is capable of self-reflection and can see the Survival Self. But the question as to why the client is here often does not originate from the Healthy Self but rather from the Survival Self. If that is the case, one can be sure that the Survival Self will continuously be very hard at work to keep things as they are. For the client, a long time ago, this used to be the best way to handle things. By getting to know the Survival Self and by understanding its protective role, it becomes clearer what the pain was and why it needed to be protected. From a deep understanding of the pain or a longing for wholeness, it then becomes possible to formulate a question aimed at recovery.

To explore this inner separation, the counselor should first explain to the client briefly what this inner separation consists of, where it originated, and how this separation can be felt in daily life.

The following questions can then be helpful for exploring the three parts.

- The question with which the client seeks counseling stems from a longing for wholeness when coming from the Open Heart:
  - To whom is the client able to show his open heart?
  - What does the client long for?
  - With whom can the client share his or her longing?

- The gatekeeper guards the border of the Wounded Heart:
  - When does the gatekeeper close the gate?
  - When does the client become (too) agitated?
  - When is the door opened or left ajar?
  - When does the client feel secure enough?
  - What does the client need to leave the door ajar for someone else?
  - How can the client console the gatekeeper from his or her own open heart?

- The Closed Heart:
  - What pain, abuse, and suffering are stored here?
  - What is it like for the client when others come close to his or her pain?
  - How can the client benefit from letting others come near the pain?

Instruction: Counsel each other in groups of three (A is the counselor, B is the client, and C is the observer) in a dialogue on Inner Separation, as described by the exercise above. Evaluate each round briefly and switch roles.

Exercise—Mindfulness: Grounding

A mindfulness exercise can be used in counseling to bring the client into the here and now, make them aware of their body and what they feel inside. There is a wide range of mindfulness exercises available that are well suited for grief counseling. These exercises are often available as sound recordings, so that one can use them by oneself (both counselor and client) (Ankersmid, 2015b).

When using such exercises in a counseling setting, speak the words slowly and quietly, after having invited the client to do the exercise with you.

Please sit up straight in your chair and put your feet flat on the ground. Relax your hands and put them in your lap or on your thighs. Feel yourself sitting and feel your back against the back of the chair.

Let's both close our eyes now, or if that does not feel good, then just focus on a point on the floor.

Feel that your feet are planted firmly on the ground and imagine that huge roots grow out of your feet, extending deep into the ground beneath you. First from your right foot. Through the floor, branching out deeper and deeper into the earth until they are firmly anchored. Then let them grow from your left foot, through the floor, branching out deeper and deeper into the earth until they are firmly anchored.

Make your root system as deep, as large, and as broad as possible. So deep and large and broad that you feel how firmly they are planted in the ground.

Let everything you do not need, like stress, unrest and tension, move down through your body, through your legs, through your feet . . . and finally let everything you do not need disappear through the roots from your body into the ground.

Feel the space that is created inside you and the peaceful feeling that is coming over you now that you are firmly rooted in the ground. Keep breathing gently, as deeply into your belly as possible, softly inhale and exhale.

Now visualize a place where your tree is standing. A place you know, where you like being and where your tree can stand perfectly, deeply rooted. In that place, your tree takes up as much space as it needs, filling its own space. In the sun, your tree offers shade, in case of rain and during storms, it offers shelter for those who need it.

Your branches extend up and to the side. They are branching out further and on the small shoots, leaves are growing. The crown of your tree is as broad and as large as you want it to be. The wind gently rustles through your leaves and your branches move at their own pace. Feel how you take up the space and how firm you stand.

Now it is time to return to the here and now, bringing that feeling of space and peace back with you. Slowly pull the roots back in, first through your left foot and then through your right. Slowly pick up your left heel and then your left toes. Then pick up your right heel and then your right toes. Shuffle your feet. Then open your eyes and come back into the here and now.

If necessary, stand up and shake your body, stretch to the sky and shake your arms and legs. Stamp your feet and feel the ground beneath you.

> **Instruction:** Divide into pairs and let each do this mindfulness exercise while the other reads it. Evaluate briefly what it was like and then switch roles.

Exercise—Guided Visualization: What Did You Say Goodbye to This Morning?

A guided visualization exercise is a combination of a meditation/mindfulness exercise and reliving an experience. A counselor can make use of this type of exercise to either bring the client back into the here and now, or to set the mood for the counseling session and at the same time, touch on a specific theme. In this case the theme 'saying goodbye' is used. The counselor uses an unhurried tone of voice after asking the client to do this exercise with them. The client does not answer the questions in the visualization out loud, but may keep and experience the answers to and for themselves:

I would like to invite you to relax and sit up straight in your chair, with your hands loosely in your lap, and to close your eyes as I am doing if you want to or otherwise focus on a point on the floor.

As you sit in your chair, feel yourself sitting on it and feel your back against the chair. Your feet are resting on the floor. As you sit here calmly on the chair, taking slow, deep breaths, in and out, in and out, take your thoughts back to this morning: to the moment you woke up, the moment you became conscious that you were awake. Where are you lying when you wake up? Are you lying beside someone or did you wake up alone? If you were lying beside someone, did they wake up too, or did they carry on sleeping? If you woke up alone, are you no longer lying next to someone, did someone lie beside you in the past, is there a loss? Or perhaps you were not yet lying beside someone and there is a longing?

What is the first thought that comes to mind when you wake up? Which is the very first thought to come up in your awakening consciousness?

How does this thought influence your day, how do you fit this thought into your day?

As you follow your morning ritual, the moment of departure for work comes closer. When you go to work, who or what do you say goodbye to? How do you go about that? How is goodbye said to you? At the moment you close the front door behind you, who or what are you leaving behind? What does that mean to you?

Then you go on your way. While traveling to work or an appointment, what thoughts are going around in your mind? What's on your mind and how does that influence your day, how does it influence you?

Then you arrive at work, or here at this session and just before you go inside, what sensation can you feel inside your body? Where in your body, before you come through the door? Which memories, which events from the past come up? At which point did you have such an experience in the past? What does that memory mean to you?

Then you enter this room and take a seat on the chair in which you are now sitting. As you breathe out, in and out, in and out, you bring your awareness to this moment. You are sitting on your chair in the here and now and when you are ready, you can open your eyes.

Instruction: Form pairs and exchange thoughts on the effect this exercise had on you. Give attention to each of the following:

- Waking up—beside someone? Which thoughts, mood, influence?
- Saying goodbye—to whom or what, which event?
- Traveling—which thoughts, mood, influence?
- Arrival—which sensations, memories, meaning?

Exercise—Growth After Loss

Using a major loss from the lifeline as example, check together with your client if and in which way there is growth after loss. Ask questions like:

- How does the client describe the growth?
- How did the client benefit?
- What qualities did the client discover in themselves after the loss?
- In what way can the client relate to others who are struggling since the loss experience?
- Looking back, what can be said about anger versus forgiveness?
- Looking back, what can be said about guilt versus reconciliation?

Instruction: Counsel each other in groups of three (A is the counselor, B is the client, and C is the observer) on growth after loss based on a personal loss, as in the exercise above. Evaluate each round briefly and switch roles.

Note

1. Active approach/confronting, palliative approach, avoidance, social support, passive response, expression of emotions, reassuring thoughts.

9

GRIEF IN THE CONTEXT OF WORK

A Case Study

From a very young age, Amber loved to read. She learned how to spell when she was only three years old, and from the moment that she could read, she read everything she could lay her hands on. She went on to study English to learn more about literature and took a teaching job at a high school shortly after her graduation. During the first years she focused mainly on her profession. As a young teacher, she needed to focus all her attention on teaching the curriculum to teenagers with raging hormones who much preferred keeping themselves busy with each other than with literature. But she loved her line of work so much that she did everything she could to convey her love of language, poetry, and literature to the students—with success. Soon she was not only teaching but also organizing poetry readings, inviting writers, and even managing to set up a writing project together with a well-known writer. She became a source of inspiration to students and colleagues. The school management asked her to take on a coordinating and advisory position, so that she could advise her colleagues too. She did well at that too and it did not take long before she was appointed team leader. She took great pleasure in her work. She dreamt of a school that would encourage the students to use their talents and of a building that would offer the best possible space for that. Step by step she was making her dream come true. The team she led took its own course more and more clearly, which was different from the rest of the school. They were happy as a team and the students were enthusiastic. Even the results improved. Amber was content. Until one day, when she was called in to the new principal's office. In short but clear phrases, it became clear that everything she had built up and invested in was to be reversed. She was expected to step back and fall in again with the rest of the school. For each project and every adjustment, she had to request his permission. It was causing too much unrest among the rest of the staff and the parents had complained about the differences in approach within the school. All arguments that Amber put forward were brushed aside. The decision had been made. It felt as though her world fell apart. For the rest of that week, Amber functioned on auto-pilot, as if she were numb. She did not tell anybody about the conversation. She could not believe it. Until a friend dropped by unexpectedly that weekend and asked how she was doing. Then she broke down.

Loss and Grief at Work

Loss at work merits special attention. Firstly, because people take themselves and thereby all kinds of loss with them to work, so that work and their personal life can never be completely separated. Secondly, because work in itself can also become a source of experiences of loss, as had happened to Amber, introduced at the beginning of this chapter. Reorganizations, mergers, being discharged, demotion, being passed over for promotion, changes in teams, the departure or death of a colleague, redundancy, transfer, retirement, bullying and so on, are all types of losses at work. It is often a surprising and new point of view (but then quickly recognized and acknowledged) for both counselors and clients that profound changes at work, and certainly the loss of a job or position, can lead to (intense) grief. In this chapter, we will give special attention to these types of loss.

The Loss of a Colleague or Coming to Work After a Loved One Has Passed Away

When an employee, or a loved one of an employee, dies, loss and grief will intrude on the work place. Most organizations seem to face a challenge when having to deal with grief. There are of course exceptions, but mostly there is difficulty in responding in a good way to loss and grief. At work, most often a business-like, professional environment, it can be difficult to show emotions, especially those of anger, fear, or sadness. Also, not wanting to discuss the loss for fear of the consequences on job security can make things even more difficult. Common complaints in grief, such as difficulty concentrating or memory impairment, can make it difficult to fully function at work. Not every manager will be sensitive to this, especially when the complaints persist and last longer than what is considered 'normal.'

Giving an employee who has just suffered a loss sick leave can be a way out. The employee will not have to appear at work and the manager can avoid having the difficult conversations with his or her employee, at least for a while. This is a temporary solution that is sometimes used by organizations. In the period immediately after the funeral, there is usually enough empathy when things are not yet as they were or should be. Although sick leave seems obvious, grief is not a disease. However, figures from 2010 show that those who have lost a loved one, on average, report in sick for work for about one hundred days at work. In men, absenteeism due to grief is 92 days, while women spend an average of 105 days after a death. It should be noted that much of the absenteeism is not noted in the records to be formally due to grief. Newer figures show that the absenteeism figures for grieving are even higher: up to 170 days. Targeted counseling of grief at work could decrease the duration of absence by 28% (Neijenhuis et al., 2012).

Even though we assume that the social support for loss is mainly found in the private environment, the research by Neijenhuis et al. (2012) shows that 50% of employees with grief actually indicate colleagues as an important source of strength. For example, 45% of this group indicates the manager as an important source of strength. These experiences in the work environment scored even higher than the 'acquaintances' category. Colleagues and managers are therefore in many cases part of the social network of the employee with grief. An employee usually benefits from being in contact with the work environment and it helps if he or she finds an emotional connection with close colleagues and is given time and opportunity by the employer to express grief. If the workplace cares for sorrow and joy in the lives of the employees, a climate is created where energy can be more adequately focused on creativity and constructive action. The employee still feels sorrow but, when allowed to express this, will be able to focus his or her attention on other matters. We cannot stress enough the importance of support in the workplace for someone who is dealing with a loss.

Work can make a major contribution to recovery provided that the relationships are healthy and the employee took pleasure in work before the loss. Going back to work then offers routine and familiarity and often helps the employee feel the support of something that is bigger than themselves. It does not have to be laid on thick. The art is to be a beckoning manager, giving the colleague the feeling that it is a good thing to be among colleagues and making such an empathetic connection that the employee is given the space needed and at the same time, stimulated to take necessary steps towards recovery.

Organizations as Sources of Loss

In addition to loss at work due to the death of an employee or the loved one of an employee, loss also occurs inside the organization, such as (imminent) dismissal, redundancy, organizational change, mergers, and the like. As Anatole France puts it: *All changes, even the most longed for, have their melancholy; for what we leave behind us is a part of ourselves; we must die to one life before we can enter another*. These are transitions: 'the psychological process that people go through as they internalize and come to terms with the details of a new situation' (Bridges, 2017). As an organizational advisor and author of management books, William Bridges is one of the first to describe work as a potential cause of experiences of loss. He makes an important distinction between situational and formal change within an organization, such as a reorganization, where structure, hierarchy, or location are changed, and transition—the psychological and emotional aspect of the reorganization, where employees have to adapt to the changed situation and environment. It is precisely this distinction that can help us articulate the themes of loss at work. The workplace still is often a place where people will not easily show their emotions around disappointment and loss. Bridges identifies three transition phases during major changes at work:

1. Ending, Losing, Letting Go
2. The Neutral Zone
3. The New Beginning

Understanding these transition phases and the psychological aspects that play a role in profound change can help people negotiate change more successfully.

Phase One: Change Starts With an Ending

Bridges starts with a striking observation. Changes begin with an ending: the ending of the old and familiar situation. It is a loss that calls for the conclusion of a period and for letting go of expectations about the future that are based on the past. The only way to enable this is to recognize and to acknowledge the loss, as this type of loss is related to the violation of the psychological contract (Argyris, 1960; Schein & Schein, 2016). Employees are asked to relinquish the bond, the attachment; security changes into uncertainty. Loyalty is fumbled with, and it is unclear what the new situation will bring. As a result, when the organization that is going through change most requires trust, that trust is most difficult to muster.

Along the Lines of Steady Progress?

How should we interpret this Bridges model? When set in time, we will always have to deal with three overlapping phases as shown in Figure 9.1. The height of the lines shows the number of people that (still or already) identify themselves with the named phase. In the beginning, the majority will be confronted with the ending and will be in the process of trying to leave the familiar situation behind. A small part will consist of forerunners who are already mainly concerned with giving shape to the new situation, usually the change team itself. Another small part will already have progressed to the neutral zone. Without knowing exactly what the future will bring, they already have let go of the past and are on their way to what is to come.

The number of people in a certain phase follows a smooth curve, over time. However, at each moment in time there will be people in different phases. For example, a project leader who is actually looking forward to the upcoming developments and mostly in the third phase suddenly realizes that the change will give him a different position causing him or her to return to phase one. In the approach to and communication on changes, it helps when organizations are aware of this. No turning points can be indicated. The transition phases indicate psychological processes of bonding, attachment, and detachment. These psychological processes do not care about deadlines and planned or fixed dates on a calendar or spreadsheet. The definition of the curves is never as beautiful in reality as in the illustrated model. This is the ideal picture. There appear to be many similarities between Bridges's Transition Model and the Dual Process Model (see Figure 9.2).

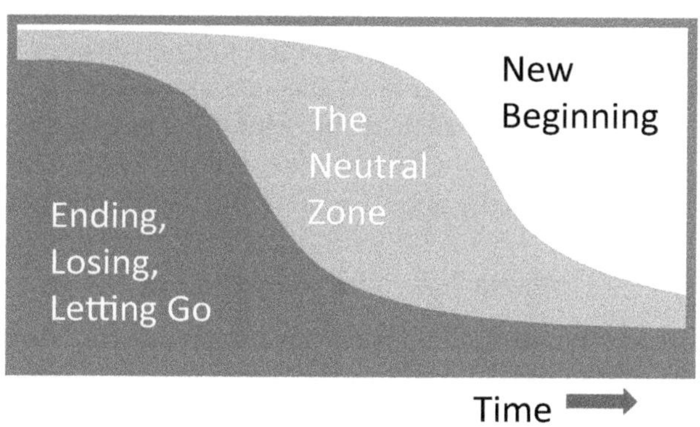

Figure 9.1 Transition Phases According to Bridges

Source: *Managing Transitions: Making the Most of Change*, by William Bridges and Susan Bridges, 2017, NB Limited

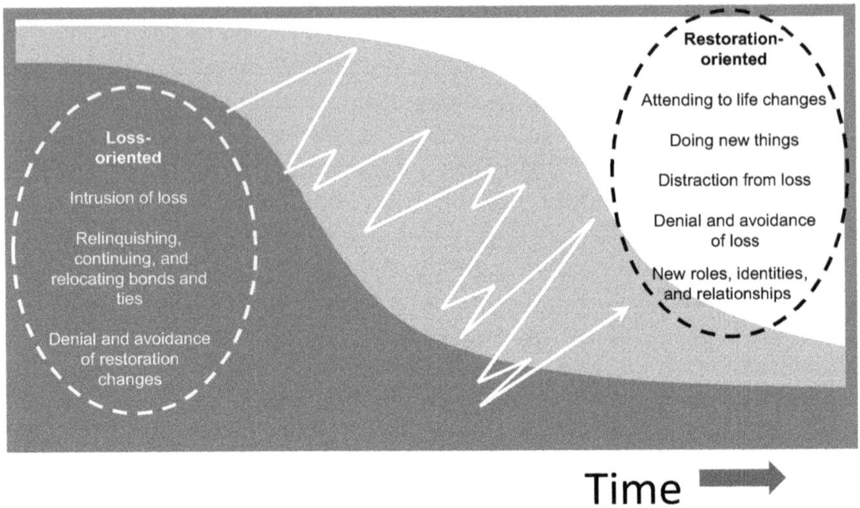

Figure 9.2 Transition Phases and Duality

Reflecting On What Is and Was

The organization implementing the change should guard from moving too fast. As described in the Transition Cycle, at the theme 'saying goodbye,' people may attempt to take a shortcut because of their discomfort. It is however impossible to skip any of the themes without paying the price. In the same way, the organization implementing the change cannot skip any transition phases without it evoking resistance in the organization. They cannot praise a new beginning without first daring to reflect on or say goodbye to the old situation. Employees will only be prepared to join them on their journey towards a new future, through the uncertain Neutral Zone, if they are empowered to leave the old behind. A symbolic ending, a ritual, can be helpful. It creates a milestone, a border post. Something of the old will have to be included in the new for employees to be able to connect to the new. The old is over, but should not be banned.

Phase Two: The Neutral Zone

We often first ask for directions before we start moving. In this context, Ben Tiggelaar (2011) likes to refer to the 'Silly Olympiad' sketch by Monty Python[1] with the '1500 meters for the deaf' and '100 yards for people with no sense of direction.' The pictures painted are as humorous as they are striking: the deaf do not hear the starting gun and do not move. The people with no sense of direction do move, but do not make it to the finish line because they all run in different directions. The one cannot exist without the other, but the chicken-egg discussion about what should come first is not solved here.

Ancient Israelites had to wander through the desert for 40 years in the biblical story to escape the oppression in Egypt and to arrive in the Promised Land. There were many struggles during the journey. At the beginning of the journey, trapped between the pharaoh's army and the sea, there was much grumbling and longing for the past: 'Was it because there were no graves in Egypt that you brought us to the desert to die?[2] What have you done to us by bringing us out of Egypt? Did we not say to you in Egypt, "Leave us alone; let us serve the Egyptians?" It would have been better for us to serve the Egyptians than to die in the desert!' We are always quick to choose the suffering we know above a promise or enticement of an unknown better world. Many a change agent would probably like to make use of a 'deus ex machina' to escape from such resistance as at the time of the passage through the Red Sea. But it was not so simple then either. It is not that the waters of the sea first parted, after which the Israelites could move through. The call to the Israelites was to first start moving, after which the waters parted. So, first trust that there will be a result even before the outcome is realized. Behold the challenge of the neutral zone.

Between the Old and the New

If you imagine yourself hanging from a trapeze at the top of a circus tent, swinging back and forth, you will also become aware of the depth below you.

> *It's not so much that we're afraid of change or so in love with the old ways, but it's that place in between that we fear. It's like being between trapezes. It's Linus[3] when his blanket is in the dryer. There's nothing to hold onto.*
>
> (Marilyn Ferguson, American futurist cited in Bridges, 2017, p. 48)

With or without a safety net, it requires a lot of courage to let go, to fly, confident that you can reach the trapeze on the other side. What happens when you let go? This disheartening question certainly does not make it easier to actually let go. To leave the familiar environment behind you on your way to a new and unknown world.

Then it is indeed important for there to be someone to show the way, who has an ideal in mind that is achievable. The route does not even have to be completely clear, there is still room for adjustment along the way. However, as the people of Israel followed a pillar of cloud during the day and a pillar of fire at night, employees need someone with vision that invites them to travel with them—someone who gives them room for personal input, in the same way the neutral zone offers opportunities for creativity. The problems in the old situation that gave rise to the change require new solutions. Solutions that can also come from the people who come along on the journey. That can be the invitation to the neutral zone, to help build the new reality. To commit to the new vision.

It is also about letting the new reality sink in. To master the new situation. To internalize the new situation, with respect for the past, for the memory.

Everyone has a free choice in that. The choice to enter the neutral zone and to follow through, to lead the change together. To take responsibility.

Phase Three: The New Beginning

The transition from the Neutral Zone to the New Beginning will not come without a fight, just like the initial transition from the Ending to the Neutral Zone. On the one hand, this transition is no more a moment that can follow an implementation schedule, although symbolic moments can help to mark the transition, be it sometimes only in retrospect. On the other hand, a New Beginning will not just happen. A struggle may be necessary.

We return to the biblical story about the exodus of Israel from Egypt. After 40 years of wandering through the desert, the Israelites stand on the border of the Promised Land. The story then tells about the twelve spies who come back with rumors about giants. This makes the people grumble again. 'If only we had died in Egypt! Or in this wilderness! Why is the Lord bringing us to this land? . . . Would it not be better for us to go back to Egypt?' And they said to each other, 'We should choose a leader and go back to Egypt!'[4] The transition from the Neutral Zone to the New Beginning does not happen without a struggle either.

Celebrating Successes

New Beginnings are about celebrating new successes. For this to happen, people need to recognize that they share the joint goals and joint values that have yet to be realized. This can only be attained after the Neutral Zone, because people must be given the chance to connect with these new values and goals.

As mentioned earlier, the New Beginning is not so much marked as the moment in which, for example, the new stationary with the company logo is being introduced with a lot of pomp and ceremony. It is the moment that someone picks up the phone and says the new company's name without having to think about it, perhaps to their own surprise. And then it appears that the new logo has turned out to be quite nice after all.

The New Beginning Ushers In a New Ending . . .

This could be the moment that the news comes from management that there is a new merger coming. A merger that will further expand the company's position in the market and will increase turnover, profitability, and shareholder value. Or there are political changes that require a different organizational structure. This is the moment of a new change, a New Ending, just as everyone was beginning to get accustomed and attached to the new situation. The only constant factor is change.

Secure Bases at Work

George Kohlrieser focuses on the development of leaders who want to initiate transition in their organizations and their employees (Kohlrieser et al., 2012). Actual movement can only occur when there is sufficient real connection and there is a challenge stemming from that connection. Kohlrieser connects the ideas of Bowlby with leadership development and the relationship between manager and employee. Precisely this relationship, which essentially resembles the relationship between parent and child, easily evokes old patterns. Unfulfilled desires and unspoken expectations of the past are projected onto the other in this case. An insecure attachment style, either an anxious-preoccupied, dismissive-avoidant, or fearful-avoidant, will cause, for example, too much or too little perceived distance. This can cause irritation, give rise to insecurity, and will lead to too much or too little risk- or initiative-taking. Leaders (but also counselors) who are able to see through such patterns within themselves and others and dare to discuss the patterns with their employees (or clients) are able to make the connection.

This attachment during adulthood (Mikulincer & Shaver, 2010) has effects on groups and teams at work, and in the more individual relationship between a manager and the employee he or she leads. The personal attachment style of each individual certainly contributes to this, but the group or the team as a whole, the network of different team members as well as the manager, can become new attachment figures. Employees in the organization can, through their membership or participation in a group or team, use the proximity in a similar way to how they used the proximity of attachment figures from their family of origin: as sources of support and security on the one hand and a basis from which to explore on the other—to develop and grow professionally. Psychological safety within teams refers to the conviction, shared by all team members, that the team is a safe place where they can take risks relating to interpersonal relationships (Edmondson, 1999). Just like individual attachment figures who serve as a secure base, groups can also encourage people to acquire new skills. Group cohesion, an aspect of group dynamics, offers an entryway to connect attachment theory and group processes. The stronger the cohesion in a group, in terms of coordination, cooperation, agreement, and mutual support, the more the members of the group will feel protected, supported, and encouraged by the group. In other words, the more cohesion there is in the group, the more members of the group will be able, from their own working model, to enter into secure attachment relationships with the group. From a group with predominantly secure attachment relationships, members with less secure attachment styles, who have less positive expectations about the group based on their working models, will be able to become more securely attached.

The individual manager can also act as a secure base for his or her employees, by being accessible, available, and sensitive and receptive to the needs of the employees. By providing appropriate advice, giving direction, and offering moral and emotional support to meet challenges, the secure base manager enables his or her employees to fully develop themselves and expand their professionalism. Here too, experiencing threat plays an important role in activating old attachment strategies. When employees perceive developments as threatening, they will be able to approach the manager who is seen as a safe attachment figure in an effort to reduce their unrest. Depending on the attachment styles of employees and managers, their working models about themselves and others, whether their own attachment style is secure, avoidant, anxious, or ambivalent, needs and strategies may, however, clash:

1. Securely attached managers are able to deal with the different needs of the employees. Based on his or her secure attachment, the manager can act as a so-called strong-enough leader and give trust and hope to the employees. Also, insecurely attached employees can best connect with a securely attached manager.
2. On the other hand, insecurely attached managers and insecurely attached employees are at high risk that the cooperation and the giving and receiving of leadership will not go well. Certainly, the combination of an avoidant-attached supervisor who does not address the need for proximity of an anxious-attached employee creates tension. The combination of an anxious-attached manager who closely watches over the shoulder of an avoidant employee stemming from the need for grip and control can lead to great tension.

However, when both the manager and the employee are avoidantly attached, they can allow each other freedom to a certain extent and maintain a good business relationship based on a mutual need for autonomy and space. Equally, a manager and an employee who are both anxiously attached are able to achieve excellent cooperation in business based on a mutual need for support, although this might seem suffocating to another person.

Change After Change

There will be room for connection to the new beginning at the end of the change, only when there has been room for goodbye. The reason 70% of the changes in organizations do not go well is partly because organizations do not make room for their people to say goodbye.

> *On the one hand, employees are invited and pressed to put all they have into their work, . . . working creatively together with colleagues*

> *on the basis of openness and trust for maximum productive use of their work energy. On the other hand, . . . their person and their emotions hardly carry any weight in mergers and reorganizations.*
>
> (Kunneman, 2009, p. 24)

When avoiding talking about the feelings and needs relating to the ending and saying goodbye to a part of the organization, when avoiding that sore spot, resistance will rise up. This resistance is however not aimed at the change itself, it is aimed at the pain of the change, a pain that is being denied and ignored and therefore disappears below the surface. It is possible to make room for a new connection by looking at resistance from a different perspective, by seeing the employee's loyalty and connection with the old familiar situation behind the resistance and giving employees the opportunity to say goodbye to this situation. Leaders who are willing to show vulnerability and talk about what they find difficult in saying goodbye, in the change, in the reactions of the environment, and who are willing to talk about this with others in the organization, are able to make the connection. Bonding cannot be forced, it can only occur in a dialogue between individual and organization about vulnerability and discomfort on both sides.

With every change where there is insufficient opportunity to say goodbye, a number of employees remain 'behind' in the old situation. On the outside they seem to go along with the new way of working, but emotionally and psychologically they are no longer connected. With every change, the organization runs the risk of losing the involvement of more and more employees. There is an accumulation of losses, comparable to the forming of sedimentary rock: layer by layer (see Figure 9.3). If a cross-section were to be done of the

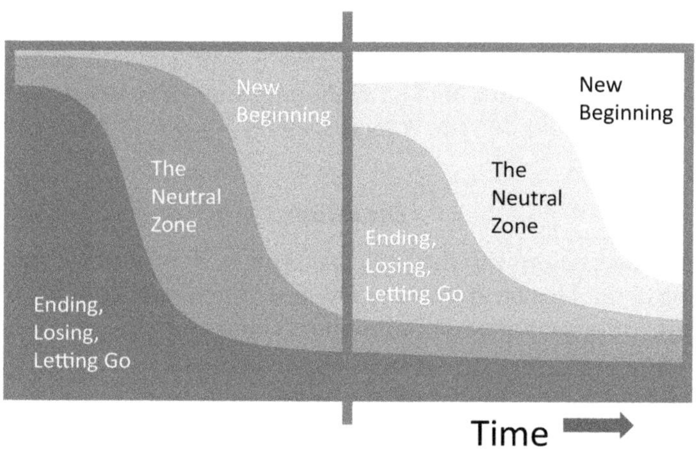

Figure 9.3 Accumulated Losses When Change After Change Occurs in an Organization

workforce by an 'organizational geologist' or an 'organizational archaeologist,' they would find all the failed changes from the past as solidified organizational grief among the employees or, in other words, solidified grief.

The main question with changes, especially accumulated changes, is whether there are any practical things managers can do to lead employees through the different phases. Most important is taking time to reflect, despite the ever-present time pressure, by consciously looking back at where the organization has come from and what the changes mean for and to the employees (Brockner, 1988), and by looking at resistance differently, not as unwillingness or inability, but as an expression of the difficulty of letting go of the attachment and loyalty to the old familiar environment. If managers want to help employees deal with the loss that comes with change, they cannot ignore the themes of farewell and loss on the Transition Cycle during the reorganization. These themes need to be given attention too, if necessary, after the fact; managers can retrospectively recognize that employees have suffered losses and, where appropriate, facilitate saying goodbye by their employees. A ritual can be used to mark the moment symbolically in time.

Rituals are a tribute to the past and are therefore effective in transitions (see also Chapter 5). Rituals provide a certain degree of continuity between the old and the new organization, for instance, when objects with a symbolic meaning from the old organization are given a visible place in the new organization. Such objects then serve as transitional objects (Winnicott, 1951). A transitional object (a concept from child psychology) refers to 'an object that, objectively and in our perception, belongs exclusively to the external reality, but is just as much a part of the child and of its inner world as a part of the outside world' (Witte, 1980). Typical transitional objects from childhood are cuddly toys and blankets that carry the nest odor and thus symbolize the secure attachment. It turns out 'that transitional phenomena never actually disappear from our lives; the 'transitional area of experience' continues to exist in adult life and is the meeting point between the inner and outer world' (Kets de Vries & Balazs, 1997).

Dialogue

After the conversation with the principal, Amber, from the case study at the beginning of this chapter, decided to follow up on the advice of her friend, to have a few conversations with a counselor (Laura).

Laura: Hi Amber, it is good to see you again.
Amber: Good morning. Yes, thank you for being able to see me again so soon.
Laura: What would you like to talk about today?
Amber: I keep asking myself, what did I miss? That question keeps coming to mind, over and over again. What did I miss?

Laura: The question 'What did I miss?' keeps coming to mind, you say. Are there answers that come to mind when you ask the question?
Amber: I just keep searching again and again whether I missed a clue somewhere. I think back to conversations, incidents. I also think about whether there were any staff members who complained behind my back or something.
Laura: So, in your mind you are searching for answers and you are examining all the possible scenarios in your head. But you can't get a grip on it, nor find answers. Is that correct?
Amber: Yes, I get stuck, it is like I keep going around in circles.
Laura: Apparently you can't find any answers by looking at it from the perspective that you have always had, time and again.
Amber: What do you mean by that?
Laura: Every person looks at her environment from her own framework. From her own background. We have all developed a way of interpreting the environment through education and experience. And we respond to that environment, to other people, to situations, from our framework. This is convenient, because that gives an overview and also a certain degree of automation. But it can also get in the way. Like now, for example. From what you indicate, I get the idea that your framework, your perspective, can't give you an answer to the situation that has come up at your work.
Amber: I can follow what you are saying, but I believe that I don't quite understand.
Laura: Is it okay if we explore together whether we can broaden your framework, so that you can look at the situation differently?
Amber: Yes, that sounds like a good idea, although I am not quite sure how to do that.
Laura: I will show you how. I have a pile of colored mats here. We are going to work with them to get a better understanding of it. Please choose and place a mat that represents your vision.
Amber: I will take this blue one then. Should I just put it down on the floor?
Laura: Yes, where you feel that it should lie. And then choose mats for yourself and for your team. And put the mats down in relation to your vision.
Amber: Um, I will put this red one down for my team and I choose this orange one to represent myself.
Laura: I see that you place yourself very close to your vision and your team very close to you.
Amber: Yes, I think that I stand closest to my vision. And that the team is looking at me.
Laura: How does it feel to look at it like that?
Amber: It gives me a warm, fuzzy feeling. This feels nice.
Laura: Now I would like you to put mats down for the old principal and the new principal, and the other staff members.

Amber: That is a lot harder. Especially the other staff members, because they are not actually one single group.
Laura: How are they divided up?
Amber: There is a group that is driven and wants innovation and a group that mainly just wants to get on with their lessons and does not want too much hassle.
Laura: Okay, then take two mats for the staff.
Amber: A yellow one for the staff that want innovation and a green one for the other group.
Laura: And now one for the school's vision.
Amber: The school's vision? Hmmm, that a good one. I will take this white one for that.
Laura: And then possibly the two most important ones: the students and their parents.
Amber: Yes, that's what we do it for. The purple is for the students, which I will put close by and this grey is for the parents. They are lying slightly further away.
Laura: Now there is a whole playground in front of us. What do you notice as you look at all this? (See Figure 9.4.)

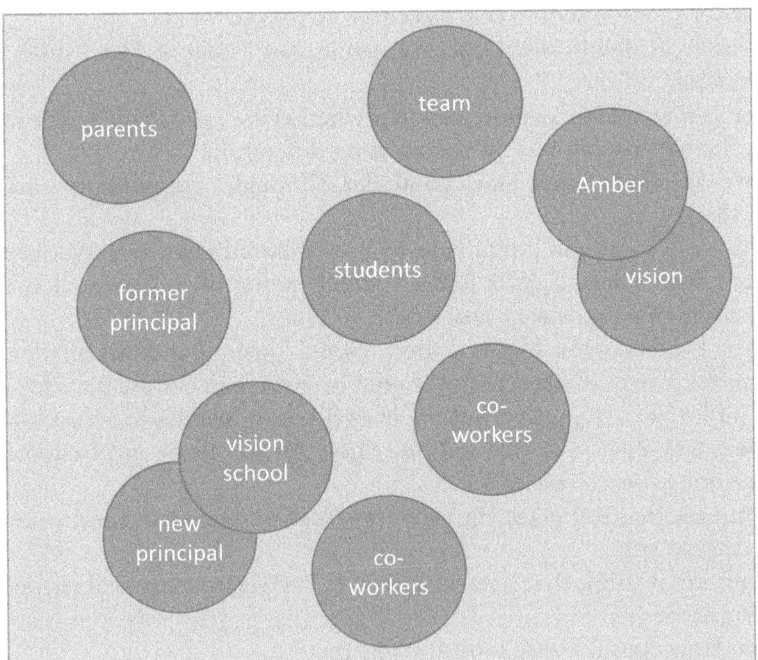

Figure 9.4 Gaining Perspective Using Mats

Amber: It is strange to look at it like that. What I immediately notice is that one side is much more colorful than the other. And that it almost looks like two separate camps. That's crazy actually. Almost as if there is a gap.
Laura: What does that say?
Amber: I never realized that there was such a distance. I also see that I am actually the furthest away from the principal and the school's vision. And the students and one group of colleagues are in between the two visions. It almost seems like there is a fight going on or something. That frightens me a bit.
Laura: What frightens you most?
Amber: Suddenly I understand! I never realized that there was a fight, but suddenly that makes it quite clear. I was totally preoccupied with my own vision and never realized that this (she points to the side where the old principal, the school's vision, the new principal, and the parents stand) was there at all. How could I have missed that! Unbelievable!
Laura: You could say that your perspective was focused mainly on this part (points to the group of mats with Amber, her vision, the team, the students, and staff members) and that you could not see that part (pointing to the other mats). You will notice that if you stand on the mats and actually look at the setup from the different perspectives, you get even more insight. We will do that next time. And then I will also tell you a bit more about the Bridges model of transitions.
Amber: In any case, I am feeling much calmer already. I look forward to next time!

Questions for Self-Reflection

- Which losses can you identify in your own (education) career?
- What attention was given by your education/work to these losses?
- When have you ever felt resistance to change in the past?
- What helped you to lessen the resistance and what increased it?
- What or who are your secure bases in your education/work?
- What does your education/work mean to you? In what way is it influenced by loss?
- What do you need to mark an ending, to say goodbye?
- What is it that you need in the neutral zone?
- How do you celebrate the transition to a new beginning?

Exercises

Exercise—Symbol for Work

Which object symbolizes the client's relationship with his or her job? What does this object mean to the client? How does this object fulfill the function of an attachment object, of a transitional object?

Instruction: Counsel each other in groups of three (A is the counselor, B is the client, and C is the observer), in a dialogue on the meaning of a transitional object using the questions as described above. Evaluate each round briefly and switch roles.

Exercise—Transition on the Lifeline

Which transition periods can the client identify on his or her lifeline?

Instruction: Counsel each other in groups of three (A is the counselor, B is the client, and C is the observer), in a dialogue on transitions you recognize on your lifeline as per the instructions in Chapter 1 and which you worked out further in Chapter 5. Use the questions for self-reflection from the previous section of this chapter. Evaluate each round briefly and switch roles.

Notes

1. This video can be viewed on YouTube at https://www.youtube.com/watch?v=n6w2tXAj0M4 (last visited on 12 May 2019).
2. Exodus 14: 11–12. Quoted from: www.biblegateway.com.
3. Linus van Pelt, from the comic book series *Peanuts* about Charlie Brown and his friends, by Charles M. Schulz. Linus is one of the youngest in the series and almost always has his precious blue blanket with him, while he is sucking on his thumb. This blue blanket fulfills the function of attachment object, or *transitional object* from child psychology (Winnicott, 1951), as loveys are often for children. In the Flemish comic series *Spike and Suzy* or *Willy and Wanda* from Studio Vandersteen, the rag doll Molly (or Sawdust or Muffin) fulfills this function for Suzy (Wanda).
4. Numbers 14: 2–4. Quoted from: www.biblegateway.com.

10

DIALOGUE

Putting Loss Into Perspective

A Case Study

Ben is an experienced counselor. He has his own grief counseling practice. He loves his work and is successful at it. But at the moment he has landed in a difficult patch with a client. It's a woman in her fifties. She has come to sessions a few times, but Ben has lately started dreading new sessions with her. He finds her stubborn and gets the feeling that she will not take much advice from him. After each session, she emails him with all kinds of questions that came up afterwards. He tries to answer the questions meticulously and kindly, but he is becoming increasingly annoyed about the time it costs him. In an open conversation with a colleague and friend to blow off steam, he becomes aware of how much of an impact it is having on him. Although it helps temporarily to vent his anger, it still does not change anything. Only when he attends a supervision session does it become clear how often he feels insecure about what he has to offer and he begins to understand the problem. This client does not validate him. Her pattern of asking things time and again, elicits the response from him that he is not giving enough. And instead of setting boundaries for himself and deciding what he can and wants to give her, he wears himself out and tends to withdraw. This pattern is not unknown to him. He has worked on this theme before. Now it requires attention again. He thinks back on his youth and his mother. She has since passed away. As a child he had wanted to do everything to see her happy. But even as a little boy, after spending months saving his pocket money, when he bought a bunch of red roses for her, she had preferred yellow. He feels a stab of pain to his heart thinking about it. Time and time again, he is forced to accommodate this pain before he is able to say: 'No further. This is what I have to give but no more.'

Professional Counseling Is a Transitional Encounter in the Here and Now

In the counseling process, saying goodbye always addresses several layers. The client wants to leave something behind and move on to something new. He or she wants to say goodbye to ineffective behaviors, emotions, conflicts, worrying, and so on. Moving on to a new situation requires a goodbye. The client's attachment history and earlier moments of loss on his or her lifeline resonate in that goodbye. Counseling loss is a collaborative effort by counselor and client. Together they explore, by acknowledging and recognizing, which obstacles hinder the integration of the loss in the client's life story and must be negotiated. The counselor takes on the role of (temporary) secure base (see Chapter 3) or attachment figure. Even though people can learn to be a secure base for themselves, the necessity of having external secure bases always comes to the fore in times of loss and transition (Bowlby, 1988d; Kohlrieser et al., 2012; Van der Kolk, 2015; Kosminsky & Jordan, 2016).

The underlying attitude of a capable counselor consists of a reliable presence, acknowledgement, and listening. The counselor is curious about the story and context of the client. This is only possible if the counselor also dares to accept 'everything' that occurs within him- or herself in the encounter with the client.

> *Learn your theories as well as you can, but put them [underneath things somehow] when you touch the miracle of the living soul. Not [reducing] theories but your own creative individuality [should be in the front seat then].*
>
> (Jung, 1928, p. 361)

The counselor needs to stay curious to his or her own sensitivity, attachment patterns, life story, and obstacles and needs to be willing to share these discoveries and sensations with the client if it serves the process. So, we can say that the inner curiosity (of the counselor towards him- or herself) is just as important as the outer curiosity (towards the other). As a counselor, you are prepared to be fully present as you are. That will allow the other to accept that they are also worthy of being fully present. Carl Rogers speaks of 'unconditional positive regard' (Rogers, 1957). That experience in itself is already healing, because it teaches the other person to accept and appreciate themselves and all their experiences more, just as they are.

The relationship between counselor and client even makes it possible to bring about changes at a neurological level. Good counseling actually enables changes in the wiring of the brain. The relationship, the trust between counselor and client, is more important than the underlying theory or the applied techniques. In order to explore whether there are underlying attachment issues, the counselor must experiment and not theorize. The counselor should open themselves to what is presented in the encounter. 'The truth lies in the client, not so much in psychological theories. It is therefore important to use methods that bring the clients implicit learning experiences clearly into consciousness, without imposing our own external interpretations' (Ecker et al., 2012, p. 100).

Presence in a counseling or therapeutic conversation is used to convey unconditional acceptance thereby validating the inherent value of the other person. It gives the client permission, as it were, to explore their inner self without reservation and gives them an opportunity to experience not being in danger of being rejected or criticized in the conversation with the counselor (Pos et al., 2014). This creates a space for counseling, also called the transitional space (van Wielink, 2014).

Within the transitional space that results from the connection between the counselor and the client, the client can start to explore. The instruments used by the counselor (in the form of exercises and dialogue) are essentially ritual work: they help promote the transition from old to new (behavior, perception, experience). This ritual work, done where necessary also with respect to events that took place earlier on the lifeline, promotes the resilience and the autonomy of the client. It frees up choices and frees the client from being held hostage by the 'then and there.'

The encounter cannot simply be forced, nor is it 'fixable.' There are no tools or tricks for that, only a framework of set conditions within which the encounter could take place. In this sense, an authentic encounter, in which healing can take place, also has an air of mystery surrounding it.

Core Skills of the Counselor

When we say there are no tools and tricks available that will 'work' in the encounter, that does not mean that there are no instruments available. We like to call these core skills. But these comprise more a part of the basic attitude of the counselor than a collection of techniques (Kosminsky & Jordan, 2016). By using these core skills, counselors can truly meet with their clients. After having found the right balance between these skills, they can use their knowledge and experience and do interventions.

1. Promoting Security and Trust in the Relationship

 The therapeutic relationship is the most important factor for success in counseling a client. The extent to which the counselor is able to create a basis of security and trust is essential. By adjusting the support (in the beginning) to the attachment style and the client's need, a relationship can be built whereby the client feels comfortable. It makes a big difference to the tempo and the structure of the counseling whether the client is securely or insecurely attached. When the client is securely attached, the bond of trust will generally be in place faster and there will quickly be a basic feeling of security from which to work. A fearful-avoidant client will probably need more time to show the necessary openness. Anxious-preoccupied clients can be claiming and dependent, so initially it seems as if there is security and trust very quickly, but at a later stage, it may become clear that the real fear has been concealed. This requires the counselor to observe and take note of his own attachment dynamic and, perhaps beyond his first tendency, to be caring and daring for the client

 The counselor assumes the role of temporary attachment figure and secure base. With the term *temporary*, we refer to the duration of the counseling period, which per definition is limited in time. The perceived effect of the relationship between client and counselor, in the form of a powerful memory, can also serve as a secure base far beyond the counseling relationship.

2. The Paradox of 100% Caring and 100% Daring

 A secure attachment can be achieved when sufficient caring and sufficient daring are offered. This certainly applies to the counseling relationship. A counselor who is caring when in contact with the client, offers safety, a sense of welcome, confidentiality, and consolation. The client feels accepted, seen, worthwhile. In this setting, the client builds trust in the environment and in themselves. The counselor and client build a comfort zone, as it were. A safe space from which the client can then take new steps. The counselor's attitude is daring when encouraging the client to look further, dig deeper, jump higher than the client initially wanted to, dared to, or could go. This is how the client builds the trust and confidence in themselves.

 The counselor offers 100% caring and 100% daring. One without the other gives either a lot of warmth, but little movement (especially caring and little daring), or a lot of action, but little real change or risk of crossing boundaries (with a lot of daring, but little caring).

 We would carefully compare this with the Dual Process Model from Chapter 6. Counseling loss is about making movement possible between the loss and restoration orientation. Sensing how to keep this balance is

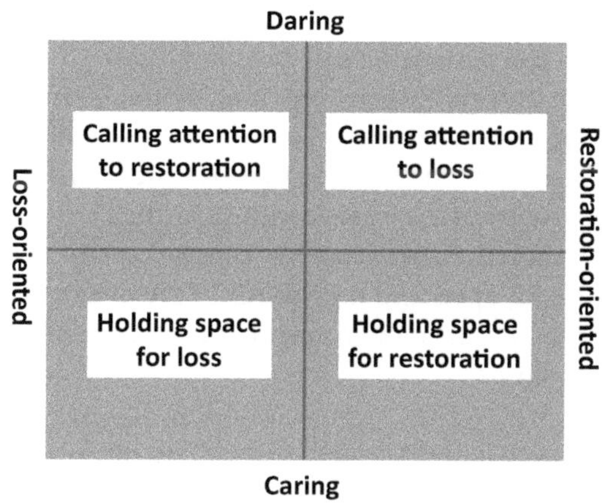

Figure 10.1 Balance Between Caring and Daring and the Dual Process Model

also facilitated by making your approach with the client open to discussion (see Figure 10.1).

3. Empathy

The human brain has 'mirror neurons,' neuronal activity that is activated by the observation of actions or feelings of another (Iacoboni, 2009). This ability is called empathy. In the relationship between counselor and client, the same mirror neurons are activated as in the connection between caregiver and child in the attachment relationship. Empathy therefore plays a significant role in the counseling relationship. Empathy has an emotional and a cognitive component. The feelings that the counselor perceives within in response to the feelings perceived in the other form the emotional component. The counselor experiences the same feelings as the client at that moment. Through the cognitive component, the counselor is able to distinguish between self and the other and can then, from his or her own perspective, determine where the emotional reaction of the other person comes from. This cognitive aspect helps counselors keep their emotions to themselves while supporting the other. From this cognitive aspect, they, despite their own feelings, can explore with the other what lies beneath or behind their primary reaction.

4. Presence- and Relationship-Oriented

Between the client and the counselor transference patterns can be elicited due to the attachment styles at play. Transference means that the response in the here and now is based on old patterns or situations. In the old situation, the reaction was helpful or appropriate but is no longer so in the current situation. And yet the reaction is elicited. Not only the client but also the counselor can respond from a transference pattern (called countertransference in the case of the counselor). In fact, the question is not whether that happens, because it will, but how it is dealt with. The counselor who is able to perceive the transference in the client and in him- or herself, can work with it in the counseling relationship, even when the relationship between counselor and client comes under pressure. By being open and mild, both to the client and to him- or herself, the counselor can make room in which to explore and still guard personal boundaries.

5. Enduring Your Own and Someone Else's Discomfort and Suffering

   The quality of a counselor in enduring his or her own sensitivity and in dealing with his or her feelings of inaptitude and inadequacy, knowing that the suffering of the client cannot (simply) 'be solved' by staying close to the client, often does not come naturally. By taking good care of him- or herself, paying attention to his or her own needs and desires and seeking support from colleagues, the counselor gives him- or herself a solid foundation on which to stay present and endure.

6. Knowledge of Self and Attention

   The counselor can only be and remain really close to the other person if he or she can stay close to him- or herself and has good knowledge of personal patterns. As mentioned in the introduction, this is about 'working from the inside out.' The self-knowledge gained from examining one's own experiences of attachment, connection, parting, and loss, provides the ability to truly meet the other person face-to-face and heart-to-heart.

Dialogue as a Starting Point and Grounds for Connecting

The dialogue is one of the most important, if not the most important, vehicles for counseling. No matter which intervention the counselor chooses, it will start, be accompanied by, and end with forms of dialogue. William Isaacs defined dialogue as seeking a greater truth by thinking together, a shared inquiry (life experience), a way of thinking and reflecting together (Isaacs, 1999). A greater truth in the context of guiding loss is, for example, that consolation is possible, that you can learn to deal with loss, that you can practice reconnecting, that you can learn to deal with conflict, and so on.

'Dialogue' comes from the Greek words 'dia,' meaning 'through,' and 'logos,' meaning 'word.' We use words to convey meaning. Love disappears when we cannot transmit and experience meaning in our dialogue (Bohm, 1996). Words are, as it were, containers for underlying experiences, thoughts, and feelings. In a dialogue between the counselor and the client, these containers are exchanged. The dialogue is a shared quest, a way of thinking and reflecting. Dialogue is something you do together. It therefore requires curiosity about the story that wants to emerge, that wants to be told. As you do not judge a book on a single chapter, the client's story is not 'done' after describing an experience.

In a dialogue, the focus is on discovering something new together. The depth of a dialogue takes both the client and the counselor to a different level: learning and discovering goes back and forth.

The dialogue is a special combination of listening and talking. Elisabeth Kübler-Ross introduced an approach through four quadrants to express the completeness of human beings in dialogue. These elements are given shape with words in dialogue (see Figure 10.2):

1. Emotion—feeling.
2. Cognition—thinking.
3. Physical—the body and the physical sensations.
4. Spiritual—philosophical, sense-making and meaning.

These quadrants are not separate parts within a human being, but help to make the aspects visible. In a major event such as a loss, people are inclined to respond from the quadrant where they feel most secure. The coping and surviving strategies determine which quadrant will then 'take over':

1. When reacting from the emotional quadrant, that person can be overwhelmed by feelings.
2. When reacting from the cognitive quadrant, that person can resort to rationalization.

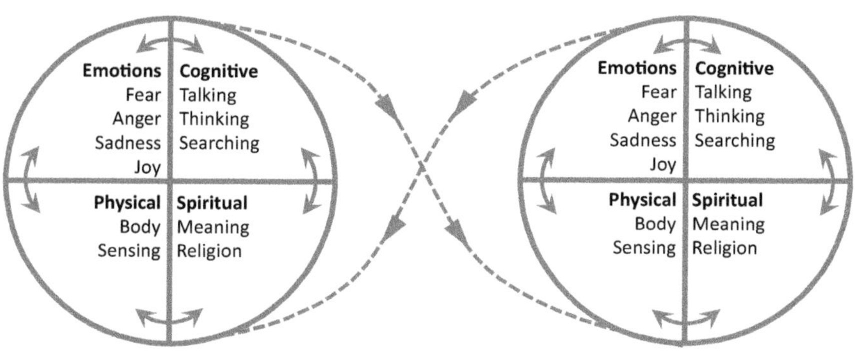

Figure 10.2 George Kohlrieser's Dialogue Model, Based on Elisabeth Kübler-Ross

Source: George Kohlrieser, 2006; copied with permission from John Wiley

3. When reacting from the physical quadrant, that person can find an outlet in sports, exercise, labor, drinking, or substance abuse.
4. When reacting from the spiritual quadrant, that person can seek refuge in religion or 'higher meaning.'

The role of the counselor is to address all quadrants in a dialogue with the client proportionately and to allow all four of his or her quadrants to be present too. This reciprocal communication between two or more people is about sharing thoughts, physical sensations, ideas, ideals, dreams, and feelings. This is about sharing back and forth all experiences that occur in life (Lynch, 1979).

Words have energy and impact. But how do clients express what goes on inside them and how do they find the words, so that the counselor understands the meaning of these words?

Because clients often do not know what they are feeling or because, out of fear or shame, they block the reality of what is going on inside them, it is often difficult to communicate about loss. Clients who cannot verbalize the pain and grief inside are much more likely to get sick, show aggressiveness, become or are addicted, become depressed or get burned out, and have a lot of stress or struggles in their relationship or at work (Lynch, 1979; Kohlrieser, 2006).

As you can see in the various case studies in this book, there are many questions that can be asked. Practicing asking questions is a lifelong journey for the counselor. It requires of you to continue exploring which questions you are inclined to ask both yourself and the other person and which you avoid asking.

About Consolation in Dialogue

Wanting to console someone who has suffered a loss is a deeply human, primary need. Just like a client's need to be consoled. But how can someone be consoled if the situation of loss, causing the pain, cannot be changed?

According to the dictionary, consolation means 'to ease pain or suffering.' However, the dictionary is less clear in how this can be achieved. In counseling, consolation is to fully acknowledge someone in his or her emotions and feelings. Facilitating someone's reconnection with their emotions will have a soothing effect, but not before it has first become seemingly 'worse.' The client, for example, seems helpless, shows violent emotions (many tears or anger with corresponding sounds), or becomes apathetic, silent. David Boadella (1973) described five phases in the development of emotions up to and including their dissipation: charge, tension, discharge, relaxation, and flexibility.

Acknowledgement of emotions brings relief and relief may be a beginning for its softening. Many clients will confirm that it is difficult, annoying, and painful to connect with the emotion. In fact, it can result in evasive behavior or cancelling or moving counseling sessions. And often after having expressed the emotion, the client will say that he or she feels relief, or is able to breathe more easily, or able to focus again.

For the counselor, it is a case of not 'covering up,' 'appeasing,' or 'rescuing' the client. Healing consolation is the ability to sit on your own hands and keep them there for as long as is needed. This is often quite 'daring' for the counselor. A secure base, says John Bowlby in perhaps one of his most telling statements, 'is largely a waiting game' (Bowlby, 1988d). Consoling is not a goal in itself for the counselor, but at most a (very welcome) additional dividend from the counseling process.

Healing consolation makes it possible to learn, see new perspectives. And clients are only capable of real contact and taking in (new) information if the brain is calm and can do its work (Fiddelaers-Jaspers & van Wielink, 2015; Reijmerink & van Wielink, 2016).

Our desire to console and be consoled is inextricably linked to our very first experiences with secure bases. In reaching out to these first secure bases, we have developed inner voices at a very early age with respect to consolation. Two of those voices are listed below:

- *The Inner Consoler* is the internal representation of one's own secure attachment, the inner proximity of the attachment figures. The Inner Consoler allows the presence of grief, fear, and shame. The Inner Consoler knows that proximity heals, and that the proximity does not have to be physical, it can also be emotional or psychological. The Inner Consoler relies on experiences with secure bases in the past that have been internalized.
- *The Inner Critic* tells the person that he or she should not make a spectacle of him- or herself. The Inner Critic is a consequence of one's (experiences with) insecure attachment, the voice of negative critical parental norms, values, and convictions.

The counselor invites the Inner Consoler and the client to join in. In this way, the client can learn to make contact with this part of themselves intuitively, or learn to do so in the counseling session. A playful way to do this is to work with symbols, for example cuddly toys, images, or stones during counseling and, to take it a step further, to invite the client to make a similar symbol available to themselves at home.

The Inner Critic does not offer consolation. In spite of that, the client may have difficulty silencing the Inner Critic to allow for solace. Also, the counselor can consciously or unconsciously address this critic, but also intentionally or unintentionally. The attachment experiences of both the client and the counselor play an important role here. It requires a conscious effort from the counselor to stay alert and deal with this.

Each person finds solace in a different way/place. Words are often unnecessary. The fact that there is someone there for you may already be enough for the client. Music, poetry, nature, playing children. There is so much that can offer solace and can serve as a secure base.

Within the context of counseling of loss, we list the following recommendations regarding consolation below (Boswijk-Hummel, 2003):

- To console is to communicate, both verbally and non-verbally.
- To console starts with being available and listening.
- Consolation is (sometimes) followed by questions (and not by the issue being solved or filling in the answers for the client).
- Consolation implies acknowledgement of the other person's feelings and of their being human.
- Consolation implies proximity, connection, and intimacy; consoling is thus a relational activity. Being there is more important than what you have to say.

Dialogue and Old (Parental) Messages

As they grow up, children develop frameworks or patterns, called working models by Bowlby. These working models give them a perspective on themselves and on their environment. This gives support, because it makes reactions from the environment more predictable for them. In a family, for example, asking for candy can be punished, while pain or sadness may be distracted with candy. A child can then develop a pattern in which they do not directly ask for what they need, but will use emotions to demand attention. Patterns like these (for both counselor and client) can have a major influence on communication, both on the daily communication at work or in private, and in the conversations with the counselor. A powerful model for exploring patterns comes from Transactional Analysis (TA) (Berne, 2016; Koopmans, 2014). The term *transaction* refers to the communication between two individuals.

An important principle of TA is that the personality has three ego states: The Parent Ego State, the Adult Ego State, and the Child Ego State. Both the Parent and the Child State also have a subdivision in Nurturing Parent and Critical Parent and Free Child and Adapted Child.

1. Parent
   In this ego state, a person will display mainly the behaviors, thoughts, and feelings that are copied from parents or caregivers. The Parent consists of two parts:

a. Nurturing Parent
This is the parent's nurturing and supporting role. In a positive sense, this is the role where the child is fed and supported physically and mentally. However, a possible distortion of this role is when too much care has a suffocating and obstructive effect on the development of the child.

b. Critical Parent
This is the limiting role of the parent. In a positive sense, this is the role where healthy structure is offered to the child, where the parent is powerfully present and serves as an inspiring example. Within this role, however, there is also a distortion in which the criticism can be used as punitive and controlling.

Both parent roles contain, in both positive and negative senses, all behaviors of people who also position themselves, though in different contexts, as parents. For example, when a manager at work approaches employees as capable adults and dares to set firm goals with confidence. Or the counselor who makes it too easy for the client because he or she assumes that the client is not ready for a 'next step,' without bringing this assumption into the dialogue.

2. Adults
This is the neutral, rational, norm-free position in which a person formulates their own choices not obstructed by convictions. It is the position from which observation is possible and feedback can be given.
3. Child
In this ego state, behaviors, thoughts, and feelings from childhood are repeated. The Child Ego State consists of two parts:

a. Free Child
This is the autonomous condition in which the child is free to play, discover and learn, separate from parental rules or restrictions. In a positive sense, this state contains the life force of the child, playfulness, and creative ability. The possible distortion would be having no boundaries, a narcissistic focus on the self and dramatically forcing one's own opinion on others.

b. Adapted Child
This is the situation where the child is limited by the boundaries and the rules within the system. The child is not entirely free to make their own choices, because it runs the risk of being rejected by the parent(s), being punished, and losing the love and care of the parents. In a positive sense, this state contains the obedient, friendly, and docile side of the child, where the child obeys according to social rules. The possible distortion consists of a scared child who no longer displays any initiative, waits, becomes overly dependent, and asks for permission constantly.

> From birth this is the position that the child unconsciously occupies, and it is part of the reaching out for care and protection. Depending on the availability and reactions of the attachment figure, the child will develop within the positions of the free or adapted child and possibly even occupy an extreme position. In addition to the genetic predisposition, the largely unconscious choice for this position is always based on the experience that the behavior from that position towards these specific attachment figures offers the greatest chance of the needs being met.

From their early years, children already learn to make unconscious decisions about how they should behave in order to 'survive,' to get or retain the (implicit) approval and appreciation of their parents. Incidentally, 'approval' and 'appreciation' can sometimes be expressed in very different ways in practice. Negative attention is sometimes better than no attention. So even patterns that seem destructive are aimed at bonding with the parents. This strategy can even determine their further adult life. Obstructive beliefs are often shaped like parental commands and prohibitions, also called 'injunctions' (Berne, 2016; Koopmans, 2014). These are negative messages that children receive from their parents, educators, or teachers, whether or not literally and whether or not consciously. These injunctions are associated with an unsafe part of an attachment style. On the other hand, children are given positive and empowering messages, also known as 'permissions,' when their parents, educators, or teachers are secure bases for them. These permissions belong to the secure part of an attachment style.

The three ego states exist within the personality. As such they are represented in every person. In each situation and with each conversation partner, one of the ego states is more prominent than the others. For example, a person can mainly respond to his or her counselor from the ego state of Adjusted Child and, in contact with the teacher of his or her child's school, speak mainly from a Critical Parent. Inside the person, the ego states can also be in 'discussion' with each other. For example, someone can reprimand him- or herself about a wrongly placed remark.

Clients can get insight into their inner dialogues by examining which permissions and which injunctions they have accepted as becoming part of themselves. A list of injunctions and permissions has been developed in TA. Sometimes it becomes immediately clear whether and how they are present. If not, going through this list, and testing and feeling what the message conjures up in you, it is possible to trace which contains 'truth' for you. This conviction can then be challenged by comparing the original cause in the past with the situations in the present where the same reaction occurs. Then other choices can be made by allowing permissions to take the place of the injunction.

Examples of permissions:

- It is okay to be (to exist)
- It is okay to be you.
- It is okay to grow up.
- It is okay to be a child.
- It is okay to be successful.
- It is okay to do/learn/experiment/make mistakes.
- It is okay to be important.
- It is okay to belong.
- It is okay to be close.
- It is okay to feel.
- It is okay to think.
- It is okay to be healthy.

Examples of injunctions:

- Do not be (do not exist).
- Do not be you.
- Do not grow up.
- Do not be a child.
- Do not be successful.
- Do not do anything, do not make mistakes.
- Do not be important.
- Do not belong.
- Do not be close.
- Do not feel.
- Do not think.
- Do not be healthy/normal.

In addition to these permissions and injunctions, there are also the so-called driver messages, a translation that children make in order to get approval for their behavior despite parental prohibitions:

- Be strong.
- Hurry up.
- Do your best.
- Give (others) pleasure.
- Be perfect.
- Be the best.

If the client manages to get these usually unconscious convictions out in the open, it can help with new beliefs and the client can practice new behaviors. However, that is not easy. There is often a deep loyalty to the patterns, the ways, and the rules of the family of origin. By doing it differently, this loyalty is threatened. To question convictions, even when they are hindrances, can therefore cause guilt towards the system of origin. It requires a solid basis of security and trust in counseling. This basis can be laid in the counselor's approach that is adapted to fit the client's attachment style and is permissive towards loyalty to the system of origin.

Attachment Dynamics in Dialogue

Early in children's development, convictions about themselves and the people around them are developed (Berne, 2016). A positive self-image leads to the conviction 'I am OK' and a positive image of someone else to the conviction 'you are OK' (Harris, 2012). The opposite images lead to the beliefs 'I am not OK' and 'you are not OK.' By combining these four images, four quadrants are created and form a matrix. These quadrants can be matched to the four attachment styles that Bowlby distinguished (Kohlrieser et al., 2012) (see Figure 10.3).

The convictions or images that people have about themselves and about others dictate the type of communication (the transactions in which they relate to others).

> *The encounter with the 'dark side' of the other evokes reactions from our own dark side. We, as counselors, should take on the challenge to examine our own dark side and be aware of our own old pain, our patterns, pitfalls and allergies. After all: you can only bring your client as far as where you are yourself!*
>
> (van Wielink et al., 2012, p. 20)

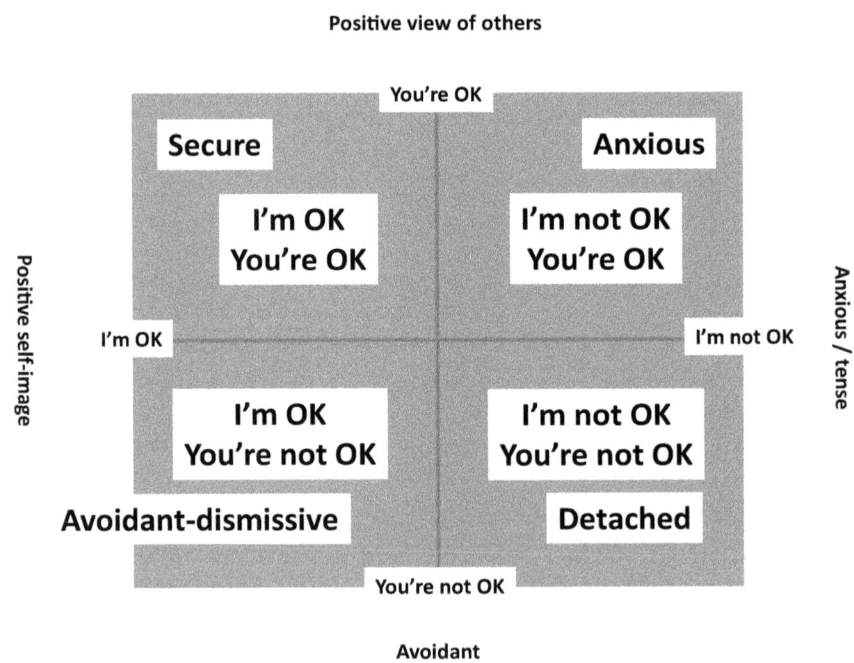

Figure 10.3 Attachment Styles Plotted on the 'I'm OK, You're OK' Matrix

Source: Kohlrieser et al., 2012; copied with permission from John Wiley

Becoming aware of convictions and the emotions evoked in situations and contact with others helps someone get an insight into themselves and their behavior.

The feeling is not in itself the cause of the behavior, but it is a reaction to an event. Different people can respond differently to the same event. How that event is perceived dictates the reaction, which in turn is driven by the thoughts that someone has about that event. It is well summarized in the ABC model from Rational Emotional Therapy (RET) (Ellis & Baldon, 1993):

Activating Events (A) + Beliefs (B) ➔ *Emotional + Behavioural Consequences (C)*

The feeling is not the cause of the behavior, but rather one of the consequences of the event. To take it a step further: the event itself did not cause the feeling, but was at most an inducement for prompting it. What mostly determines the feeling and therefore the behavior is the thought about the event: the conviction. This thought is an ingrained conviction about what should happen in an ideal situation. Unconsciously people repeat fixed, ingrained patterns. Patterns that have once helped them a long time ago, but are no longer appropriate or fitting for who they are nor for who they want to be. Their unconscious mind has taken control, it has become survival behavior. They show old, adaptive behaviors (Stewart & Joines, 2012; Koopmans, 2014).

The ingrained patterns make it look, at that moment, like someone has no choice, at least not the freedom of choice to show other behavior, let alone to feel anything differently. He or she then experiences the infamous 'amygdala hijack,' the kidnapping of a small piece of the brain, the amygdala, through which people are taken hostage by their learned behavior from the past (Goleman, 2013; Kohlrieser, 2006). Grief can in such a way also take us hostage.

There is a fixed link between (basic) needs and (basic) emotions (Koopmans, 2014):

- Fearful—needs security
- Angry—needs boundaries
- Sad—needs support
- Happy—needs others

People do not consciously choose their needs themselves, they are given to them in the mix of genes (nature) and upbringing (nurture). At birth and while growing up, the composite of hereditary transfer and systemic contextual transfer (transfer in family of origin, one's own family, school, etc.) ensures that children receive baggage during their upbringing. They learn unconsciously and very quickly in what ways they can get their educators to meet their needs. Babies learn to literally survive, they learn to attach themselves and they learn how to bind others to them. They respond instinctively to get their needs met by showing their emotions and using them to communicate and manipulate.

With this, children lay the foundation for their behavior. They learn unconsciously and rapidly to adapt to the other important person, the parent, educator or other secure bases they meet as they grow up.

Children learn which behavior gets what results; they learn to estimate the effects of their behavior on the other person. During later education, these lessons will become more and more explicit and take the form of a social code or etiquette. But even in their earliest childhood, children unconsciously learn what works and what does not, what is and what is not allowed in their system. These rules and restrictions can also consciously or unconsciously take the shape of sentences like 'boys don't cry,' or 'girls may not get angry.' With this they learn to suppress expression of their emotions. But the underlying needs do not go away. There are therefore no 'good' or 'bad' emotions.

Structure of a Counseling Program

A counseling trajectory consists of a number of sessions, starting with an intake. During the encounters, the themes on the Transition Cycle are pivotal. It is impossible to indicate in advance which theme will be discussed at what time. The client's request is leading, as is the client's pace of recognition and acknowledgement that are necessary to explore the themes together. The original question will deepen and possibly change in every session, through the dialogue. This means that every new session begins with a new (mini) intake, a new invitation to look at the question (behind the question) and to determine which theme is important in this respect. The backgrounds to these themes as described in the previous chapters, the accompanying questions and the exercises can all be used by the counselor during his work.

The approach according to the themes of the Transition Cycle can thus serve as a framework for the counseling process. However, the order and priority of the themes are not fixed in advance and require coordination with (the development of) the client's request.

Throughout this book you have been able to read and experience how counseling people during change always requires customizing. There are no standard recipes, no techniques that always work or theories that can take away discomfort. At the end of the day, good counseling depends solely on the degree to which the counselor is actually able to 'hit it off' with his or her client. In this way counseling loss is also a journey on which one has to go the distance, practice, look at what fits, continue to gather knowledge to keep up with developments, and have sufficient supervision and peer group moments with colleagues.

You can trust that when you do the things listed above, it will be fine. It is also a good idea to check with colleagues which approach has worked for them, and to incorporate that into your work in your own way. This section therefore contains a number of suggestions for a possible general approach to a series of sessions with a client.

1. Introduction and Intake
   At the introductory session and the intake, it is firstly necessary to determine whether there is a mutual connection, and whether a basis of safety and trust develops in order to be able to work on the themes of the client's question. As a counselor you explain your working methods and together with the client you take a first look at the question that is put forward.
   Immediately in the first contact, a foundation is laid for the psychological contract and for the relationship contract. As a counselor, you are aware of what the contact with this client evokes in you. Which subjects are easily discussed during your session and where do you notice that you are reluctant? Which questions are hard to ask this client? What do you plan to bring forward and what will you still keep to yourself?
   During this first interview, the client tells you his or her reason for coming. As a counselor, you offer a direct framework to further deepen and broaden the client's request. Where does this question originate from? What would the client like to achieve by means of the counseling? What resources are there?
   Have your client make a short report every session and ask him or her to send it to you by email prior to the next session. After the first time specifically, make sure the client includes the counseling question in this report. Maybe after the first session, something will already change surrounding the client's question.
2. Contact and Welcome
   During the first contact between the counselor and the client, the theme of 'contact and welcome' is immediately touched on. As a counselor, you have an impact. Your experiences with the themes welcome and connection influence the way you welcome the client. Conversely, the client immediately will display many of his or her own experiences during the first contact. Maybe the client will try to see which way the wind blows and seem a bit reserved. Or there is immediate connection and friendliness, or maybe some resistance. Observe how that affects you as a counselor.
   You can work with the client on feeling welcome. For example, you can have your client make his or her own birth announcement (see the exercise in Chapter 2). A wonderful occasion to start with at the

beginning. And to have conversations about how welcome the client felt at the beginning of his life. How this has travelled with him since and is expressed in how he feels welcome in new places and with new people.

The genogram (see the exercise in Chapter 2) is a good way to place this welcome in a broader (systemic) perspective. You can easily create and explore the genogram together.

Give your client a homework assignment to make his lifeline as you learned about in the exercise in Chapter 1. Invite the client to make his or her lifeline on a large sheet of paper, which you can put on the floor the next time he comes.

3. Attachment

During the next session you use the lifeline as a starting point. You explore the periods together, the events above and below the line. You explore what your client became attached to, and what he or she lost. What are the big themes in your client's life? What does your client see when looking back? Which story is told? And which story (still) needs to be told?

You also explore what secure bases there are in this session. You explain what they are and how it works. About caring and daring. As homework for the next session, ask your client to create a secure base map (see the exercise in Chapter 3). Again, it is a good idea to have this done on a large sheet of paper.

Clients often do the agreed upon homework. But sometimes they do not. That is an interesting fact. First of all, it is important for you as a counselor to be aware of how the client's not doing his homework affects you. Maybe you do not have the feeling that you are being taken seriously and your reaction is stern, or maybe you will choose to ignore it and will not discuss it with your client, or maybe you think that it is because you thought you made the mistake and were unclear. There are many other thoughts and feelings that you can have when this happens. Be aware of your own patterns at such a moment, so that you can have a clear look at the client's pattern and examine together with him what made him not do the homework. Often old attachment dynamics can be hidden underneath. And that gives the input for this session, which will be about attachment.

4. Intimacy

This session will be about being able to allow someone to come close. The secure base map is a good way to access that theme. How was it to make the map? You will discuss what your client has been able to experience with these secure bases. With what did he or she connect well on the subject of intimacy? What made it go so well with this secure base? In which secure base was this missing and was there perhaps fear or shame?

In the meantime, you have already had a number of conversations together. How is the intimacy between you? How close can you and do you dare to come as a counselor? How does the client respond to proximity? Once again, be aware of how you, as a counselor, move around the theme intimacy. What do you let others see, and can you be vulnerable? Maybe you find it difficult when people really get close or do you like to be reserved. The contact between counselor and client is an important source to work with. So, if the client tells you about intimacy in contact with secure bases, you can also ask how that reflects in the counseling sessions. What does and what does he or she not show. What is different or perhaps the same as in the contact with others.

Next, you can also use the lifeline to continue talking about loss. The counselor can, for example, ask the client: if you look at the lifeline and the secure base map, what is your greatest loss? And what would you like to say goodbye to?

For homework you can ask your client to write a 'goodbye letter' (see the exercise in Chapter 5) and to bring it to the next session with you. This letter is only written as an exercise. There is no intention to actually send the letter.

5. Loss and Goodbye

During this session, saying goodbye is pivotal. You can reflect on the homework first. What was it like for the client to write the goodbye letter? Which steps were easy for them to take, and which were not? Did the client perhaps encounter any inner resistance?

Make time so that the client can read the letter out loud. Let the client imagine that you are the thing or the person to whom the letter is addressed. Sit across from each other. The client reads at a quiet pace. You listen. You are silent together. Then you tell him what you experienced while listening. The client also tells what it was like to read the letter.

The reading of the letter can be very intimate and also evoke shame. And that not only applies to the client, but also to the counselor. Again, it is important that you are aware of your own thoughts and feelings. Maybe you can tell something about it. Often it helps the client to also bring up his deeper feelings or thoughts.

For homework you can ask the client to have a frank dialogue with two people in his or her inner circle about saying goodbye. A dialogue in which your client tells about experiences (using the letter) and asks how the other person is familiar with these themes. In this way the client practices making contact with secure bases around a theme that can add depth to the relationship.

Of course, just like after the previous sessions, you will receive a short report from the previous session and prior to the following session. But this time the client also briefly tells you in the report about how the encounters went with the two people.

6. Grief

First there is time to look back. What has happened since last time? What did your client experience during the dialogues with the two people? What went well, and what (if any) obstacles did the client encounter?

In this session about grief you can use the Dual Process Model. By placing the opposite poles 'loss orientation' and 'restoration orientation' as anchors on the floor of the room, the client can explore which orientation feels familiar and which feels less familiar. What is it like to be at one pole and what is it like at the other? What could the client do to take a step further on both poles? By actually moving and standing on the poles, a different perspective arises than by talking about it.

After this exploration of the poles you could put on your coats and go outside. By taking a walk and standing still now and then, you put the theory of the poles into practice. And while you are walking together you practice being silent and listening and looking at what is happening around you. Back in your counseling room you check what is going on inside you yourself and whether you want to give something back to your client, and which questions you still want to ask.

You ask him to write a 'travel report' in preparation for the next session (see the exercise in Chapter 6). A letter in which your client describes his journey. About falling, getting up, learning, growing, and discovering themselves and what they stand for. And what they dream about.

7. Meaning and New Connection

A final session. To harvest and look beyond. Of course, your client will read his or her travel report to you. And maybe you hear music, as it were, echoing through the words. Halfway through, you ask the client to stop reading. You have this beautiful song on your phone. What you are hearing from your client makes you think of this song. You let your client hear it. And then the client carries on reading.

Your client has practiced and discovered. You let your client identify the harvest in a few short sentences. You can also look back together: on the lifeline and secure bases. What has changed? What remained the same? Which questions are still open-ended, to be explored in the future? You tell the client what you have observed during the journey. You express your gratitude for the client's trust. And you give the client encouragement for the next steps that will be taken.

Maybe you had bought a pretty postcard. You wrote something on it, from your heart. You give that card to the client when you say goodbye to each other. And you tell the client that you will be available, if needed.

And now this counseling journey has come to an end. Experiencing loss requires, as we have seen throughout this entire book, a (counseling) space in which questions about vulnerability are explored in order to be able to reconnect them with a life that goes on and that reconnects with the lives of others whose lives also continue in their own way. We talked about the micro- and macro-narratives in that context. The counseling space is thus also a place in which it becomes possible to seek to connect the client's stories to sources that come from the outside in. For example, we cannot ignore inspirational texts from fairy tales, music, religious writings, literature, and poetry. The starting point in the counseling room is that the client, with and despite everything, can fully reaffirm life, so that the client, in terms of Viktor Frankl, can 'Trotzdem ja zum Leben sagen' (Nevertheless, say yes to life) (2004). In this way, client and counselor give meaning to events together, in the space that we call the Transitional Space (refer to De Roos & van Wielink, 2015).

In the counseling space one can work with constellations, make drawings, write songs, silently meditate, make an action plan, walk through the forest, and so on. Everything that the counselor uses is essentially ritual labor: it is designed to promote the transition from old to new (behavior, perception, experience) (van Wielink, 2014).[1] The counseling space can thus also be seen as a symbolic space in which change is 'consciously, deliberately and purposefully' pursued. The transitional space is therefore also a ritual space. Counselors work with markings that act as transition rites. They reflect on breakthroughs and new steps. They emphasize and celebrate these new steps and (small and big) successes. In this way, counselors and clients mark transitions to new insights or other behavior.

Dialogue

Ben from the case study at the beginning of this chapter has often been to see his counselor Ruby. This time he wants to explore the dynamics of his contact with a female client.

Ben: Hi, Ruby, thanks for seeing me!
Ruby: Hi Ben, glad you are here.
Ben: Yes, I thought it is time to pay you a visit again, because I can't seem to solve this myself. It is about a client. I will call her Heather for now. I just don't know what to do about it. She irritates me immensely. And I realize that reflects on me too, but I just can't seem to solve it on my own.
Ruby: You really want to get on with it! First, try to relax a bit, sit down and put both feet on the floor. Take a deep breath. Close your eyes for a moment. Concentrate on your breathing. If you feel tension, let go of it (sigh a few

times). So, when you are ready, you open your eyes and come back to focus on the present again.

Ben: Thank you. This feels nice. I feel so agitated all the time.

Ruby: What could be causing you to feel so agitated? Do you know?

Ben: I don't exactly, but I suspect it has something to do with the client I was telling you about. I seem to be building up enormous stress from my sessions with this client. And I just can't manage to get rid of it. I would like to look at the reasons why I can't get rid of that stress. I feel such irritation towards her. On the one hand she keeps me at a distance and on the other hand, she claims me.

Ruby: So, on the one hand she keeps her distance and on the other hand it feels like she claims you. What irritates you about that?

Ben: It takes up so much of my time. If she were to just say what she wants from me!

Ruby: What do you think it is that she wants?

Ben: I think she wants me to have all the answers for her. That I can solve it for her. I can't seem to get through to her that I can't. That she needs to do the work. That I can't do it for her.

Ruby: What is it like for you to not have the answers?

Ben: (Is quiet for a moment.) In itself, I think that I am fine with that. But in one way or the other, she makes me feel like I am failing.

Ruby: What makes you think that?

Ben: Well, it is hard to say really. She keeps asking for explanations about things that were discussed in earlier sessions. As if I didn't explain it properly, or something like that.

Ruby: So, because of her questions, you get the feeling that you didn't explain it properly.

Ben: Yes, that's correct.

Ruby: And, say it is true that you didn't explain it properly. What is so bad about that?

Ben: It makes me feel like I have failed. I want her to see what her patterns are so badly and I want her to know that she has a choice. It is hard for me to see that it is not helping. And I get the feeling that she blames me for that.

Ruby: Who from your past does this remind you of? For whom were you always doing your best?

Ben: Immediately, my mother comes to mind. She was often down and disappointed with life. Even though I tried my hardest, she was never really cheerful. I have explored this topic so often, but it is still painful.

Ruby: So, in the past you so often tried your hardest to cheer your mother up. What effect is it that you want to achieve with this client?

Ben: I really want her to take a step forward. So that she can feel she has a choice to shape her life the way she wants to, even now that her husband has passed away.

Ruby: Why does this affect you like this?

Ben: I feel her sorrow and it is so painful to me that she feels her life is meaningless. I want so much for her to feel hope and options. But no matter what I do, she seems to stay completely in her own world. As if she refuses to give me access.
Ruby: How is that painful for you?
Ben: If she does not give me access? Well . . . then I am left standing alone . . . I can feel that I am standing alone empty-handed. That is most painful. That we are both alone and that I can't do anything about it. (Sighs.)
Ruby: (Remains silent for a moment.) In a way that is also the best you have to offer. That you remain present in solitude. Empty-handed. That your pain and her pain coexist.
Ben: Yes . . . I think that's true. . . . Thank you. I feel much calmer now.

Invitation to Develop a Personal Vision on Grief

It is not the critic who counts; not the man who points out how the strong man stumbles, or where the doer of deeds could have done them better. The credit belongs to the man who is actually in the arena, whose face is marred by dust and sweat and blood; who strives valiantly; who errs, who falls short again and again, because there is no effort without error and shortcoming; but who does actually strive to do the deeds; who knows great enthusiasms, the great devotions; who spends himself in a worthy cause; who at the best knows in the end the triumph of high achievement, and who at the worst, if he fails, at least fails while daring greatly.

(Theodore Roosevelt, quoted by Brené Brown, 2015)

This book builds on the oldest and the most recent insights, theories, and models of grief and counseling loss. These insights, theories, and models could only arise because of previous insights, theories, and models. All these building blocks are of significance to our profession, both from a historical perspective as well as for our daily practice.

Inside everybody there is a deep longing to be seen and accepted. A longing and maybe even a necessity to feel secure. Especially when we are in need. Fear is incited and subconsciously we are inclined to prepare for the worst and to ready all protective mechanisms.

This is the state in which most clients turn to a counselor. A counselor they can explore their needs with, whom they can learn to trust again to take new steps. A counselor who can be a secure base for them.

In this book we assert the need for secure bases. People, objects, places, and animals we can rely on for support in loss and transition, who encourage us to engage in new connections.

A counselor willing to be a secure base for his or her clients, starts with him- or herself. The counselor investigates their own inner attachment dynamics, connects to their own loss, feels their own emotions, and acknowledges the impact of their own life story. That way the counselor can be present in the story of the client. From that state of being, the counselor is caring and daring. The client can learn to trust anew, both in themselves and in others.

All models, insights, and theories on loss and grief provide secure bases for our work. From this solid foundation, laid by many predecessors, we can continue to build. We would like to extend this invitation to you too, to explore your personal relationship with loss and grief and to develop your own view of loss and grief based on your own unique experiences and everything we offer in this book.

Questions for Self-Reflection

- What was the dialogue between your parents like in your view? Was there real dialogue, or was there more discussion and debate?
- What questions were put to each other and to you?
- Which questions were avoided?
- What happened when you asked questions that your parents did not know the answer to?
- What question or questions would you have wanted to ask?
- What question or questions should others ask you more often?
- How do you explain your view of grief and loss to a potential client?
- How does your view of grief influence your counseling? What does a client notice about this?

Exercises

Exercise—Which Questions Were Asked?

Let your mind take you back to the kitchen or dining table at your home. Think of difficult or emotional situations, involving you or your family members. From that position, answer the questions for self-reflection above.

> **Instruction:** How did the answers to the self-reflection questions influence your ability to conduct the dialogue, develop your curiosity, and ask questions? What impact does this have on you as a counselor?

Exercise—Symptoms of Grief

Identify as many different symptoms of grief as possible that you can find or suffer from.

Instruction: Everyone has a preferred quadrant from which he or she works as a counselor and from which he or she personally deals with losses. This preference finds its origin in the family of origin. This preference becomes visible in the exercise in the ease with which phenomena are named in a specific quadrant. The counselor is also inclined to want to counsel a client while in this quadrant. In order to be able to connect with clients in counseling, however, the counselor must be able to work from all quadrants.

Pair up and discuss your lists of symptoms with your partner. What differences and similarities do you notice?

Then link all the symptoms from the exercise to the four quadrants:

- Emotions
- Thoughts
- Spiritual
- Physical

Then discuss:

- How easy or how difficult is it for you to name phenomena in a quadrant?
- How easy is it for you to link a symptom to a specific quadrant?
- Why do you think that is?

Exercise—Letter of Consolation

In what way are you inclined to offer consolation? What is your inner reaction to this? With a consolation letter you get the chance to focus attention on this. It is a letter you write to someone close to you who has suffered a loss.

Keep in mind what was stated in an earlier section of this chapter (About Consolation in Dialogue):

- To console is to communicate, both verbally and non-verbally.
- To console starts with being available and listening.
- To console is followed (possibly) by questions (in any case instead of solving or filling in).
- To console implies recognition: of the feelings of the other person and of the other person as a person.
- To console implies proximity, connection and intimacy; consoling is thus a relational activity. Being there is more important than what you say.

Be concrete, and say what you have to say. Of course, you do not have to send the letter if you do not want to.

> **Instruction:** Write a letter of consolation to someone close to you who has suffered a loss. Form pairs, read the letter, and discuss what it is like to write a letter of consolation.
>
> What consolation would you (still) like to receive?

Exercise—Transactions

Think back to a time when you came home as a child with a bad grade for a test or for your report, or when you were caught skipping class, getting up to mischief, or kicked out of class. How did your parents respond? How did that reaction affect you? How did you react?

> **Instruction:** Use the situation in the exercise and try to identify with each of the following positions:
>
> - Nurturing Parent
> - Critical Parent
> - Adult
> - Adapted Child
> - Free Child
>
> Form pairs (A and B).
>
> - What response would you give while playing each role?
> - A speaks out loud to B.
> - In which role does A try to address B with this reaction?
> - In which role does B feel he or she is being addressed?
> - What effect does this have on A and B?
>
> Discuss briefly and then switch roles.

Exercise—Script Decisions

What internal dialogue do you use during moments of discomfort? What do you say to yourself? Use the list of injunctions from earlier in this chapter. Which injunctions do you recognize and what situations from the past or present do they remind you of? Which permissions help you to challenge this negative belief?

Instruction: Determine on the basis of the injunctions which script decisions you made yourself and which behavior you show. Find out what your reasons were in the past to make these decisions and think about how you want to deal with them in the present. What permissions do you need to internalize?

Form groups of three (A is the counselor, B is the client, and C is the observer) and counsel each other on the script decisions, injunctions, driver messages and permissions. Evaluate each round briefly and then switch roles.

Exercise—Intake

When a client comes for counseling, there is always a reason for seeking help, but not always a clear question. Often the question will not even be specifically about loss or grief. The intake involves the first exploration of the request for help and equally the exploration of the personal connection between the counselor and the client. It is precisely in this exploration of the question and the themes that play a role here that the themes of safety and trust become visible.

Instruction: Divide into groups of two (A is supervisor, B is client). B comes for an intake with A and has a provisional request for help. A does an initial exploration of this question, in which, besides the content of the final question on which the counseling would focus, the approach of A during counseling and the vision from which A works, becomes clear.

At the end of the intake, the question for B is whether B would go to A on the basis of this intake. Why or why not?

Change roles.

Exercise—The Structure of a Counseling Program

Based on the intake in the previous exercise, create an individual framework of a counseling program. Pay specific attention to the work forms you would like to use with your client per theme.

Instruction: Divide into groups of two and discuss each other's structure for a counseling program. Answer the following questions:

- What do the chosen teaching methods say about you as a counselor?
- Which methods do you avoid?

- What does that say about where you now stand as a counselor?
- How 'daring' are you towards your client?
- How do you manage the balance between 'caring' and 'daring?'

Note

1. In addition to the rituals in 'narrow sense,' as described in Chapter 5, the rituals described here are to be seen in a broad sense.

BIBLIOGRAPHY

All methods, exercises, and theory are justified with references to both national and international sources. For titles not available in English, a translation of the title is provided.

Albert, L.S., D.G. Allen, J.E. Biggane & Q. Mab (2015). Attachment and Responses to Employment Dissolution. *Human Resource Management Review* 25: 94–106.

Anderson, C. (1949). Aspects of Pathological Grief and Mourning. *International Journal of Psycho-Analysis* 30: 48–55.

Ankersmid, M. (2015a). *Verlaat verdriet—bij mensen die als kind een ouder hebben verloren*. Antwerpen: Witsand Uitgevers. (Belated Sorrow—For Those Who Lost a Parent During Childhood)

Ankersmid, M. (2015b). *Mindful omgaan met verlies*. Antwerpen: Witsand Uitgevers. (A Mindful Way to Deal with Loss)

Argyris, C. (1960). *Understanding Organizational Behaviors*. Homewood, IL: Dorsey Press.

Baart, A. (2004). *Een theorie van de presentie*. Den Haag: Boom Lemma. (A Theory of Presence)

Baumeister, R.F. (1992). *Meanings of Life*. New York: Guilford Publications.

Berne, E. (2016). *Games People Play. The Psychology of Human Relationships*. London: Penguin Books/Houten: Aula (Spectrum).

Boadella, D. (1973). *Wilhelm Reich: The Evolution of His Work*. Chicago: Vision Press.

Bohlmeijer, E. (2012). *De verhalen die we leven. Narratieve psychologie als methode*. Amsterdam: Boom uitgevers. (Stories to Live by Narrative Psychology as Method)

Bohm, D. (1996). *On Dialogue*. London and New York: Routledge.
Bonanno, G.A. (2010). *The Other Side of Sadness*. New York: Basic Books.
Bonanno, G.A., M. Westphal & A.D. Mancini (2011). Resilience to Loss and Potential Trauma. *Annual Review of Clinical Psychology* 7: 1.1–1.25.
Boswijk-Hummel, R. (2003). *Troost vragen, geven en ontvangen*. Haarlem: De Toorts. (Seeking Comfort, Giving and Receiving)
Boszormenyi-Nagy, I. & G.M. Spark (1984). *Invisible Loyalties. Reciprocity in Intergenerational Family Therapy*. London: Taylor & Francis.
Bout, J. van den (1997). Rouwsluiers. *De Psycholoog* 37: 21–26. (Veils of Grief)
Bowlby, J. (1988a). *Attachment: Attachment and Loss*. Vol. 1. London: Pimlico, Random House.
Bowlby, J. (1988b). *Separation, Anxiety and Anger: Attachment and Loss*. Vol. 2. London: Pimlico, Random House.
Bowlby, J. (1988c). *Loss Sadness and Depression: Attachment and Loss*. Vol. 3. London: Pimlico, Random House.
Bowlby, J. (1988d). *A Secure Base: Parent–Child Attachment and Healthy Human Development*. Tavistock Professional Book. London: Routledge.
Bridges, W. (2017). *Managing Transitions. Making the Most of Change*. London: Nicholas Brealey Publishing.
Brockner, J. (1988). The Effect of Work Layoffs on Survivors: Research, Theory, and Practice. In: B.M. Staw & L.L. Cummings (eds.) *Research in Organizational Behavior*, Vol. 10. Greenwich, CT: JAI Press.
Brown, B. (2015). *Daring Greatly. How the Courage to Be Vulnerable Transforms the Way We Live, Love, Parent and Lead*. New York: Penguin Books.
Calhoun, L.G. & R.G. Tedeschi (1989–1990). Positive Aspects of Critical Life Problems: Recollections of Grief. *Omega* 20: 265–272.
Calhoun, L.G. & R.G. Tedeschi (1996). The Posttraumatic Growth Inventory: Measuring the Positive Legacy of Trauma. *Journal of Traumatic Stress* 9 (3): 455–471.
Calhoun, L.G. & R.G. Tedeschi (1998). Posttraumatic Growth: Future Directions. In: R.G. Tedeschi, C.L. Park & L.G. Calhoun (red.) *Posttraumatic Growth: Positive Change in the Aftermath of Crisis*. Mahwah, NJ: Erlbaum.
Calhoun, L.G. & R.G. Tedeschi (2001). Posttraumatic Growth: The Positive Lessons of Loss. In: Robert A. Neimeyer (red.) *Meaning Reconstruction & the Experience of Loss*. Washington, DC: American Psychological Association.
Cozijnsen, B. & J.P.J. van Wielink (2012). *Over de rooie. Emoties bij verlies en verandering op het werk*. Alphen aan den Rijn: Kluwer. (Going Beserk: Emotions as a Result of Loss and Change at Work)
Cozolino, L. (2010). *The Neuroscience of Psychotherapy: Healing the Social Brain*. New York: W.W. Norton & Company.
Delfos, M.F. (2008). *Verschil mag er zijn. Waarom er mannen en vrouwen zijn*. Amsterdam: Bert Bakker. (Differences Allowed. Why There Are Men and Women)

Denderen, M.Y. van (2017). *Grief Following Homicidal Loss*. PhD Dissertation. Groningen: Rijksuniversiteit.

Deutsch, H. (1937). Absence of Grief. *Psychoanalytical Quarterly* 6: 12.

Dijk, R. van (2017, 4 Februari). Viel mijn broer of sprong hij? *Trouw*. (Did My Brother Fall or Did He Jump?)

Dohmen, L.J.M.C. (red.) (2002). *Over levenskunst. De grote filosofen over het goede leven*. Amsterdam: Ambo. (About the Art of Living. The Great Philosophers on the Good Life)

Doka, K.J. (1989). *Disenfranchised Grief: Recognizing Hidden Sorrow*. Lanham: Lexington Books.

Doka, K.J. (2002). *Disenfranchised Grief: New Directions, Challenges, and Strategies for Practice*. Champaign: Research Press, Inc.

Draaisma, D. (2011, September). It's Alright, I'm a Doctor: Grensoverschrijding in de wetenschap. *De Academische Boekengids* 88: 10–12. (It's Alright, I'm a Doctor: Unacceptable Behaviour in Science)

Dweck, C.S. (2017). *Changing the Way You Think to Fulfil Your Potential*. London: Little, Brown and Company.

Ecker, B., R. Ticic & L. Hulley (2012). *Unlocking the Emotional Brain. Eliminating Symptoms and Their Roots Using Memory Reconsilidation*. New York: Routledge.

Edmondson, A. (1999). Psychological Safety and Learning Behavior in Work Teams. *Administrative Science Quarterly* 44 (2): 350–383.

Ellis, A. & A. Baldon (1993, February). *Ret: A Problem Solving Workbook*. Unknown: Albert Ellis Institute.

Evers, D. & N. van Miltenburg (2011, 15 September). *Volkskrant.nl, Vrije wil meet je niet met een hersenscan*. www.volkskrant.nl/vk/nl/3184/opinie/article/detail/2907160/2011/09/15/Vrije-wil-meet-je-niet-met-een-hersenscan.dhtml, geraadpleegd op 17 November 2011. (Free Will Cannot Be Measured with a Brain Scan)

Fiddelaers-Jaspers, R. (2006). *Gedeeld verdriet. Het opzetten en begeleiden van rouwgroepen voor jongeren*. Budel: Damon. (Shared Loss: Setting Up and Guiding Support Groups for Grief and Bereavement for Young People)

Fiddelaers-Jaspers, R. (2010). *Mijn troostende ik; kwetsbaarheid en kracht van rouwende jongeren*. Utrecht: Uitgeverij Ten Have. (My Soothing Self: Vulnerability and Strength of Grieving Young People)

Fiddelaers-Jaspers, R. (2011a). *De rouwende school; handboek voor kinderopvang, primair en voortgezet onderwijs en mbo*. Heeze: In de Wolken. (The Grieving School: Manual for Day-Care, Primary, Secondary and Vocational Education)

Fiddelaers-Jaspers, R. (2011b). *Met mijn ziel onder de arm; tussen welkom heten en afscheid nemen*. Heeze: In de Wolken. (Wandering with a Wounded Heart: Between Welcoming and Saying Goodbye)

Fiddelaers-Jaspers, R. (2014). *Jong verlies; rouwende kinderen serieus nemen.* Utrecht: Uitgeverij Ten Have. (Young Losses: Taking Grieving Children Seriously)

Fiddelaers-Jaspers, R. & S. Noten (2015). *Herbergen van verlies: Thuiskomen in het Land van Rouw*. Heeze: In de Wolken. (Accommodation of Loss: At Home in the Land of Grief)

Fiddelaers-Jaspers, R. & J.P.J. van Wielink (2015). *Aan de slag met verlies. Coachen bij veranderingen op het werk.* Utrecht: Uitgeverij Ten Have. (Working with Loss: Coaching of Changes at Work)

Frankl, V. (2004). *Man's Search for Meaning*. London: Ebury Publishing.

Freud, S. (1917). Trauer und Melancholie. *Internationale Zeitschrift für Ärztliche Psychoanalyse* 4: 277–287.

Geelen-Merks, D. van & J.P.J. van Wielink (2015). *Met zoveel liefde heb ik van je gehouden. Woorden bij persoonlijk verlies.* Antwerpen: Witsand Uitgevers. (That's How Much I Loved You. Words for Personal Loss)

Goleman, D. (2013). *The Brain and Emotional Intelligence: New Insights*. Florence, MA: More Than Sound.

Grunberg, A. (2016, 7 Mei). *Als ik gekwetst word, glimlach ik.* Interview door Toef Jaeger in NRC. (When It Hurts, I Smile)

Hagman, G. (ed.) (2016). *New Models of Bereavement Theory and Treatment.* New York: Routledge.

Harlow, H. (1959, June). Love in Infant Monkeys. *Scientific American* 200: 68, 70, 72–74.

Harris, T. (2012). *I'm Ok, You're Ok*. London: Cornerstone.

Hart, O. van der (red.) (2003). *Afscheidsrituelen. Achterblijven en verdergaan.* Amsterdam: Pearson.

Heyvaert, M., S. van Mechelen, B. Maes & P. Onghena (2012). (Farewell Rituals. Staying Behind and Moving On) Begeleiding van rouwprocessen bij personen met een verstandelijke beperking: Een kwalitatieve metasynthese van case studies. *Nederlands Tijdschrift voor de Zorg aan Mensen met Verstandelijke Beperkingen* 38 (4): 247–268. (Counselling of Grief Processes in the Mentally Challenged: A Qualitative Meta-Synthesis of Case Studies. *Dutch Journal for the Care of People with Mental Challenges*)

Iacoboni, M. (2009). *Mirroring People: The Science of Empathy and How We Connect with Others.* New York: Picador.

Isaacs, W. (1999). *Dialogue and the Art of Thinking Together*. New York: Currency.

Jung, C.G. (1928). *Contributions to Analytical Psychology*. New York: Harcourt, Brace and Company.

Kabat-Zinn, J. (2003). Mindfulness-Based Interventions in Context: Past, Present, and Future. *Clinical Psychology: Science and Practice* 10 (2): 144–156.

Kahneman, D. (2012). *Thinking Fast and Slow*. London: Penguin Books.
Kahneman, D. & A. Tversky (1979). Prospect Theory: An Analysis of Decision Under Risk. *Econometrica* 47: 263–291.
Kastenbaum, R.J. (2015). *Death, Society and Human Experience*. London: Routledge, Taylor & Francis Group.
Kastenbaum, R.J. & P.T. Costa, Jr (1977). Psychological Perspectives on Death. *Annual Review of Psychology* 28: 225–249.
Katz, R.S. & T.A. Johnson (eds.) (2016). *When Professionals Weep: Emotional and Countertransference Responses in Palliative and End-of-Life Care*. New York: Routledge, Taylor & Francis Group.
Keirse, M. (2015). *Vingerafdruk van verdriet. Woorden van bemoediging*. Tielt: Lannoo. (Fingerprint of Grief. Words of Encouragement)
Kets de Vries, M.F.R. (2016). *Mindful Leadership Coaching Journeys into the Interior*. Basingstoke: Insead Business Press.
Kets de Vries, M.F.R. & K. Balazs (1997). The Downside of Downsizing. *Human Relations* 50 (1): 11–50.
Klass, D., P.R. Silverman & S. Nickman (2014). *Continuing Bonds: New Understandings of Grief*. London: Taylor & Francis.
Kohlrieser, G. (2006). *Hostage at the Table. How Leaders Can Overcome Conflict, Influence Others, and Raise Performance*. San Francisco: Jossey-Bass.
Kohlrieser, G. (2015). *How to Turn Loss into Inspiration*. TEDx Lausanne. www.youtube.com/watch?v=RNwKV_Rk-TU, visited on 22 January 2017.
Kohlrieser, G., S. Goldsworthy & D. Coombe (2012). *Care to Dare—Unleashing Astonishing Potential Through Secure Base Leadership*. San Francisco: Jossey-Bass.
Kolk, B. van der (2015). *The Body Keeps the Score. Mind, Brain and Body in the Transformation of Trauma*. New York: Penguin Books.
Koopmans, L. (2014). *Dit ben ik! Worden wie je bent met transactionele analyse*. Zaltbommel: Thema. (This Is Me! Becoming Who You Really Are with Transactional Analysis)
Kosminsky, P.S. & J.R. Jordan (2016). *Attachment-Informed Grief Therapy. The Clinician's Guide to Foundations and Applications*. New York: Routledge, Taylor & Francis Group.
Kübler-Ross, E. (2014). *On Death and Dying: What the Dying Have to Teach Doctors, Nurses, Clergy and Their Own Families*. New York: Simon & Schuster.
Kübler-Ross, E. & D. Kessler (2014). *On Grief and Grieving. Finding the Meaning of Life Through the Five Stages of Loss*. New York: Simon & Schuster.
Kunneman, H. (2009). *Voorbij het dikke-ik, bouwstenen voor een kritisch humanisme*. Utrecht: Humanistic University Press. (Moving Past the Fat-Me, Building Blocks for Critical Humanism)
Lamme, V. (2010). *De vrije wil bestaat niet: Over wie er de echt baas is in het brein*. Amsterdam: Bert Bakker. (There Is No Such Thing as Free Will: Who Is Really the Boss in Your Brain)

Leader, D. (2008). *The New Black. Mourning, Melancholia and Depression.* London: Penguin Books.

Lent, W. van (2016). www.demannenboom.nl. (*The Tree for Men*).

Lilgendahl, J.P. & D.P. McAdams (2011). Constructing Stories of Self-Growth: How Individual Differences in Patterns of Autobiographical Reasoning Relate to Well-Being in Midlife. *Journal of Personality* 79 (2): 391–428.

Lindemann, E. (1944). Symptomatology and Management of Acute Grief. *The American Journal of Psychiatry* 101 (2): 141–148.

Lipton, B. & D. Fosha (2011). Attachment as a Transformative Process in AEDP: Operationalizing the Intersection of Attachment Theory and Affective Neuroscience. *Journal of Psychotherapy Integration* 21: 253–279.

Lommers, H. & H. van Amsterdam (1992). *Het Is Stil in Huis; afscheid nemen van je huisdier*. Lisse: Etiko Uitgevers. (The Silent House: Saying Goodbye to Your Pet)

Lookeren Campagne, F. van (2010). Te hard gewerkt, te lang gewacht. Per ongeluk kinderloos. *Intermediair* (14): 18–23. (Worked Too Hard, Waited Too Long. Accidentally Childless)

Lynch, J. (1979). *The Broken Heart: The Medical Consequences of Loneliness.* Baltimore: Bancroft Press.

MacLean, P.D. (1990). *The Triune Brain in Evolution: Role in Paleocerebral Functions.* Berlin: Springer Science+Business Media.

Main, M. (1996). Introduction to the Special Section on Attachment and Psychopathology: 2. Overview of the Field of Attachment. *Journal of Consulting and Clinical Psychology* 64 (2): 237–243.

Main, M., E. Hesse & S. Hesse (2011). Attachment Theory and Research: Overview, with Suggested Applications to Child Custody. *Family Court Review* 49: 426–463.

Marks, M.L., P. Mirvis & R. Ashkenas (2014). Rebounding from Career Setbacks. *Harvard Business Review* 92 (10): 105–108.

McGonigal, K. (2016). *The Upside of Stress: Why Stress Is Good for You, and How to Get Good at It.* New York: Penguin Books.

Meeusen-van de Kerkhof, R., H. van Bommel, W. van de Wouw & M. Maaskant (2001). *Kun je uit de hemel vallen? Beleving van de dood en rouwverwerking door mensen met een verstandelijke handicap.* Utrecht: Landelijk KennisNetwerk Gehandicaptenzorg. (Can You Fall Down from Heaven? Perception of Death and Grief Among the Mentally Challenged)

Mikulincer, M. & P.R. Shaver (2010). *Attachment in Adulthood. Structure, Dynamics, and Change.* New York: The Guildford Press.

Murphy, K. (2017, 7 Januari). Yes, It's Your Parents' Fault. *New York Times.* https://www.nytimes.com/2017/01/07/opinion/sunday/yes-its-your-parents-fault.html, visited on 14 May 2019.

Neijenhuis, J., J.P.J. van Wielink & L. Wilhelm (2012). Rouw is geen ziekte, maar je kunt er wel goed ziek van zijn.' *ArboMagazine* 10: 20–21. (Grief Is No Disease, But It Can Make You Really Sick)

Neimeyer, R.A. (2005). Complicated Grief and the Quest for Meaning: A Constructivist Contribution. *Omega* 52 (1): 37–52.

Neimeyer, R.A. (2006). Bereavement and the Quest for Meaning—Rewriting Stories of Loss and Grief. *Hellenic Journal of Psychology* 3: 181–188.

Neimeyer, R.A. (ed.) (2016). *Techniques of Grief Therapy: Assessment and Intervention*. New York: Routledge, Taylor & Francis Group.

Neimeyer, R.A. & B.E. Thompson (eds.) (2014). *Grief and the Expressive Arts. Practices for Creating Meaning*. New York: Routledge, Taylor and Francis Group.

Norton, M.I. & F. Gino (2014). Rituals Alleviate Grieving for Loved Ones, Lovers, and Lotteries. *Journal of Experimental Psychology: General* 143 (1): 266–272.

Noten, S. (2015). *Stapeltjesverdriet; stilstaan bij wat is: Een onderzoek naar de invloed van verlies op zeer jonge leeftijd*. Heeze: In de Wolken. (Stacks of Sadness; Attention on What Is: Research on the Influence of Loss at a Very Young Age)

Oaklander, M. (2016, 7 March). Why We Cry. *Time*: 68–72.

Ogden, P. & J. Fisher (2015). *Sensorimotor Psychotherapy: Interventions for Trauma and Attachment*. New York: W.W. Norton & Company.

Ongenae, C. (2015). Brené Brown: 'Als we met hart en ziel willen leven, moeten we onze angst voor de donkere kant van het leven loslaten.' https://catherineongenae.com/2015/01/02/brene-brown-als-we-met-hart-en-ziel-willen-leven-moeten-we-onze-angst-voor-dedonkere-kant-van-het-leven-loslaten, visited on 11 January 2017. (If We Want to Live with Heart and Soul, We Will Need to Release Our Fear of the Dark Side of Life)

Parkes, C.M. (1970). The First Year of Bereavement. A Longitudinal Study of the Reaction of London Widows to the Death of Their Husbands. *Psychiatry* 33 (4): 444–467.

Parkes, C.M. (2006). *Love and Loss: The Roots of Grief and Its Complications*. London & New York: Routledge.

Parkes, C.M. (2015). *The Price of Love: The Selected Works of Colin Murray Parkes*. London and New York: Routledge, Hove.

Pol, I.G.M. van der (2012). *Coachen als professie; fundamenten voor begeleiding naar heelheid*. Amsterdam: Boom uitgevers. (Coaching as Profession: Fundamentals for Guiding Towards Wholeness)

Popper, K. (2002). *The Logic of Scientific Discovery*. London and New York: Routledge Classics.

Portzky, M. (2015). *Veerkracht. Onze natuurlijke weerstand tegen een leven vol stress*. Antwerpen: Witsand Uitgevers. (Resilience. Our Natural Resistance to a Life Filled with Stress)

Pos, K.J., J.P.J. van Wielink & L. Wilhelm (2014). Maakbaarheid als het grote verhaal. *Tijdschrift voor Coaching* (2): 6–11. (Engineering Is the Whole Story. Magazine for Coaching)

Rando, T.A. (1991). *How to Go on Living When Someone You Love Dies.* New York: Bantam Doubleday Dell Publishing Group, Inc.

Reijmerink, M. & J.P.J. van Wielink (2016). De Transitiecirkel—George Kohlrieser.' http://canonvanhetleren.overmanagement.net/artikel/de-transitiecirkel-george-kohlrieser, visited on 15 January 2017.

Remen, R.N. (2006). *Kitchen Table Wisdom.* New York: Penguin Group (USA), Inc.

Rogers, C. (1957). The Necessary and Sufficient Conditions of Therapeutic Change. *Journal of Consulting and Clinical Psychology* 21: 95–103.

Roos, S. de & J.P.J. van Wielink (2015). Religieuze aspecten van coaching: De pastor en de coach. *Tijdschrift voor Coaching* (4): 4–9. (Religious Aspects of Coaching: The Pastor and the Coach)

Rosenberg, M.B. (2015). *Nonviolent Communication: A Language of Life.* Encinitas, CA: Puddledancer Press.

Rubin, S.S., R. Malkinson & E. Witztum (2012). *Working with the Bereaved: Multiple Lenses on Loss and Mourning.* New York: Routledge, Taylor & Francis Group.

Ruppert, F. (2008). *Trauma, Bonding and Family Constellations. Understanding and Healing Injuries of the Soul.* Steyning: Green Balloon Books.

Russac, R.J., N.S. Steighner & A.I. Canto (2002). Grief Work Versus Continuing Nonds: A Call for Paradigm Integration or Replacement? *Death Studies* 26 (6): 463–478.

Samuel, J. (2017). *Grief Works: Stories of Life, Death and Surviving.* London: Penguin Life.

Sandberg, S. (2017). *Option B: Facing Adversity, Building Resilience, and Finding Joy.* London: Ebury Publishing.

Schein, E.H. & P. Schein (2016). *Organizational Culture and Leadership.* San Francisco: Jossey-Bass.

Schildkamp, V. (2017). Gered uit een eindeloos rouwproces. *AD.nl*, www.ad.nl/dossier-nieuws/gered-uit-een-b-eindeloos-b-rouwproces~a187754a, visited on 19 January 2017.

Schore, A.N. (2001). The Effects of a Secure Attachment Relationship on Right Brain Development, Affect Regulation, and Infant Mental Health. *Infant Mental Health Journal* 22: 7–66.

Schore, A.N. (2012). *The Science of the Art of Psychotherapy.* New York: W.W. Norton & Company.

Schreurs, P.J.G., G. van de Willige, J.F. Brosschot, B. Tellegen & G.M.H. Graus (1993). *Utrechtse Coping Lijst (UCL).* Amsterdam: Pearson. (Utrecht Coping List)

Segal, Z.V., J.M.G. Williams & J.D. Teasdale (2002). *Mindfulness-Based Cognitive Therapy for Depression: A New Approach to Preventing Relapse*. New York: Guilford Press.

Spuij, M. (2017). *Rouw bij kinderen en jongeren; over het begeleiden van verliesverwerking*. Amsterdam: Nieuwezijds. (Grief in Children and Other Young People: Counselling in Dealing with Loss)

Sroufe, L.A., E.A. Carlson, A.K. Levy & B. Egeland (1999). Implications of Attachment Theory for Developmental Psychopathology. *Development and Psychopathology* 11: 1–13.

Stevenson-Hinde, J., P. Marris & C.M. Parkes (eds.) (1991). *Attachment Across the Life Cycle*. London and New York: Routledge.

Stewart, I. & V. Joines (2012). *T A Today. New Introduction to Transactional Analysis*. Chapel Hill: Lifespace Publishing.

Stichting Jonge Helden (2016). www.voorjongehelden.nl. (*Foundation for Young Heroes: Children Who Are (or Will Be) Dealing with Loss*).

Stigchel, S. van der (2019). *How Attention Works: Finding Your Way in a World Full of Distraction*. Cambridge: MIT Press.

Stroebe, M.S. & H. Schut (1999). The Dual Process Model of Coping with Bereavement: Rationale and Description. *Death Studies* 23: 197–224.

Stroebe, M.S. & H. Schut (2010). The Dual Process Model of Coping with Bereavement: A Decade On. *Omega* 61 (4): 273–289.

Stroebe, M.S. & W. Stroebe (1991). Does 'Grief Work' Work? *Journal of Consulting and Clinical Psychology* 59 (3): 479–482.

Swaab, D. (2011). *We Are Our Brains From the Womb to Alzheimer's*. London: Penguin Books.

Swieringa & Jansen (2005). *Gedoe komt er toch. Zin en onzin over organisatieverandering*. Schiedam: Scriptum. (There Will Be a Fuss, No Matter What. Sense and Nonsense of Organizational Change)

Tiggelaar, B. (2011, 27 May). Deze managementlessen haal je uit Monty Python. *Intermediair*. (Management Classes According to Monty Python)

Toebosch, T. (2012, 30 April). Verlies verwerken volgens Claudius Galenus. *NRC Handelsblad*. (Dealing with Loss According to Claudius Galenus)

Veenbaas, W., et al. (2007). *Passe-Partout*. Utrecht: Phoenix Opleidingen. (The Skeleton Key)

Veenbaas, W. & J. Goudswaard (2011). *Vonken van verlangen; systemisch werken: perspectief en praktijk*. Utrecht: Phoenix Opleidingen. (Sparks of Longing: Systemic Approach, Perspective and Practice)

Vonk, R. (2013). *Liefde, lust en ellende*. Schiedam: Scriptum. (Love, Lust and Misery)

Vough, H.C. & B. Barker Caza (2017). Where Do I Go from Here? Sensemaking and the Construction of Growth-Based Stories in the Wake of Denied Promotions. *Academy of Management Review* 41 (1): 103–128.

Weijers, A. & P. Penning (2016). *Het leven duurt een leven lang*. Eigen beheer: www.hetlevenduurteenlevenlang.nl. (Life Lasts a Lifetime)

Weisfelt, P. (1996). *Nestgeuren; de betekenis van ouder-kind relaties in leven*. Soest: Uitgeverij Nelissen. (The Smells and Sounds of Home: The Meaning of Parent–Child Relationships in Life)

Wentink, M. (2014). *Je verlangen: Dwaallicht of kompas?* Eeserveen: Akasha. (Your Longing: Marsh Fire or Compass?)

Werner, E.E. (2005). Resilience and Recovery: Findings from the Kauai Longitudinal Study. *Research, Policy, and Practice in Children's Mental Health* 19 (1): 11–14.

Wielink, J.P.J. van (2014). Kwetsbaar leven. Over desoriëntatie en heroriëntatie (Interview Met Prof. Christa Anbeek). *Tijdschrift voor Coaching* (4): 6–11. (Vulnerable Living. About Disorientation and Reorientation)

Wielink, J.P.J. van & L. Wilhelm (2011). Ben ik, vrij onverveerd? Over de vrije wil en de keuze om je talenten te ontplooien. *Tijdschrift voor Coaching* (4): 91–93. (Am I Really Free and Fearless? About Free Will and Choice in Talent Development)

Wielink, J.P.J. van & L. Wilhelm (2012a). Transitie en de betekenis van werk. Loopbaanontwikkeling en veranderingsprocessen. *LoopbaanVisie* (1): 24–27. (Transition and the Meaning of Work. Career Developments and Change Processes)

Wielink, J.P.J. van & L. Wilhelm (2012b). Interne en externe zingeving bij verlies. *Streven* (11): 907–919. (Internal and External Meaning Reconstruction After Loss)

Wielink, J.P.J. van & L. Wilhelm (2012c). 'Pink Slip'—tussen boventalligheid en ontslag. *P&O Actueel* (1–2): 36–39. (The Pink Slip—Between Redundancy and Dismissal)

Wielink, J.P.J. van & L. Wilhelm (2012d, 2 April). Medicalisering van rouw is ongewenst. *Financieel Dagblad*. (Do Not Medicate Grief)

Wielink, J.P.J. van & L. Wilhelm (2014). Organisaties als veroorzakers van verlies; Reorganisaties, arbeidsverlies en de rol van de leidinggevende. In: J. Maes & H. Modderman (red.) *Handboek rouw, rouwbegeleiding, rouwtherapie; tussen presentie en interventie*, 551–563. Antwerpen: Witsand Uitgevers. (Organizations as Source of Loss: Reorganizations, Job Loss and the Role of the Manager. In: Guide for Grief, Grief Counseling, Grief Therapy: Between Presence and Intervention.)

Wielink, J.P.J. van & L. Wilhelm (2015a). Een nieuw begin; over afscheid nemen in de praktijk van de professioneel begeleider. *Tijdschrift voor Begeleidingskunde* (4): 2–13. (A New Beginning: About Saying Goodbye in the Practice of the Professional Counsellor)

Wielink, J.P.J. van & L. Wilhelm (2015b). *Rouwregels. Handvatten voor organisaties rond overlijden en terminale ziekte*. Antwerpen: Witsand Uitgevers. (Tools for Organizations Pertaining Death and Terminal Illness)

Wielink, J.P.J. van, L. Wilhelm & A. Bakker (2019). *Voice Dialogue*. In: R. Neimeyer (ed.) *New Techniques of Grief Therapy: Bereavement and Beyond*. New York: Routledge.

Wielink, J.P.J. van, L. Wilhelm & D. van Geelen-Merks (2019a). *Balancing Caring and Daring*. In: R. Neimeyer (ed.) *New Techniques of Grief Therapy: Bereavement and Beyond*. New York: Routledge.

Wielink, J.P.J. van, L. Wilhelm & D. van Geelen-Merks (2019b). Memory Reconsolidation. In: R. Neimeyer (ed.) *New Techniques of Grief Therapy: Bereavement and Beyond*. New York: Routledge.

Wielink, J.P.J. van, L. Wilhelm & D. van Geelen-Merks (2019c). The Secure Base Map. In: R. Neimeyer (ed.) *New Techniques of Grief Therapy: Bereavement and Beyond*. New York: Routledge.

Wielink, J.P.J. van, L. Wilhelm & D. van Geelen-Merks (2019d). The Transition Cycle. In: R. Neimeyer (ed.) *New Techniques of Grief Therapy: Bereavement and Beyond*. New York: Routledge.

Wielink, J.P.J. van, L. Wilhelm & P. Wouters (2012). Coachen op de grens van therapie. Over het dilemma van professionele afstand en menselijke nabijheid. *Tijdschrift voor Coaching* (2): 16–20.

Winnicott, D.W. (1951). Transitional Objects and Transitional Phenomena. In: *Collected Papers: Through Paediatrics to Psychoanalysis*, 249–262. New York: Basic Books, Inc.

Witte, H.F.J. de (1980). Over de ontwikkeling van het transitional object. *Tijdschrift voor Psychiatrie* 22 (5): 296–311. (The Development of the Transitional Object)

Worden, J.W. (1991). *Grief Counseling and Grief Therapy*. New York: Springer.

Wortman, C.B. & R.C. Silver (1989). The Myths of Coping with Loss. *Journal of Consulting and Clinical Psychology* 57 (3): 349–357.

Wouters, P. (2010). Werken met verlies. De kunst van het nabij blijven. *Tijdschrift voor Coaching* (4): 62–64. (Working with Loss. The Art of Proximity)

Yu, W., L. He, W. Xu, J. Wang & H.G. Prigerson (2016). How Do Attachment Dimensions Affect Bereavement Adjustment? A Mediation Model of Continuing Bonds. *Psychiatry Research* 238: 93–99.

INDEX

Note: Page numbers in *italics* indicate a figure and page numbers in **bold** indicate a table on the corresponding page.

For Product Safety Concerns and Information please contact our EU
representative GPSR@taylorandfrancis.com
Taylor & Francis Verlag GmbH, Kaufingerstraße 24, 80331 München, Germany

www.ingramcontent.com/pod-product-compliance
Ingram Content Group UK Ltd.
Pitfield, Milton Keynes, MK11 3LW, UK
UKHW022351190926
475702UK00015B/2224
* 9 7 8 0 3 6 7 2 0 6 5 4 3 *